Golden Mondays
The Story of Cricket's Bank Holiday Matches

by
John Shawcroft

With a foreword by M.J.K.Smith

First published in Great Britain by
Association of Cricket Statisticians and Historians
Cardiff CF11 9XR
© ACS, 2011

British Library Cataloguing-in-Publication Data.
A catalogue record for this book is available from the British Library.

ISBN: 978 1 905138 96 8
Typeset by Limlow Books

Contents

Foreword

By M.J.K.Smith
Former captain of Warwickshire and England

At the time of writing I am President of the Association of Cricket Statisticians and Historians, a rather forbidding title, but it is an Association which makes a real contribution to the records and to cricket's history.

The biographies are usually of players outstanding in their time, but who have generally not reached the levels of the Graces, Hobbs and Huttons, but who had top class careers, which certainly warranted being recorded for posterity. Similarly books are produced on particular eras in the game, and now John Shawcroft has come up with another subject in the county Bank Holiday fixtures. They were not always the most obvious local derbies, for example in my time Warwickshire would have been expected to play Worcestershire rather than Derbyshire, but they were long standing fixtures, given a little extra spice by being on the Bank Holiday.

These were special fixtures in the calendars, since assuming good weather they were quite likely to be the best-attended fixtures of the season which contributed to the atmosphere. The Roses match, Lancashire v Yorkshire, would probably be the first one most people would think of, and I would suggest a good performance in this fixture would come alongside a similar performance in the Gentlemen v Players match that someone was sticking his head above the parapet and taking a step up the ladder towards representative cricket.

I consider myself fortunate to have played in the time of uncovered wickets. These produced such an interesting variety of conditions, which of course could change so much from session to session, or overnight. So the potential was there for a major turn-a-round if you were good enough to take advantage and had the nerve to carry it through. There will be a fair selection of these.

John Shawcroft has picked out a particular theme for his book – there will be some top games, dramatic changes of fortune and exciting finishes, which indicates excellent subject matter and a very interesting book.

Mike Smith

Introduction

Britain's Bank Holidays seldom fail to attract the headlines. Fine weather brings reports of traffic reduced to a crawl, with 20-mile tailbacks on West Country roads and the motorways, but there is nothing like a good old fashioned weekend washout to bring out the worst of the misery. Then people who have stayed at home can indulge in smug smiles while seaside holidaymakers and visitors to theme parks or garden centres regret decisions not to go abroad, flight delays notwithstanding.

Calls are renewed for adjustments, despite the fact that previous changes in the 1960s failed to yield much satisfaction. Whit Monday and August Bank Holiday Monday – the first Monday in the month – were introduced as part of Sir John Lubbock's Bank Holidays Act of 1871 which regulated public holidays. Whitsuntide falls seven weeks after Easter, which is a moveable feast; thus the Whit Monday holiday could occur on any date between 11 May and 14 June. The changes established Spring Bank Holiday on the last Monday in May, with August Bank Holiday moved to the final Monday of the month. The last of the old August Bank Holiday Mondays fell on 3 August 1964 and Whit Monday Bank Holiday ended on 30 May 1966. Every four or five years on average, Spring Bank Holiday coincides with the Whit weekend.

For decades, the old-style Bank Holidays – and to a lesser extent their modern counterparts – formed cornerstones of the cricket season. At league and village level the Mondays were largely reserved for knockout competitions. In the first-class game, Whitsuntide and August Bank Holiday, with the counties meeting home and away, were part of a schedule which brought order and rhythm in the summer programme. The tourists began, usually in late April, at Worcester and the season ushered itself in quietly, at Lord's where MCC met Yorkshire and at Fenner's and The Parks, with Cambridge University and Oxford University hosting county sides. May brought the first round of Championship matches, with the Whitsuntide fixtures early or late according to the Easter cycle. The tourists faced MCC and sometimes the selectors gave themselves a further glimpse of the England hopefuls with a Test trial. The series itself took a familiar path, Trent Bridge and Lord's in June, along with Ascot and Wimbledon, Old Trafford and Headingley in July and The Oval around the second week of August.

In the meantime, Oxford and Cambridge went on tour before meeting at Lord's early in July, the Varsity match being followed by Eton and Harrow and Gentlemen v Players. August began with the Bank Holiday fixtures, including Canterbury Week, and then came the festivals and seaside matches, such as Weston-super-Mare, Cheltenham, Eastbourne, and Bournemouth and, to conclude, Scarborough, Hastings and Kingston-upon-Thames. People arranged their summer holidays to coincide with these dates. Matches, with three days allocated, started on Saturdays and Wednesdays, with Tests beginning on

Thursdays. Sundays were left free for players to take part in benefit games, go for a round of golf or spend time with their families.

Whitsuntide and August Bank Holiday were focal points with the earlier holiday fixtures helping shape the course of the Championship and some of the August matches crucial to its outcome. Vast crowds saw counties at full strength, with no Test matches diluting the occasion. For generations such fixtures were virtually set in stone: Derbyshire-Warwickshire, Essex-Worcestershire, Gloucestershire-Somerset, Kent-Hampshire, Lancashire-Yorkshire, Leicestershire-Northamptonshire, Middlesex-Sussex, Nottinghamshire-Surrey and Glamorgan against the tourists. Changes had to occur, of course, but could Cardus and Thomson have come to terms with a Roses match played early in July? And they would never have imagined that because the counties were in different divisions, there might not be one at all or, indeed, no first-class cricket played on some Bank Holiday Mondays.

Much has been lost but although the future might rest in Twenty20 there are welcome signs of a revival of the old traditional fixtures. There was certainly something different about them. Seeing a match start on the Saturday and then being able to watch the second day's play instead of attending school or work counted as a privilege. Here I have been able to draw on personal recollections of golden Mondays at Derby, Edgbaston, Trent Bridge or the Roses venues, both as schoolboy and young adult. Of course, not all the Mondays were golden. A wet Whit or August Bank Holiday formed the staple diet of many a music hall comedian. Memory is littered with ruined cricket days, seaside excursions turned into endurance tests because of the cold and wet and, particularly, of one spectacular failure, an expedition to the source of Derbyshire's River Derwent on Howden Moor, aborted near to our goal as common sense prevailed. But among the disastrous Mondays, enough of them were golden to enrich the summers and earn places in cricket's heritage. Enough, too, to illuminate the new-style holidays with their magic as fresh visitors arrived at Trent Bridge, Derby and the other county grounds and first-class cricket took place at Easter and during the May Day holiday.

A personal pilgrimage over the past few seasons to see old holiday opponents clash (although seldom at holiday times} has been enlightening. Nottinghamshire and Surrey produced some excellent cricket at Trent Bridge, Gloucestershire followers found little joy in a Somerset upsurge, Yorkshire and Lancashire fought tooth and nail in the old manner at Headingley, and Grace Road, Lord's, Worcester and Edgbaston revealed stirrings of old rivalries. And one could continue, with memorable holiday battles between Derbyshire and Nottinghamshire at Ilkeston, Derby and Trent Bridge.

I must thank fellow members of the Association of Cricket Statisticians and Historians (ACS), not only for making the publication of this book possible but also for unstinting and freely-given assistance, particularly the former Warwickshire and England captain Mike Smith (who made his fair share of Bank Holiday hundreds) for kindly writing the foreword and Roger Moulton, who has acted as my editor and provided much useful information, advice and helpful comment, David Baggett. Robert Brooke, David Harvey, Andrew Hignell, David Jeater, Roger Mann and Peter Wynne-Thomas. Players past and present, notably John Clay and Jim Parks and, sadly, many, who are no longer with us, have shared their memories. I would also like to thank my wife Gill and our son and daughter-in-law Stephen and Tracey for their encouragement and support and acknowledge my late parents who, no doubt, amended Bank Holiday Monday plans of their own in response to boyhood pleas involving the County Ground at Derby or Trent Bridge. Thanks are also due to Peter Griffiths of Limlow Books for typesetting the book, Zahra Ridge for the cover design, and Chris Overson and Kit Bartlett for proofreading. I am also very grateful to Roger Mann, Andrew Hignell, Archivist of Glamorgan County Cricket Club, Rob Boddie, Librarian of Sussex County Cricket Club and Jo Miller, Librarian and Members' Liaison Officer of Surrey County Cricket Club for their help with photographs.

Chapter One
Whitsun Frolics

Izmik, a Turkish lakeside town near the Sea of Marmora, is an unlikely icon of cricket history. Today it serves as a pleasant retreat for weekenders escaping the heat and dust of Istanbul, 80 miles away. Cypress trees, cornfields, vineyards and peach orchards add to the hilly charm of an area associated with fine ceramics.

The town's unwitting link with cricket occurred during its previous Hellenistic incarnation of Nicaea. In AD325 Constantine, the first Christian Roman emperor, chose it as the location of the initial Ecumenical Council of the Christian Church. Many important theological issues were debated for several weeks until 25 July, when the Nicene Creed, a statement of the basic principles of the religion, was issued. The Council of Nicaea also brought uniformity to the vexed question of a correct date for Easter, leading to the earliest date for Easter Sunday being set at 22 March and the latest 25 April.

Nicaea's role in helping shape the course of English cricket concerns Whitsuntide, the birthday of the Christian Church. This falls on the seventh Sunday – seven weeks - after Easter Sunday and corresponds with the Jewish festival of Pentecost (from the Greek word for fifty), on the 50th day after Passover. On the first Easter Sunday, Jesus rose; on the first Whit Sunday – "when the day of Pentecost was come" – the descent of the Holy Spirit in the form of flames to the Apostles enabled the disciples to spread the message throughout the world. Therefore Whitsuntide is also a moveable feast, with 10 May as the earliest date Whit Sunday can fall and 13 June the latest. Of the 34 dates available to Whit Sunday, 21 occur in May and 13 in June. The name is said to be a variant of White Sunday, derived from the white robes of the newly baptised. The feast was officially known as Whit Sunday in the first prayer book of Edward V1 (1549) and this name has continued in the Anglican Church.

The church was the centre of life for the parish, the milestones of people's lives marked by the feasts and fasts of Christmas, Candlemass, Lady Day, Easter, and Rogationtide. Their games and leisure pursuits took place on the Feast and Holy Days - their holidays. Whitsuntide, falling on the threshold of summer and the first holiday with any realistic chance of warm weather, was such a time. It could herald a four-day occasion starting on Saturday as Whitsun Eve – which saw much preparation including buying new clothes - and finishing on the Tuesday, or a full seven days known as Whit week. As early as the 12th century the clergy had introduced miracle and mystery plays during the early part of Whit week. For centuries Whit Monday had been regarded as a general holiday. Pageants, fairs, Morris dancing, well dressings, social gatherings, ram roasting, cheese rolling, processions, singing and dancing, cudgelling contests, wrestling, foot racing, bowling, backsword play, bull baiting, cock fighting and other activities resulted in innkeepers awash with profit from the sale of food and drink.

Whit Walks found the community assembling at a certain point and parading around the town or village. People would wear their new clothes – or at least something new - with the girls clad in white, and make their way to the green or the playing fields. Another custom, Whitsun Ales – not a type of beer despite its name – consisted of country fairs with sports and competitions. After the Civil War the Parliamentarians' Puritan government banned such merrymaking but under Charles II – he was born on a Whit Monday – Whitsun Ales became a major event. Artists, too, made the most of it. Punch and Judy, thought to be a Whit Monday fair scene on a recreation ground in Carlisle, is one of LS Lowry's most valuable paintings. And little girls from the parishes would be crowned May or Rose queens.

Amidst such fun and frolics it is easy to imagine how cricket came to be played by young boys and their elders on Whit Monday after the religious duties had been observed on the previous day, when families would gather for special meals. The game had been associated with such holidays since time immemorial. There were many incidents of cricketers falling foul of 17th century laws for playing on Sundays. *The Post Boy* of 30 March 1700 advertised a match to take place on Clapham Common on Easter Monday and the diaries of a Sussex yeoman Thomas Marchant, who owned land at Hurstpierpoint, record cricket played in his parish during Whitsun week early in the 18th century. In 1744 Surrey met England at Moulsey Hurst on Whit Monday, Kent played All England at The Artillery Ground on Whit Monday 1751 and a year later teams from the Wealden villages of Withyham and Hartfield staged a match during Whit week for half a guinea a man, the announcement stating 'Every one of the gamesters to be (at least) 60 years of age'.

As the signposts of cricket's development – Slindon, Hambledon, the MCC, law revisions and the third stump – passed, more references to games being played at holiday times appeared. Hambledon's season, for example, began on the first Tuesday in May when the players came together for practice. More than 20,000 people saw a match at the Artillery Ground in Finsbury Square in which England defeated Hambledon by one wicket on Whit Wednesday and Thursday 1773. There was at least one special holiday occasion for the Small family when father and son, each named John, appeared for Hambledon against England (also styled Kent v Hampshire, each with a given man) at Sevenoaks on Whit Tuesday and Wednesday 1784.

Soon the emphasis switched from Hambledon to London as the aristocracy which patronised the sport found the city more convenient than the rural settings. Appropriately Lord's was the venue for the main Whitsun fixtures of the late 18th century. On Monday 21 May 1787 Middlesex met the White Conduit Club at the new ground; ten days later in Whit week Middlesex defeated Essex. MCC arranged a series of Whit fixtures at Lord's: Hornchurch in 1791, Brighton in 1792, Middlesex Thursday 1795 and Montpelier in 1798. Middlesex met Brighton in 1793 to complete the previous September's match and also played Kent in 1796.

An old Etonian, George Finch, Eighth Earl of Winchilsea, past player and president of Hambledon and a founding father of Lord's and MCC, was the patron of a strong Surrey team which faced England at Lord's during the 1794 Whitsuntide. He led a powerful side which included John Wells, Tom and Harry Walker, Robert 'Long Bob' Robinson and William (Silver Billy) Beldham, the finest batsman of the age. Beldham dominated the England bowlers with 72 and 102 not out. The left-handed Harry Walker surpassed this with an undefeated 115 in Surrey's second innings which was given up in those pre-declaration days at

259 for five. It was phenomenal scoring by contemporary standards and it was too much for an England team which included David Harris, the master of length bowling in the days of under-arm, whose duels with Beldham produced the high peaks of that era.

Thus Lord's in its earliest years at Dorset Square (it settled at its current home in 1814), established something of a tradition for Whitsuntide fixtures.

Chapter Two
Early Days

People flocked to Lord's, attracted by the great players of the day; Beldham, the Walkers and their ilk. Soon Beldham's star waned, his mantle taken up by the autocratic and eccentric aristocrat Rev Lord Frederick Beauclerk, the fourth son of the Duke of St Albans, who was a grandson of Charles II and Nell Gwynn. A fine, all-round amateur cricketer, he became a dominant, if somewhat hot tempered, and unscrupulous figure at Lord's and MCC, openly admitting that he could make 600 guineas a year playing matches for stakes. He preached his sermons as vicar of St Albans from a saddle in the pulpit and it is easy to imagine him haranguing his flock on Whit Sunday before playing cricket on the following day, no doubt with a wager or two thrown in.

Beldham and Beauclerk were among the vanguard of batsmen who were forced to move out to the pitch of the ball as the bowling arm was raised higher and higher. David Harris had bowled with his hand about the level of his armpit and round-arm was an inevitable, if controversial, development. John Willes tried to introduce it but in 1822 he was no-balled for throwing, leaving the ground in disgust at the umpire's ruling. A seed had been sown, however, and the Sussex bowlers William Lillywhite and James Broadbridge formed a devastating combination against batsmen unacquainted with the new style. In 1827 three experimental matches between England and Sussex – the county being permitted to bowl round-arm and the all-professional England XI not - were arranged to try it out. To add spice there was a side bet of 1,000 guineas a side.

The first trial was played at the Darnall New Ground two miles north-east of Sheffield, the three-day game beginning on Whit Monday. The ground had terrace seats for 8,000 spectators and a large brick grandstand, with an open balcony supported by seven pillars, provided rooms for the players. In July 1826, Tom Marsden, a 21-year-old left-handed batsman, made 227 for Sheffield & Leicester against Nottingham at Darnall New Ground – only the second double hundred recorded. In the trial he fell hit wicket to Lillywhite before he had scored as the Sussex bowlers took control, England losing their first five wickets for a single. Fuller Pilch's 38 brought some respectability before he was bowled by Lillywhite for what proved to be the highest score of the match. Marsden top scored with 22 in England's second innings but Sussex won by seven wickets. It is believed this match is portrayed in an aquatint of the short-lived ground, which eventually became Darnall Cemetery. Sussex won the second of the trials by three wickets but England, with their batting strengthened, edged home by 24 runs in the third at Brighton. But the round-arm revolutionaries had made their point and the bowling was legalised in 1835.

The trial was not the only important Whitsun fixture in 1827. For several years there had been a sprinkling of Cambridge University - Cambridge Town fixtures, with Herbert Jenner prominent for the former. Jenner, the first captain of Cambridge University, was a powerful figure; a fine, all-round cricketer – batsman, bowler and wicket-keeper - who became President of MCC and lived until his 99th year. He played his first match at Lord's for Eton v Harrow in 1822 and also appeared for the Gentlemen but the calls of his profession as a barrister restricted his time in big cricket. His opposite number at Oxford University was Charles Wordsworth, nephew of the poet. Jenner and Wordsworth had played against each other in the Eton-Harrow match and Wordsworth knew many players who had gone from Eton, Winchester, Rugby and Harrow to both Universities. Gradually his idea for a Varsity match took shape.

"Nothing came of my wish to bring about a match between the Universities in 1826. But in 1827 the proposal was carried into effect. Though an Oxford man, my home was at Cambridge, my father being Master at Trinity, and this gave me opportunities for communicating with men of that University," Wordsworth reflected 60 years later when he was Bishop of St Andrew's. He issued the challenge, Jenner accepted and then Wordsworth set about arranging for the first Oxford-Cambridge match to be played at Lord's.

The fixture was scheduled for Whit Monday and Tuesday, June 4-5 1827 but rain restricted the historic match to one day. Jenner drew first blood by bowling Wordsworth for eight and took five wickets, also keeping wicket at the other end. Oxford made 258, an unusually high total given the state of the pitches in those days, R.Price scoring 71. Wordsworth's left-under-arm off breaks then accounted for seven batsmen at a cost of 25 runs and although Jenner got 47 he was the only man to reach double figures in a score of 92. The match was drawn. Although some of the early Varsity games took place at the end of Whit Week, this remains the only one to be played during the actual holiday. Wordsworth also promoted and rowed in the first University Boat Race at Henley in 1829. The 1827 Whitsuntide fixtures - the first of the experimental games and the initial Varsity match – had far-reaching effects on the future of cricket but it was Lord's which was to provide the mid-19th century with its showpiece.

Chapter Three
The Best v The Best

That showpiece had its origins in the formation of the great travelling elevens which did so much to promote and develop the game. William Clarke's slow under-arm bowling brought him thousands of wickets but ambition sought wider horizons. Clarke, who laid out the Trent Bridge ground in Nottingham, created the All-England Eleven, which provided jobs for the leading professionals of the day. They journeyed the length and breadth of the country for matches against odds, popularising cricket in areas where it had seldom been seen before.

Always, though, Clarke had his one good eye on the balance sheet and his autocracy led to a schism in 1852. Under the leadership of John Wisden and Jemmy Dean, a rival combination, the United All-England Eleven, was formed. Relations between the two organisations were strained but things changed after Clarke's death in 1856. Another Nottinghamshire man, George Parr, who throughout the 1850s was the finest batsman in the country, took over Clarke's old role. Suggestions that the two elevens should meet had met with short shrift from Clarke but Parr was more receptive. He was, after all, Wisden's partner in the management of a ground at Leamington.

Friends of Jemmy Dean were keen to arrange a benefit for him involving a fixture between the two teams. The idea was put to Parr who accepted it with one stipulation. This was that the elevens should first play a match for the Cricketers' Fund Friendly Society at Lord's. The fund had three objectives. It aimed to provide members with relief if, due to old age, illness, accident or any other infirmity, they were incapable of following their profession. It undertook to make temporary assistance available to a member's widow and children if they were left destitute and it would also ensure a member had a decent burial. Members contributed an annual subscription of one guinea and had to be fully paid-up for five years to qualify for benefit. No new members over the age of 45 were allowed. The Society's treasurer, James Dark, was also the proprietor of Lord's – he sold the lease to MCC in 1864 - and he agreed to place the ground at the disposal of the two elevens.

So the eagerly awaited clash between the AEE and the UAEE – the Match of the Century – could scarcely have had a better cause, although Old Clarke was probably revolving in his grave. The AEE team was George Parr (captain), Alf Diver, Andrew Crossland, Heathfield Harman Stephenson, Julius Caesar, Cris Tinley, George Anderson, Alf Clarke, Edgar Willsher, John Bickley and John Jackson. The UAEE fielded John Wisden (captain), Thomas Hunt, James Dean, John Grundy, William Caffyn, Henry Wright, John Lillywhite, Fred Bell, Tom Lockyer, William Mortlock and William Martingell.

Most of them were young men in the cricketing sense and close to their best. Several had previous experience of Lord's at Whitsuntide, among them Martingell, Dean and notably Parr who had appeared in the Pilch's XI v Felix's XI fixture in honour of the latter in 1846 when Prince Albert spent a couple of hours at the match on the second day. And it would have been unlike Clarke to miss out on the financial aspects of a holiday game, such as Fourteen of MCC v AEE in 1851, with Arthur Haygarth of *Scores and Biographies* fame in the MCC team and the outgoing and incoming batting champions Pilch and Parr in the AEE side. Wisden and Parr had also excelled in the North v South match of 1855, a contemporary fixture then of greater importance than Gentlemen v Players. Whitsun, however, tended to miss out on the important single-wicket matches between 1800 and 1848. Three of Alton met Three of Winchester in Whit week 1833 and on Whit Saturday 1844 Pilch and Martingell opposed each other when The Lions met The Crowns in a three-a-side match at the Beverley Ground, Canterbury. But the great contests, such as Pilch and Marsden and Alfred Mynn and Nicholas Felix, took place at other times of the year.

Glorious weather greeted this making of history between the rival elevens on Whit Monday 1 June 1857, the first of three days. Spectators began arriving at 9.30am for the noon start and the crowd was estimated at 10,000, tavern staff doing a brisk trade as they sold pots of ale around the ground. Parr used a two-shilling piece for the toss and Wisden, calling correctly, chose to bat. By 3.25 United were all out for 143, Caffyn top-scoring with 38 and Jackson, 6ft and 14 stone, taking six for 31. The teams then dined on roast beef and plum pudding at Mr Dark's residence and play did not resume until 4.45pm. By the close AEE had lost seven wickets for 136, Stephenson making 51 before being caught and bowled by his Surrey colleague Caffyn. Parr, 20, at close of play, remained undefeated with 56 on the second morning when AEE were dismissed for 206. Caffyn took seven for 69 but Wisden, handicapped by a thigh injury, could only deliver nine overs. AEE led by 63 and United began their second innings disastrously, losing three wickets for 19, including Caffyn who suffered a blow in the ribs from the fearsome bowling of Jackson. Bell made 33 but the innings closed for 140, Willsher five for 45. AEE were seven without loss at the close and they reached their target of 78 for the loss of five wickets on a shower-interrupted final day. Parr, who was missed twice, finished on 19 not out and thus had the distinction of being unbeaten in both innings. Although the game did not quite live up to the hype and expectations it proved to be absorbing – more than 20,000 attended over the three days - and produced £140 for the Cricketers' Fund.

Thus the annual fixture was established, although it was 1860 before the teams met again at Whitsuntide, AEE winning a low-scoring match in which Parr made 55 and George Tarrant, who rivalled Jackson for pace, took six for 28 in United's first innings. Between 1862 and 1866 it settled as a Lord's holiday event. Robert Carpenter was presented with a new bat following his unbeaten 63 which formed half of United's first innings total in 1862 and a year later their batsmen had a torrid time against Jackson on a hard, fiery pitch parched by a lengthy drought. George 'Ben' Griffith lacked Jackson's speed but the AEE found the Surrey man's left-arm bowling a handful and his match analysis of ten for 73 had much to do with United's 70-run victory. This game was significant for the Press. Until then journalists attempted to position themselves near to the scorers and were frequently jostled by the crowd but in 1863 a room was made available exclusively for them at the St John's Wood Tavern. One of the best matches took place in 1864. United needed 204 in the fourth innings – an immense task on the Lord's pitch notorious for its poor quality. On a final day of sweltering heat they lost two wickets for 10 and a third fell before Mortlock, the Surrey Stonewall and Yorkshire's Roger Iddison staged an aggressive fightback. They carried the score to 126 before Mortlock was out for 65, including an all-run seven after hitting the ball out of the ground through the gates which had just been opened to admit a carriage. Iddison, 44, was run out at 156 and United lost two further wickets with nine runs still needed before Frank Silcock and Thomas Sewell saw them home by two wickets – and the fund £102 better off.

All was not well, however. A north-south feud developed, with Parr and the northern professionals ranged against Surrey and The Oval hierarchy. Matters came to a head when seven players resigned from the UAEE and formed the United South of England XI in November 1864. This meant the AEE-UAEE matches effectively became North v Rest of the North. The last Whitsuntide game for the Fund at Lord's took place in 1866, MCC reacting to a further row by cancelling patronage of the annual fixture and establishing the Marylebone Professional Fund, 'for the support of those professional players, who, during their career, shall have conducted themselves to the entire satisfaction of the Committee of the MCC'. England defeated Middlesex at Lord's during Whit in 1867 in the inaugural match for the latter fund, WG Grace making 75 and sharing a partnership of 151 for the third wicket with the Old Etonian Alfred Lubbock (129). A crowd of 4,000 saw a dazzling exhibition from two of the finest young amateur batsmen of the day. WG was aged 18 and Lubbock 21 but while Grace's career was to span decades Lubbock had practically given up the game by the time he was 28 in favour of a career in his family's bank.

The final match between the two Elevens for the Cricketers' Fund was played at Old Trafford in 1867, although not at Whit, when Richard Daft made the only hundred of the series. Subsequent Whitsuntide fixtures were played at Savile Town, Dewsbury for the benefits of Robert Carpenter and Tom Hayward (1868) and George Anderson (1869). After this the United All England Eleven was disbanded. Other elevens arose but were swept away by the increasing popularity and developing strength of county cricket. The AEE struggled on, playing its final first-class match in 1878 although it existed for another decade or so. By the time of its demise more than 30 years had passed since its first encounter with the UAEE. Of the 19 matches between 1857 and 1869 each of the two elevens won eight while three were left unfinished. Nine took place at Whitsuntide and again honours were even.

Much of the history of the two elevens is taken up with tortuous tales of pay rows, splits and sheer bloody-mindedness which tends to obscure the high quality of the cricket. WG Grace was in no doubt about their status. "When the two most famous elevens met reputation was at stake and both strove to put their best teams in the field. There was no half-hearted play then. Thought was put into every ball bowled, and neither batsman nor fieldsman spared himself. It was the match of the year from a player's point of view, and crowds testified to it by turning out in thousands. It was not always so in the North v South matches. More than once an eminent player cried off at the last moment, and occasionally the sides were poorly represented."

More than half-a-century later, Sydney Pardon, editor of *Wisden*, added a further tribute. "In the All-England and United All England elevens we had two highly-organised teams, and either of them, strengthened by a couple of the best amateur batsmen, would have been equal to all emergencies. Looking up the scores of the matches at Lord's between the two elevens from 1857 to 1866 I have been struck by the complete equipment of the sides at every point. Each had at least five regular bowlers – nearly every one of them first-rate according to the standard of those days."

There was a final irony. John Jackson took more wickets (107 for AEE) than anyone else in the series. He died at the age of 74 in Liverpool Workhouse Infirmary. Virtually destitute in his declining years, he became a beneficiary of the cause he so ably supported, receiving an allowance of 5s 6d a week from the Cricketers' Fund Friendly Society.

Chapter Four
St Lubbock's Day

The big crowds attending the Lord's showpiece fixtures masked a social problem. Missionary touring elevens had taken cricket beyond the railheads and introduced it to the people; the AEE-UAEE encounters lifted the game to new heights of quality before the allure of the travelling elevens began to pall. The outcome was an interregnum of sorts – a period when there was little big cricket to see and relatively few people with the time and money to watch it. And ironically, as Great Britain entered an era of unparalleled prosperity, the leisure hours of its working class had suffered.

Many people uprooted themselves from the countryside, forced to seek work in the towns after the enclosures of common land left them with no means of supporting themselves by farming or agriculture. Long and demanding six-day weeks with Sunday allowed for rest and religion, plus Good Friday and Christmas Day, left a man with few opportunities to see Pilch or Mynn should they be playing in the vicinity. His lot was to improve but it was to be a long, hard road.

Factory Acts eased the burden of labour. Those of 1819 and 1833 reduced the amount of hours children between the ages of nine and 18 were required to work; the Ten Hours Act of 1847 introduced a 10-hour working day or a 60-hour week, although employers found it easy to side-step the legislation. It was not until 1874 that the clear ten hours was secured; indeed, it was to be 1910 before miners had their underground shifts restricted to eight hours. The first major step which affected the playing and watching of cricket was the Saturday half-day, which developed from the shorter Saturday working day originally granted to textile workers and which, given an early-morning start, had allowed them an afternoon off. The half-day emerged during the 1850s, when business closed at 2pm. During the next 20 years the idea of a paid holiday also started to take root. At first this was restricted to just a few days but the gradual development of Wakes Weeks and similar mill and factory shutdowns in northern industrial towns placed the focus on local fairs and other events. As the railway system developed, so workers descended on seaside resorts such as Blackpool during Wakes Week. In the south, Brighton, Folkestone, Hastings, Margate, Ramsgate and Southend beckoned. By the 1920s, 1.5 million workers were entitled to a paid holiday, a figure which had doubled by 1938 and octupled in 1939 with the Pay Act.

In 1868, the general election had left the Liberals with 387 seats to the Conservatives' 271. The first great ministry of William Ewart Gladstone had begun and one of his early reforms was to have a major influence on cricket.

The catalyst was Sir John Lubbock who became Liberal MP for Maidstone in 1870. Lubbock, who was born in 1834, was a member of a family of bankers which had strong associations with Bromley in Kent. They bought an estate there in 1808, which originally was used for sheep rearing although the later emphasis was on dairy cattle and cereal crops. In the mid-19th century High Elms House, at

Shire Lane, Farnborough, and its gardens, were laid out as a country estate with 30 employees. Charles Darwin moved to nearby Down House in 1842, six years after returning from his voyage in the *Beagle* and it was through him that Lubbock acquired a love of nature and science. Darwin encouraged his studies, persuading Lubbock's father to give the boy a microscope. After Eton, Lubbock was taken into the bank – Robarts, Lubbock & Co which later amalgamated with Coutts & Co – and made a partner at the age of 22. At the age of 24 he drafted the country clearing system which made it possible for cheques to be drawn in one bank and processed by another without charge. His interests included geology, archaeology, anthropology and botany and he was the first archaeologist to divide the Stone Age into the Palaeolithic and Neolithic periods. Lubbock became an author – with works on the behaviour of ants and on anthropology - scientist and the president of 25 learned societies and commercial organisations. In recognition, he received honorary degrees from Oxford, Cambridge, Edinburgh, Dublin, St Andrew's and Wurzburg Universities.

Sir John's stated aim in Parliament was: "To promote the study of science, both in secondary and primary schools, to quicken the repayment of the National Debt, and to secure some additional holidays and shorten the hours of labour in the shops." He brought to the House of Commons a happy combination of a leading banker and social reformer. Bank employees at that time were the aristocracy of the clerical world, working about 48 hours per week as opposed to the 60-plus of most office staff. In the 16th century there were 58 saints' days in the English calendar but the law gave the lords of the manor power to over-ride these when they required their labourers to work. Later, the Bank of England had observed some 33 saints' days and religious festivals as holidays but in 1834 this was reduced to just four: 1 May, 1 November, Good Friday and Christmas Day. The first legislation relating to Bank Holidays was passed with cross-party support when Sir John introduced the Bank Holidays Act of 25 May 1871. It regulated public holidays: Easter Monday, Whit Monday, August Bank Holiday Monday (the first Monday in August) and Boxing Day by statute. Good Friday and Christmas Day, which, because of common observance had been customary holidays since before records began, were classed as common law holidays. Thus four extra days were added to those on which cheques and bills would not be paid by the banks – and because the banks were not open it followed that most other businesses were unlikely to operate.

Cricket was an obvious beneficiary – a thought probably not far from Sir John's mind when he began drawing up the bill. He was the eldest of eight brothers, three of whom played first-class cricket – Nevile, the third son, Alfred the seventh and Edgar, the eighth, with a distant cousin. CWS Lubbock, playing for Northamptonshire in 1938-39. Lubbock was firmly of the belief that bank employees should have the opportunity to attend or take part in matches when they were scheduled. So Easter Monday, Whit Monday and the first Monday in August dovetailed with the dates when matches were traditionally played between the villages in the region where he was raised. It was cleverly done. "If we had called our Bill the General Holiday Bill or the National Holiday Bill I doubt not it would have been opposed," he said. Instead, a move designed to benefit the British worker succeeded in its passage through Parliament by being disguised as an initiative to help the banking industry. In Scotland, the 1871 Act established New Year's Day, Good Friday, Easter Monday, first Monday in May, first Monday in August and Christmas Day as Bank Holidays.

Lubbock's initiative was welcomed by *The Daily Telegraph*. "The people may forget a great many deeds of glory and names of renown; but they will never forget him who has given them a new and universal day of repose and recreation."

In 1874, Sir John retained his Maidstone seat, (the town returned two MPs until 1885) but was defeated in the 1880 general election. He was raised to the peerage as the first Baron Avebury in 1900 and died in 1913. In 1938 the estate was sold to Kent County Council, which used it as a nurses' training centre. It passed to Bromley Borough Council in 1965 and has been preserved as Green Belt land available to the public to enjoy the nature, animal habitats and leisure opportunities. Sir John's grandson, Eric Lubbock, the Fourth Baron Avebury, served as a Liberal MP from 1962 to 1970 after winning a sensational victory in the Orpington by-election in March 1962.

High Elms House was destroyed by fire on August Bank Holiday Monday in 1967 but a blue plaque at the estate honours Sir John's name. Long before the plaque he had been in the consciousness of the working man, for some had suggested the August Bank Holiday should be called St Lubbock's Day.

Chapter Five
North v South

Peace was restored to cricket's warring factions in 1870. After prolonged negotiations the United North of England XI – which played its first match in Dewsbury at Whitsun – met the United South of England Eleven at Lord's in July for the benefit of the Cricketers' Fund Friendly Society. For some years North met South at Prince's on the fund's behalf while similarly styled elevens maintained the Lord's tradition at Whit for the Marylebone Professional Cricketers' Fund.

Thus Whit Monday 1870 saw George Parr's first professional appearance at Lord's after an absence of four seasons. North won, WG Grace opened for the South and the attendance was around 8,000 on the Monday and 4,000 on the second day. A year later, on 29 May 1871, cricket enjoyed the first benefits of Sir John Lubbock's new act. "Such a crowd (8,000 again) as which was attracted to Lord's on Whit Monday has, perhaps, never been seen on the old ground since its establishment," said the *Sporting Gazette*. "It rolled up and formed itself into a ring long before the game commenced." Play started at 12.15 and at lunch (2.30pm) Grace was 135 not out. When the lunch bells rang, people, in quest of food, dashed towards the one exit gate that was open and such was the crush that no one could get in or out. Some solace for missed lunches – the interval lasted 45 minutes - was provided by WG with 178 (three fives and 19 fours) out of a total of 328, sharing a partnership of 170 with his brother GF who made 83. Willsher, five for 52 and six for 54, emphasised South's dominance in an innings victory over a North team which included Hayward, Daft and Carpenter. In the only other important game played on that first Whitsun Bank Holiday, Oxford University entertained the Gentlemen of England and won by 114 runs.

So another Whitsuntide tradition was now established. There was a crowd of 8,000 on the Monday of the 1872 game which South won; James Southerton's round-arm slow bowling bringing him a match analysis of 14-66. The series gained in popularity with four fixtures arranged at various grounds in 1873, South winning two, North one and the other drawn. Southerton had another field day in 1874 and then, said *Wisden*: "The Whit Monday of 1875 was most enjoyably fine, the bright, hot sun that beamed down upon the millions of holiday folks out that day pleasure taking being agreeably tempered by a cool and brisk breeze from the east." Lord's was thronged with 8,342 who paid for admission, many bottles of champagne were uncorked on the pavilion balcony, there was a large Press turnout and around the ground people stood or sat five deep. "The wall top of Mr Dark's garden was covered by those 'who could climb and did not fear to fall'. It was a depleted North side, with several of their best players involved elsewhere; at Trent Bridge where Nottinghamshire were playing Derbyshire and in matches at Hallam, Old Trafford and Leicester. The match was all over in a day, Southerton taking 16-52 in North's totals of 90 and 72. Although Alfred Shaw and Fred Morley did well to restrict South to 123, they won by 10 wickets, the game ending at five minutes past seven. South won the 1876 and

1877 matches, WG Grace taking six for 77 in the North's second innings in the latter year, and in spite of the low scoring on the infamous Lord's pitches, the Whitsuntide spectators – 10,858 paid their sixpences on the 1878 Monday, North winning by three wickets – generally received value for money.

An exception was the 1879 fixture, set apart by MCC for Alfred Shaw's benefit. *Wisden* left nobody in doubt as to the reason why in an evocative description of a day when no play took place: "It was foul, very foul, for it rained heavily throughout that day, evening and night; it was the most dismal, dreary, depressing, drenchingly wet Whit Monday the oldest holidaymaker could remember; not one gleam of hope shone throughout that wretched day; all was rain, rain, rain; success was soakingly swamped out from all the many outdoor amusements arranged to attract the holiday thousands. No cricket could possibly be played at Lord's ground, and of the 1,105 cricket enthusiasts who paid their admission 6d on that wretchedly wet day, all – or all who chose to ask for them – received re-admission checks for the Tuesday or Wednesday." Nearly 2,000 turned up on a dreary Whit Tuesday to see play start at 2.45pm and the weather was fair on Wednesday when the paying attendance was 3,262. North won the match, Shaw taking six for 39 and eight for 21 – and was granted the proceeds of a later match as a result of WG's generosity.

Oxford University experienced the devastation the weather could cause when they met MCC at Cowley Marsh, Oxford on Whit Monday 1877. They were all out for 12 (albeit one man short) on a rain-ruined pitch, faring little better in their second innings which produced only 35. Morley's left-arm pace brought him a match analysis of 13-14 – seven for six and six for eight. MCC won by an innings, the match ending in a day. North were decisive in 1883, Edmund Peate's slow left-arm bowling proving too much for the South, although WG made 64 in their first innings of 128. Lancashire's Jack Crossland, with his controversial action, took 14 wickets for North in 1884 but finished on the losing side.

In the 1885 Whitsun fixture at Lord's, South defeated North by nine wickets in a benefit game played for Fred Morley's widow and children. Morley's was a sad tale. He started his career with the All England Eleven, graduated into the Nottinghamshire side and was regarded as the best pace bowler in the country by 1875. After a fine season in 1882, he was selected for Ivo Bligh's tour of Australia the following winter, which saw the creation of the Ashes. The England party sailed on the *SS Peshawur*, which, on 15 October 1882, was in collision with the Madras-bound *Glenroy* off Colombo. The *Glenroy*'s captain was later found to be at fault and after towing the badly damaged ship to Colombo, the *Peshawur* resumed her voyage with seemingly only a barman injured. Morley, however, never appeared fully fit, although he played in three of the four Test matches, and in February 1883 – four months after the collision – he was diagnosed with a broken rib. He had been treated by several doctors previously who failed to discover the injury. Morley received medical treatment at MCC's expense when he returned to England but he could play in only a couple of matches. His condition declined and he died of congestion and dropsy on 28 September 1884, aged 33. There was little doubt that the undiagnosed rib injury had been a contributory cause.

North avenged this defeat in a remarkable game in 1886. They lost nine wickets for 148 before Parnham (90 not out) and White (62 not out on his first-class debut) each made the highest score of their brief careers in a last-wicket partnership of 157. Despite WG's presence as captain, South struggled and were beaten by nine wickets. There was a similar story in 1887 when North won again, this time in a single day, but the teams were not fully representative. The lustre was starting to fade and this marked the end of the North-South Whitsuntide encounters at Lord's. WG grumbled that the fixture had become overdone, with five such matches taking place during the 1889 season, North, winning three of them, having the best of it. It was becoming difficult to choose satisfactory sides as an increasing number of counties realised the value of the holiday fixtures - another indication that the crossroads were beckoning. There had been a few gaps in the Lord's series from 1870 to 1887, such as 1880 when An England Eleven met Richard Daft's American Eleven, England winning a game notable for some splendid fast bowling by the 21-year-old AH Evans who took nine for 59 in an innings. Evans, an Oxford Blue at cricket and rugby, enjoyed a short but glittering career before the teaching profession claimed him. His son AJ Evans played in the Lord's Test against the 1921 Australians. In 1881 and 1882 Over 30 faced Under 30, each side winning once before the North-South fixture was resumed. After 1887 Lord's at Whit was given over to county cricket, although nothing was scheduled in 1888 and the Middlesex-Kent match a year later was abandoned without a ball being bowled.

For decades Lord's, despite its dreadful pitches, had been the focus for the Whitsuntide games but now Canterbury emerged as the prototype for the August Bank Holiday and festival weeks.

Chapter Six
Canterbury Week

Travelling by river and then by coach 'with time for plenty of glasses of ale at every village we passed through' seems an admirable way of going to a cricket match. Such was the journey made by the visiting cricketers, actors and their friends, who were due to entertain in the theatre at night in the first Canterbury Week of 1842. They came by river from London to Ramsgate and continued through Thanet to Canterbury.

The famous festival was inaugurated by a group of amateur actors and the old Beverley Club. The first game, between Kent and All England, was played on Beverley's ground on the Thanet road but the Week moved in 1847 when the St Lawrence ground was opened. Fuller Pilch was groundsman from 1847 to 1868. Lord Bessborough and his brother Sir Ponsonby Fane founded the Old Stagers to give theatrical performances in the evenings. In 1845, the Ponsonby brothers were among the founder members of I Zingari, the most famous of all the wandering clubs, which, with another notable amateur club, The Band of Brothers, has enjoyed a long association with the Week.

The first Week opened on 1 August 1842 and after Sir John Lubbock's initiative it coincided neatly with August Bank Holiday. By then it had been established for almost 30 years, with the cricket played amidst the most social and hospitable of settings. For a time the matches paired Kent against England in the first half and the Gentlemen of the MCC against the Gentlemen of Kent in the second. The fixtures became more varied and in the August Bank Holidays of the 1870s – the first part of the Week – North v South was featured. It was a happy juxtaposition but the Bank Holiday was subordinate to the whole of the Week. Thus the Thursday Ladies' Day of 1871: "From noon to four pm visitors arrived in large numbers. Four-in-hands skilfully tooled, old fashioned family carriages whisked along in the old fashioned four-horse postillion form, new fashioned brakes and waggonettes, dashing dog carts, tandems, busses and other vehicles, all of them fully, most of them fairly, freighted, rattled up the incline of the fine old ground one after the other in such numbers that when the rush was over and all were settled in picturesque groups, when the little slope was covered by brightly toileted ladies, when the promenade was thronged by a gay company and when the ring around the ground was fully formed, it was universally acknowledged that the big gathering was the gayest, the most numerous and influential ever seen at a cricket match at St Lawrence," said *Wisden*. Truly was this The Ladies' Day, for of the 7,000 visitors present "the better half" were ladies, whose presence so very much enhanced the beauty of that charming, animated picture of English summer life." The picture was completed by a fine, all-round performance from WG Grace who made 117 and had a match analysis of 12-144 in The Gentlemen of the MCC's victory over Kent.

Showery weather marred the 1872 Bank Holiday match in which James Lillywhite took all ten North wickets in their solitary innings but finished on the losing side. A year later *Wisden* enthused over the colours which graced the ground: the Union Jack, the rampant White Horse of Kent, the famous old buff and blue of politics, the gorgeous red, black and gold of I Zingari, the sombre black and blue of Kent's Band of Brothers, the scarlet and black of The Knickerbockers, the ever-popular red and gold of MCC, the dark blue of Oxford, the light blue of Cambridge, the blue and yellow of the RA and of the banners covering the house fronts in the High Street.

Amidst all the high society, pageantry and tradition, William Gilbert Grace was the principal attraction, illuminating the festival year in and year out. The colour, the music and the country balls continued to delight but in 1876 The Champion surpassed himself. He had failed in his opening innings of the Week, scoring only nine on the holiday Monday for Kent and Gloucestershire, who combined to meet the Rest of England from 1874 to 1876. The fixture replaced North v South and Gloucestershire was only included so WG could play. England took the field a man short and their young captain AJ Webbe was advised by Alfred Shaw to place a man between slip and third man to cover both positions. Shaw went there himself and there was great amusement when Grace sliced a ball from Tom Emmett straight to him. Their glee was not shared by WG, who marched off chuntering: "He was in no position at all." There was another moment of humour when the august figure of Lord Harris walked out to the middle and the scoreboard operator inadvertently left out the first letter of his surname. The holiday crowd, many of whom had been drinking, howled its delight at 'Arris until the mistake was corrected. WG atoned for his first innings' failure with 91and he switched sides for the following game when he represented MCC in a 12-a-side fixture against Kent. On Friday evening MCC followed on 329 behind. "Everyone believed that the match was now a hopeless thing for the old club," said WG. "I was exceedingly anxious to get off that night, so that I might reach Clifton next day and have a quiet Sunday's rest before meeting Nottinghamshire on the Monday. It was no use trying to play carefully so I made up my mind to hit. I risked a little more than usual, helped myself more freely than I would have done under different circumstances, and everything came off." When play ended at 6.45pm with MCC 217 for four, he was still there on 133. On a very hot Saturday he established a new record for an individual innings, his 344 leaving William Ward's 278 of 56 years earlier in the shade, before he caught the train to Bristol on Sunday. Grace followed this with 177 against Notts and 318 not out against Yorkshire at Cheltenham - 839 runs in eight days. The story goes that the downhearted Nottinghamshire side changed trains at Birmingham on the journey home. They met the Cheltenham-bound Yorkshire team on the station and were teased unmercifully about Grace. The White Rose smiles soon faded.

Canterbury's St Lawrence ground, with its famous lime tree, is one of the first to have had boundaries, a move made necessary by the tents which surrounded the playing area. Through all the cricketing and Bank Holiday changes its gaiety and colour remained largely unchanged. In 1998, Matthew Fleming, Kent's captain from 1999 to 2002, wrote in his *Daily Telegraph* column about the 147th Festival Week. "The 20 marquees are full to brimming. The High Sheriff, the President, the Buffs, the Conservative Club and the Lord Mayor all have marquees. The cricket, whilst keenly contested, knows its place and plays second fiddle to the ladies' hat competition, the clinking of ice, the groaning tables, polite applause and, as the day draws on, the odd nodding head and resonant snore. The Kent and Hampshire batsmen do their level best but their presence is temporary. The Festival Week is permanent."

Fleming said that participation immediately weaves you into the fabric of the county and you become part of Kent's famous cricketing history.

So the festive charm continues to this day but the eccentricities of such fixtures as Thirteen of Kent v Eleven of England did not endure and 1882 introduced a more competitive element. Kent met the Australians in the first game and Middlesex in the second. It was the first time they had played a county in the second match; it was also the Australians' first visit to Canterbury. On the Monday all the hotels in the city were full, the streets more crowded than ever and the display of bunting more plentiful than on any previous occasion. Canterbury Week 1882 was described as the best of all, the radical changes in the programme meeting with general approval. Cricket elsewhere took note.

Chapter Seven
Clash of Titans

Canterbury Week's fixtures took their modern shape in 1882 but the year marked other watersheds. The county club secretaries began to meet regularly and in May the magazine *Cricket* was established by Charles Alcock as a weekly record of the game.

Alcock was a remarkable figure. He had been secretary of Surrey since 1872 and editor of *James Lillywhite's Cricketers' Annual* and *John Lillywhite's Cricketers' Companion*, which were to merge in 1886. *Cricket* gave extensive coverage of all English first-class matches, details of overseas tours, items of gossip and weekly profiles. It existed until 1914 and performed a major role in promoting both the sport and its players. For the county game was on the rise. In 1873 it had been agreed that cricketers could represent only one county per season, the criteria being birth or residence – regulations regarded by some as the start of an official Championship. But fixtures were few, far between and somewhat hit or miss. Surrey played 14 inter-county matches that season, Middlesex three and Derbyshire only two.

Holiday engagements had been spasmodic: Yorkshire and Kent at Hyde Park, Sheffield in 1849, Cambridgeshire-Surrey in 1861 and so on. Curiously Derbyshire, one of the poor relations of county cricket, were in the vanguard. Sixteen of Derbyshire beat Eleven of Nottinghamshire at Trent Bridge in 1874, a defeat avenged by Notts a year later in an eleven-a-side game, but a burgeoning East Midlands' Whitsuntide event was nipped in the bud. The 1876 fixture should have been played at Derby but Nottinghamshire wanted it at Trent Bridge. Derbyshire refused and the fixture was cancelled, Derbyshire meeting Hampshire instead. Derbyshire found some consolation with matches against the Australians in 1880, when large crowds saw Spofforth take 13 wickets and in 1884 (Spofforth 12 victims) when the tourists won by an innings. The value of the Australians as an attraction in those times must be placed in context. In 1880 it was late spring before anyone knew for certain that they were coming and at one time they had to actually advertise for fixtures. Yorkshire (1879) and Kent (1881) visited the bleak County Ground at the Derby Racecourse at Whit. August Bank Holiday opponents were provided by Lancashire at Chesterfield's Saltergate in 1874 and Yorkshire at Derby in 1878 and 1881. Elsewhere sets of August fixtures began to emerge, Surrey meeting Sussex from 1877 and Gloucestershire entertaining the 1880 Australians. Then in 1882 a significant step was taken. The secretaries of Nottinghamshire and Surrey agreed that the counties should meet over both the holiday periods.

Matches between Surrey and Notts dwarfed all other county rivalries in the 19th century and the 1882 fixtures laid a cornerstone of the Championship programme. For 84 years Whitsuntide found Surrey at Trent Bridge, with Notts at The Oval during the August Bank Holiday. Only the war years of 1914-18 and 1939-45 intervened until the tradition was broken after the Trent Bridge match of 1966. The teams had first met in 1851 and high quality cricket was sometimes punctuated by acrimony. Quarrels involving the All-England Eleven, George Parr and the north-south schism spilled over into the counties. They did not meet in 1863 and ill-feeling followed Surrey's one-wicket victory in 1865. Parr was still refusing to play at The Oval and his absence tilted the balance. Surrey needed 14 when Sewell, the last man, joined Stephenson and Notts were incensed when he was given not out when they felt he was clearly stumped. As a consequence they declined to meet Surrey during the next two seasons. Fences were mended and by the eve of the Bank Holiday tradition their lengthy association was re-established.

Nottinghamshire were on the threshold of a golden era. Richard Daft had retired, a pay strike clouded 1881 but Arthur Shrewsbury, William Scotton, William Gunn, William Barnes, John Selby, Wilfred Flowers, William Attewell, Alfred Shaw and the wicket-keeper Mordecai Sherwin formed the backbone of a formidable combination. By contrast Surrey were in something of a trough. Notts won both of the 1882 games, Morley taking ten wickets in a Trent Bridge fixture of low scores, but it was a different story at The Oval, where the visitors made 352 for two in front of a large August Bank Holiday Monday crowd. Oscroft was caught at 26 but Shrewsbury and Barnes survived chances to add 289 for the second wicket before Barnes fell to a catch at short leg when he had made 130. Shrewsbury, 182 overnight, went on to 207 and a total of 501 was enough to bring victory by an innings, Flowers and Shaw doing the damage with the ball. The match ended on Wednesday 9 August 1882; on Tuesday 29 August – the second day of the match - Australia defeated England by seven runs at The Oval, the famous spoof obituary placed in *The Sporting Times* by Reginald Brooks giving rise to the birth of The Ashes.

These were halcyon days for Nottinghamshire. They beat Surrey by an innings in two days at Trent Bridge in 1883 in spite of a brave effort from Bobby Abel, run out for 45 in a first innings' total of 87. Alfred Shaw, Nottinghamshire's captain, could do little wrong: top score with 33 and seven for 22 in the visitors' second innings of 43. In 1884 Nottinghamshire's nine victories from ten fixtures left the outcome of the unofficial Championship in no doubt. The draw was at The Oval, when Nottinghamshire were in a strong position after a hundred from Shrewsbury. The spectators flocked in; 15,663, 10,126 and 2,839 on the three days and, on Whit Monday, 8,000 at Trent Bridge.

Surrey, however, were emerging as Nottinghamshire's principal rivals. In 1885 rain prevented any play before 4pm on Whit Monday and The Oval game was also drawn, where large crowds - 15,000 on Monday – had to tolerate some tedious batting. Muscles were being flexed and although Notts were acknowledged as unofficial champions for the fourth consecutive season in 1886 it was seriously disputed south of the Thames. They were unbeaten in 14 matches, winning seven of them while Surrey had 12 wins in 16 with three defeats. Least- lost suggests Nottinghamshire, a contemporary opinion shared by *Wisden* and *James Lillywhite's Cricketers' Annual*, but *Cricket* listed Surrey. The southern county's match-winning ability gives their argument a sound basis yet Notts had the best of things when the teams met. Rain affected the Trent Bridge match, where Surrey made 282 before some fine bowling by George Lohmann (six for 69) had the home side on the rack. Nine were down for 180 when Sherwin joined Scotton, who had opened, and the pair added 43, Scotton remaining undefeated with 110. So to The Oval, with Nottinghamshire unbeaten and Surrey having lost only once. "Probably no county match had ever been looked forward to with keener interest," said a contemporary report. Unfortunately Monday was cloudy and dull, although 12,136 paid for admission. John Shuter won the toss and Surrey were dismissed for 99, Attewell, operating unchanged from the pavilion end, taking eight for 56 in 44.2 overs. Nottinghamshire gained a lead of 173 and despite 74 from Walter Read, the visitors won by seven wickets.

If Surrey felt hard done by, they made no mistake in 1887. Again they won 12 out of 16 but now, with one point awarded for a win and half for a draw, the outcome was clear. Shaw's Trent Bridge days were over, Sherwin taking on the captaincy, but it was Shuter who found himself in the spotlight during the Whitsun fixture. Surrey led by 26 on the first innings and at the start of the final day they were 157 for three. By one o'clock they had carried this to 264 for four and with declarations not permitted at that time a draw appeared certain. Shuter then deliberately hit his own wicket and the remaining five men got themselves out in order to finish the innings. Nottinghamshire needed 316 but failed against Lohmann (five for 66) and despite William Gunn's 72 were beaten by 157 runs. It was Surrey's first win at Trent Bridge since 1870. Bobby Abel wrote: "Surrey v Nottinghamshire were the great matches of that season. The first game at Trent Bridge was the epoch making one which eventually led to the institution of the closure rule. Lohmann had a giant's share in winning the remarkable game for us by 157 runs. He bowled nearly all afternoon, sending down 60 overs for 66 runs and five wickets, always keeping a perfect length and breaking both ways."

By the August Bank Holiday return, each side had played six matches and lost once. A vital game if ever there was one; in fact the Surrey club received 110 telegrams on the final afternoon requesting the result. There was a record crowd of 27,000 on Monday and they saw Surrey establish an early ascendancy by reducing Nottinghamshire to 143 for eight. Then Henry Richardson, a medium pace bowler who made his debut that summer, scored an unbeaten 54, sharing partnerships of 26 with Joseph Sulley and 79 for the last wicket with Sherwin (34). Faced with a total of 248, Surrey lost Abel before the close in scoring 14. There was a price to pay for Sherwin's innings for he sprained a wrist, Gunn, so brilliant in the outfield, taking over behind the wicket. Nottinghamshire gained a lead of 36, Sulley taking four for 66, but several chances were missed. Needing 205 in the fourth innings, Surrey reached 77 for one with Shuter and Key going well before Sulley had Key caught by a recovered Sherwin. Barnes, brought on at the pavilion end, struck with three wickets and half the side was out for 127. Lohmann and Maurice Read then took Surrey to the brink of victory before Read was caught for 38. The winning run came at 4.40pm, the spectators being "hugely elated" over Surrey's success. *Cricket* said there was a scene of excitement which The Oval had not seen in a long time, cheers following cheers until the various members of the winning team had dispersed. In total, 51,607 paid for admission over the three days. With few police present there was some unseemly behaviour – *Wisden* describing it as "a great deal of bottle-throwing and other playful eccentricities." The victory put daylight between Surrey and their rivals. These included Yorkshire, beaten by an innings by Surrey at Bramall Lane but in tremendous form over the holiday at Canterbury. They made 559, forced Kent to follow-on but had to be satisfied with a draw after Frank Hearne's 144. Certainly the August Bank Holiday fixtures of 1887 make nonsense of any school of thought which dismisses county cricket as irrelevant before the Championship was officially formed in 1890.

The financial aspects of such games are evident from the balance sheets – in 1887 receipts from the Surrey match at Trent Bridge were almost four times the expenditure. But another balance, that of power, had shifted to The Oval and after a depressing 1888 season Nottinghamshire appointed John Dixon as captain, thus ending the reign of professionals at the helm. Dixon, who held the post for eleven years, led an ageing side in 1889 but he could hardly have got them off to a better start. At Whitsun Gunn (118) and Dixon (54) helped Nottinghamshire to a total of 308. Richardson and Frank Shacklock then routed Surrey for 98 and 57, the home side winning in two days to the delight of a match attendance of 16,870. By the time of the return at The Oval, Nottinghamshire were still unbeaten. On Monday, when the gate was 20,863, play was restricted to three hours because of rain. Only 13 runs separated the teams on the first innings and Shuter set Nottinghamshire 219 in 180 minutes on a drying pitch after Bill Lockwood had struck 83 against his native county. Lohmann (six for 22) ended their hopes, only Shrewsbury (25) resisting for long in a total of 84. The attendance of 49,935 was only about 2,000 fewer than the 1887 record.

The 1889 season produced a triple tie at the head of the table between Lancashire, Nottinghamshire and Surrey. The counties then agreed to regulate the competition themselves for the 1890 season, with losses deducted from wins and drawn games ignored. Again, it appeared all hinged on the August Bank Holiday match. At Whitsun, 11,366 paid on Monday, Nottinghamshire winning by 108 runs and Frank Shacklock having a match analysis of 10-145. Half-a-century later, Sydney Santall wrote of sitting in the pavilion and watching Lohmann bowl. "I can see him now, in my mind's eye, running in to bowl with his fair hair fluttering in the breeze and that slight touch of labour in his otherwise beautiful action – a great artist and the hero of many a schoolboy in those far-off days." Both teams had lost only once by the time The Oval match came around and it was Surrey who came out on top, winning by seven wickets after enforcing the follow-on. A Surrey double in 1891 was notable for Lockwood's bowling at The Oval and the recall to Nottinghamshire's colours of the 55-year-old Richard Daft after ten years in retirement to play in the same side as his son HB.

Nottinghamshire's eclipse was only temporary. They recovered much of their old form in 1892 and the rivalry touched new heights. By August Bank Holiday the two clubs were neck and neck at the top of the table, each having seven points. Nottinghamshire were unbeaten in nine matches, Surrey had played one more game but had been beaten at Trent Bridge earlier in the season. It was reflected in the August gate: 34,010 on Monday. "For nearly six hours this assemblage sat or stood doggedly watching every ball that was bowled, every stroke that was made, stolidly smoking all the while and all together," said *The Daily Graphic*. Surrey struggled to 129 all out at little more than a run per over, Shacklock taking eight for 59. Nottinghamshire fared little better, 123 for eight at the close and all out for the addition of a single on the second morning. Lockwood, bowling unchanged, wrecked the innings with eight for 67. Surrey led by five but failed to recover from a bad start in which their first three wickets fell for 21. Shuter made a positive 43 but the bowling of Attewell, Shacklock and Flowers was too much for the others. Surrey, before a crowd of 29,370, were dismissed for 159. Needing 165 to win Notts made a poor start as the balance of this bitter struggle swung once again. Shrewsbury and Dixon were back in the pavilion with only 12 scored but Gunn and Barnes added 94 and Nottinghamshire closed at 109 for three. Seven wickets left, only 56 required on the final day but Surrey were not yet done. At 120 for five there was a sniff of victory but although Lockwood and

Lohmann proved a handful, Nottinghamshire got home by four wickets. They followed their win at The Oval with victories over Kent and Middlesex but their last four matches brought two defeats and two draws, Surrey taking the title.

Surrey now began to dominate the holiday fixtures, mainly due to some high quality fast bowling from Tom Richardson, although half the Nottinghamshire side thought he threw his quicker ball in 1893. His rights to flying bails were not exclusive: in the 1896 match at Trent Bridge two Notts bowlers, Attewell and Guttridge, despatched them 20 and 30 yards respectively. In 1898 Nottinghamshire, after following on 172 behind at The Oval, made 548 for nine at their second attempt, William Gunn (236 not out) having the better of his duels against Richardson (one for 120) and Lockwood (one for 110). Digby Jephson bowled 23 overs of lobs but Gunn, all 6 feet 4 inches of him, was undisturbed. This was the first match of a week of holiday cricket at Surrey's headquarters and there could scarcely have been a greater contrast in the second match, Yorkshire being routed by Richardson and Lockwood in two days after Surrey had made 536. A year later there was an even more remarkable game. The Nottinghamshire match was drawn and then came a truly titanic encounter between Surrey and Yorkshire. Both teams were in the running for the Championship and neither was prepared to give an inch. Yorkshire made 704, Wainwright (228) and Hirst (186) sharing a fifth wicket partnership of 340. Surrey responded with 551 for seven, Abel (193) and Hayward (273) piling up 448 for the fourth wicket. A crowd of 14,000 watched the final day's play on Saturday, Abel and Hayward being at the crease for all but 40 minutes. In three full days' play only one innings was completed, 1,255 runs being scored for the loss of 17 wickets. Tom Richardson emerged from the fray with figures of 53.1-15-152-5.

The greatest years of crucial Championship fixtures in the Nottinghamshire-Surrey series were now in the past, although Surrey took the title in 1899 and 1914 and Nottinghamshire in 1907. Nevertheless the people still came on the Mondays: 24,970 in 1895, 28,220 in 1896, 18,702 in 1899 and 20,332 in 1901 at The Oval; 9,000 in 1904 and on a chilly day in 1907 9,000 at Trent Bridge. In Nottinghamshire's Championship year - 15 victories in 19 undefeated matches - Albert Hallam and Tom Wass carried all before them in a wet summer. Hallam, a medium pace right-arm bowler and Wass, posing problems with his medium fast leg breaks, won match after match. They were too much for Surrey at Trent Bridge but respectability was restored at The Oval, where the home team made 283 and 313 for two declared. In this match, Surrey's popular captain Lord Dalmeny, son of a former Prime Minister and the future Sixth Earl of Rosebery, made 87 in Surrey's first innings, Wass taking five for 122.

This contest between batsman and bowler typified the feudal amateur-professional relationship of those days. Their paths were never likely to cross socially yet in the middle there was a degree of respect. The one was a rough hewn coal miner from Sutton-in-Ashfield, albeit with a little polish applied by his skippers, first Dixon and then Arthur Jones. The other, born in Mayfair and an old Etonian, was to become a celebrated figure in the world of horse racing, a soldier, politician and administrator of distinction. He was 92 when he died at Mentmore House in Buckinghamshire, leaving £9,650,986 net. It was as a result of Dalmeny's approach to the Prince of Wales in 1905 that the county club adopted the Prince of Wales's feathers on their crest. He was always proud of the fact that he awarded Jack Hobbs his county cap after only two matches; no doubt in the comfort of his armchair in later days he sometimes recalled the occasion when he made 87 against Topsy Wass. Officials at The Oval also had cause to remember Wass. He once arrived at the ground accompanied by his wife and was told by a gateman that she would not be allowed in without payment. "Oh," said Wass grimly. "If this beggar doan't come in, this beggar" – indicating himself – "doan't play." Mrs Wass was admitted without further argument. Figures, alone, could have done the talking: nine for 91 in the first innings at The Oval in 1902 and a career-total of 141 Surrey wickets at 21.53 apiece.

There were some outstanding individual performances; hundreds for the Gunns, William and his nephews John and George, and for Joe Iremonger, Jones and Joe Hardstaff senior on the Nottinghamshire side and for Abel and Hayward from the Surrey ranks. Hayward took a heavy toll of the Nottinghamshire bowlers during his record-breaking season of 1906. He finished with 3,518 runs in all first-class matches, with 13 hundreds and an average of 66.37 – 2,814, average 70.35 in the Championship. At Trent Bridge, Wass hit back after Notts had been dismissed for 174, getting rid of Hobbs and Hayes at a personal cost of four runs but he then had to retire with a strain. Six wickets for down for 36 before Hayward and Lees added 71. Hayward made 144 not out in a total of 225 and followed this with 100 in Surrey's five-wicket victory, the first and second of four hundreds in a week. He was less successful at The Oval, falling to Wass for 22 and then scoring 28 not out as the game ended in a draw. In 1907 Jack Hobbs was dismissed for 0 and 1 at Trent Bridge – the nearest he came to a pair in his career. He made the Nottinghamshire bowlers pay with 3,378 runs, average 51.18 and eleven hundreds, the first in 1908 and the last 25 years later. Six of these were in Nottingham but he could do little in 1909 when he began the Trent Bridge fixture needing 81 to reach a thousand in May. Nottinghamshire won the toss and batted all day, the final one of the month.

Hobbs and George Gunn forged a strong friendship which says much for the character of both men. Arthur Jones captained a below-strength MCC party which toured Australia in 1907-08. Hobbs was included in the team while Gunn made the trip for his health. He was available for selection as a replacement should he be needed and also acted as scorer. Jones fell ill just before the first Test and, with Hobbs having suffered from seasickness and lack of form and Hayes achieving little, Gunn was selected. It was a controversial choice, Len Braund, in particular, being unimpressed. Hobbs had good reason to feel he had been given less than a fair opportunity but he demonstrated what a great sportsman he was, helping Gunn prepare by bowling all afternoon to him in the nets. "Let me make it quite clear that no friction existed between Gunn and myself, either then or at any other time. We were real friends throughout the tour and have remained on the best of terms down to the present day," he wrote. Gunn made 119 and 74 on his Test debut, clinching his place for the remainder of the series. Hobbs made a successful return and at the close of play in the final match at Sydney there was time for reflection. England were 116 for one in reply to Australia's 137, Hobbs being undefeated with 65 and Gunn 50. "George and I felt at peace with the world," Hobbs wrote. "We sat in the hotel lounge together, puffing our cigars luxuriously. Skipper Jones popped his head round the corner and greeted us: "Ah, yes, this is the time to enjoy a cigar isn't it?" England lost the match by 49 runs and the rubber 4-1 but Gunn and Hobbs finished first and second in the batting averages.

At Whitsuntide Hobbs and his wife would stay at the Gunns' home in West Bridgford, the cricketers walking to the ground together. When the day was done, Hobbs chatted about the game from what became a favourite fireside chair. The rest of the Surrey team usually stayed at the Black Boy Hotel. The pair might have become colleagues for Gunn had worked as a nursery attendant in Surrey, where he played club cricket. He was offered terms by the county but after talking to his uncle Billy he signed a three-year contract with Nottinghamshire. George Gunn made his county debut in the 1902 Whitsun match. He said when he first went in to bat he tried to play attacking shots. Arthur Shrewsbury, who was at the other end, came down to him at the end of the over and said: "Stick to thy defence and leave the attacking shots to me."

The Hobbs-Gunn friendship was a feature of the holiday games, when players stayed in each other's homes and saved the hotel expenses. The crowds, too, were pleased to see familiar faces. A cornet-playing spectator heralded Nottinghamshire's Championship success in 1907. When Surrey arrived he greeted Tom Hayward with a blast of *See The Conquering Hero Comes* and played *Goodbye Tommy* when he was out.

If the matches were celebrated in music at Trent Bridge then poetry – of a sort – held sway at The Oval. Albert Craig, the Surrey Poet, was a familiar figure for many years. The Surrey-Nottinghamshire match was an irresistible subject, as in *The Oval, August Bank Holiday.*

> Darling Old Oval, once again we meet
> One clan to triumph, one to bear defeat
> Notts, dear old Notts, appear in all their pride
> We greet them warmly to the 'Surrey Side'

Craig honoured past and present players in his verse: Shrewsbury, Shaw, Walter Read, Hayward, Richardson, Lockwood, Walter Lees, Neville Knox, Ernie Hayes, Herbert Strudwick among them. The poem concluded:

> Long may the Notts and Surrey favourites meet
> In cordial fellowship each other greet
> And when the victors have been laurel crown'd
> May warm and kindly feeling still abound

John Gunn recalled the rivalry when, in the harsh winter of 1963, I visited his West Bridgford home and spent a memorable afternoon. He was an old and frail man but the memories remained sharp, the recollections of long-ago games easily verified by a glance in *Wisden*. The names resonated from the Golden Age. A left-handed allrounder, Gunn appeared in six Test matches and toured Australia. The feeling of awe that I was in the company of a cricketer who played against WG Grace remains to this day. He had good cause to remember the Surrey matches for in 1903 at The Oval he made 46 and 32 and took eight for 63 and six for 69 with his slow medium bowling, following this with 52 and six for 53 and eight for 121 at Leyton – 28 wickets in one week. Gunn said the fastest bowler he ever faced was Charles Kortright, although, of the pacemen, he thought Tom Richardson – even though his best years were over before Gunn began his career – and Bill Lockwood were better bowlers. One delivery from Kortright struck him in what is euphemistically described as the lower groin, although Gunn put it a little more colourfully. "He was tremendously quick. I once went out to bat against him in poor light at Lord's. He soon sent my stick flying . . . and I wasn't sorry either!"

"The matches against Surrey were always special. We all knew each other well and I was in the same Players' side as Bobby Abel, Bill Lockwood, Tom Hayward, Ernie Hayes and Jack Hobbs and so on over the years. Another very fast bowler was Neville Knox, who took a lot of wickets for the Gentlemen in one match I remember."

The weather was bitterly cold on that February day, the nearby Trent Bridge ground covered in snow. One of Gunn's former captains, Arthur Carr, had just died at 69, collapsing after shovelling snow at his Yorkshire home. Giving the roaring fire a poke (Nottinghamshire provided him with an allowance to buy coal) he expressed regret but added: "What did he think he was doing, shovelling snow at his age?" Gunn, himself, died in August that year at the age of 87, a legacy being his 2,646 runs off the Surrey bowlers, his average of 40.70 superior to George's 37 and William's 31. The trio amassed nearly 8,000 runs, John taking 106 wickets to boot.

On August Bank Holiday Monday 1914, 15,000 people saw Surrey reach 472 for five, Hobbs making 226 and sharing a third wicket partnership of 202 with Donald Knight. It was highly entertaining but insignificant when placed in the context of wider events. Across the river crowds thronged in Whitehall as the crisis in Europe deepened. Surrey's innings closed at 542 on Tuesday and the spectators barracked some dour batting by George Gunn and Joe Hardstaff senior, police being called to eject some of the offenders. That day Great Britain declared war on Germany and in the evening Nottinghamshire's captain Arthur Carr was called away for military duty. It hardly mattered for only 45 minutes play was possible on a rain-affected final day.

Chapter Eight
Roses in Bud

Nottinghamshire and Surrey inherited the mantle of North against South in their 19th century battles for supremacy but a greater rivalry was developing on either side of the Pennines. Matches between Lancashire and Yorkshire – the Wars of the Roses, red for the Lancastrians, white for the Yorkists - came to epitomise the Bank Holiday fixtures, not least because of the gifted pens of Sir Neville Cardus and AA Thomson. Epic tussles described by Cardus in *The Manchester Guardian*, and Thomson, frequently through his step-uncle Walter, enriched cricket's literature and captured the flavour of one of the game's oldest feuds.

The fixture came relatively late to the holiday calendar, a decade after the Nottinghamshire-Surrey encounter. Earlier clashes date from 1867 and the scorecards of old reveal bowlers' matches and the development of Lancashire's great AN Hornby-RG Barlow opening partnership. Standards touched the heights. Martin Bladen Hawke, later the Seventh Lord, was captain of Yorkshire from 1883 until 1910 and president from 1898 until his death in 1938. Tom Emmett, William Bates, George Ulyett, Edmund Peate and Bobby Peel of Yorkshire and Hornby, who was England's captain in the Ashes match of 1882, Barlow, AG Steel, Johnny Briggs and Richard Pilling from Lancashire - such quality ensured outstanding cricket. Yorkshire faced Derbyshire over six consecutive August Bank Holidays from 1878 to 1883 before they were succeeded by Lancashire for the next couple of years. Kent enjoyed fixtures with both Roses counties before, in 1892, the foundations were established. That season Yorkshire won the Whitsuntide game and Lancashire exacted satisfying and impressive revenge at Old Trafford.

Appetite was whetted but nobody was prepared for the remarkable struggle at Manchester during the 1893 August Bank Holiday, witnessed by Thomson's step-uncle Walter. Lancashire had won at Headingley but by the time of the return fixture they were second to Yorkshire in the Championship table. The match started on Monday and 22,254 people passed through the turnstiles, the attendance being estimated at 25,000. The pitch was slow and difficult and each side had completed an innings by the close: Lancashire 64, Yorkshire 58, rain having held up play for a time. It was a nightmare for batsmen and there were bowlers of high calibre to exploit the misery: George Hirst, Peel and Ted Wainwright for the visitors and Briggs and Arthur Mold on the home side. After Lancashire were put out for 50 in their second innings, Yorkshire, needing 57 to win, started their quest just after one o'clock. Arthur Sellers and Stanley Jackson began with 24 in 16 minutes before Jackson was run out. The ball hit his pad, an appeal for lbw was rejected and Jackson, having run halfway up the pitch, found Sellers rooted at the other end thinking his partner had been given out. Six wickets were down for 42 at lunch and the tension mounted during the afternoon until, with six needed, Yorkshire had one wicket left. Their chief tormentor was Briggs, who found the deteriorating pitch ideally suited to his left-arm spin. Their hopes rested on Ulyett, long-serving all-rounder, Ashes veteran and, although in the twilight of his career, still a hard-hitting batsman. Audaciously Briggs tossed the ball up, "a ball which, as Uncle Walter said would have tempted the Archangel Gabriel." Ulyett relished the challenge and the opportunity to end the match with a single blow. Away it soared, aimed to clear the long-on boundary, only for Albert Ward to lean back and hold probably the most crucial catch of his career. Lancashire thus won a remarkable match by five runs. Briggs had figures of six for 35 and five for 25 while his great rival Peel, second in the line of Yorkshire's remarkable succession of slow left-handers which also included Peate, Rhodes, Verity and Wardle, took four for 15 and six for 24. But Yorkshire had the last laugh, winning the title with Lancashire runners-up. Briggs and Peel were granted the Old Trafford and Bradford matches for their benefits in 1894 and the crowds flocked in during the following season: nearly 20,000 at Bramall Lane on Whit Monday, a record paying attendance of 25,331 at Old Trafford on August Bank Holiday Monday.

Such drama and high gate receipts seemed to have permanently established the fixture over the two holidays but six years elapsed before the Whitsun crowds saw it again. Yorkshire gave their 1896 Whit dates to the Australians and found themselves without opponents in August as Lancashire and Kent exchanged visits. Canterbury proved a happy hunting ground for Archie MacLaren, 226 not out on his first appearance there in 1896 with 34 boundaries and 244 (38 boundaries) in 1897 when Briggs took six for 55 and seven for 80 in an innings victory. MacLaren made 76 in Alec Hearne's benefit of 1898, when Johnny Tyldesley scored a hundred. Manchester lived up to its rainy reputation for three consecutive years, the 1899 Whit match being abandoned without a ball being bowled, but Cuthbert Burnup made 200 for Kent in 1900. For Yorkshire it seemed to be a case of who they could get: Warwickshire in 1897-98, a rain-ruined Sheffield to mar the Australians visit in 1899 at Whit with an August visit from Worcestershire offering some consolation, and nobody at all in 1900.

It was 1901 before the Roses matches were restored to the holidays. This was a period when Yorkshire were supreme; three consecutive titles in 1900-02 and only two defeats, both at the hands of Somerset in 49 matches. Lancashire smarted in the wake of defeat at Old Trafford in 1901 and drew blood at Headingley two months later. The match, JT Brown's benefit, was drawn but MacLaren and Ward made hundreds and Yorkshire had the worst of it. Things threatened to get out of hand on Monday when 30,891 packed the ground. Shorter boundaries were marked out to ease the congestion but it was 3.30pm before play could resume after lunch.

Some writers, Thomson amongst them, cite 1902 as the most colourful and dramatic season in the history of the game. Yorkshire stormed to the Championship, 13 victories in 25 matches, defeated only by Somerset at Bramall Lane. Lancashire were fifth and received a thorough drubbing in the Whitsun match at Sheffield. The pitch was dire and Yorkshire's 148 was enough for victory by an innings and 22 runs, Stanley Jackson enjoying a match analysis of eight for 13 in 10.2 overs with his lively medium pace and sharp off breaks and making the game's highest score, 33. He fell to a catch at the wicket off the bowling of Sidney Barnes, plucked out of the Lancashire League and taken to Australia the previous winter by MacLaren. In the August return – Albert Ward's benefit – Yorkshire were again in a strong position when the Old Trafford rain ruled out play on the last day. They dismissed Lancashire for 243, Schofield Haigh taking five for 62, and replied with 499 for five. David Denton and George

Hirst made hundreds, sharing an unbroken partnership of 178 for the sixth wicket. Barnes, so effective at Bramall Lane, was reduced to 46-18-124-1. Cardus wrote: "Old Trafford was in those days the 'country', surrounded by fields; Stretford a village. No women or girls were to be seen in the crowd, except in the Ladies pavilion, a black and white timbered seclusion."

Archie MacLaren was now at the height of his powers. An immaculate batsman in the grand manner, he lives in history through his 424 at Taunton in 1895 and five hundreds against Australia. After finishing four years at Harrow as captain, he skippered Lancashire from 1894 to 1896 and again from 1899 to 1907. Twice in the 1890s he toured Australia with Andrew Stoddart and took out a side himself in 1901/02. Opinions differed as to his ability as captain, pessimistic and unlucky, perhaps, but a rigid disciplinarian, skilled tactician and one who sometimes found himself at odds with the selectors, Hawke in particular. Reggie Spooner and Walter Brearley rated him highly and John Gunn described him as "the best captain I ever played under." MacLaren was England's captain in that epic 1902 series, which Australia won 2-1, although it might just as easily gone the opposite way. The England team at Edgbaston which dismissed the tourists for 36 before the weather intervened, and in the rain-ruined Lord's game, can still make a case for being the best-ever: MacLaren, Fry, Ranjitsinhji, Jackson, Tyldesley, Lilley, Hirst, Jessop, Braund, Lockwood and Rhodes. Five of the golden eleven were Roses men.

Although they won the Championship in 1904, remaining undefeated, Lancashire found the days long as far as the Roses matches were concerned. Both were drawn – at Headingley Hirst's benefit attracted an attendance of 78,792 over the three days, the crowd reputedly consuming 135,000 bananas. Eleven such matches had now passed without a Red Rose victory but the run was halted in emphatic fashion during the 1905 Whitsuntide fixture at Old Trafford, Lancashire won by an innings after some fine bowling by Brearley and Kermode on a treacherous pitch enlivened by second-day rain. Earlier a Monday paying attendance of 24,661 had been treated to some superb batting by Tyldesley and Spooner who added 213 for the second wicket. They had some luck, Tyldesley being missed by John Tunnicliffe at slip when 14 and Spooner on 37 surviving a ball which hit the stumps and failed to dislodge a bail. Yorkshire won the August match at Sheffield in the face of some magnificent fast bowling from Brearley, who took seven for 35 and six for 122. Fine batting from Denton and Rhodes's all-round skills saw them home. It was AA Thomson's first visit to Bramall Lane, its gloomy skies reminding him of the biblical 'pillar of cloud by day' which floated above the Israelites in the wilderness. Yorkshire won the Championship, although Lancashire were first in mid-August. It would be another 21 years before the Roses counties occupied the top two positions in the table.

George Hirst was now at his peak. Short, thick-set and tenacious, he was a hard-hitting right handed batsman and left-arm bowler a shade faster than medium, who was described as the father of modern seam and swing bowling. Hirst was all the more deadly because his swerve took place in the last two or three yards of flight. His contemporary, Wilfred Rhodes, was the greatest slow left arm bowler in the country at the turn of the century: later his bowling was set aside as he became a batsman good enough to forge a successful opening partnership for England with Hobbs. Hirst, in 1906, scored 2,385 first-class runs and took 208 wickets. At Bradford he took six for 20 in Lancashire's first innings and made 58, the highest score of the match, which Yorkshire won by six wickets in two days. The return, Johnny Tyldesley's benefit at Old Trafford, saw Hirst take five wickets in the first innings and then set up another Yorkshire victory with a fighting 85 on a difficult pitch.

The Roses fixtures were a favourite choice for a professional's benefit: Hunter, Wainwright, Brown, Ward, Tunnicliffe, Hirst, Haigh, Johnny Sharp and Rhodes. In 1908 at Old Trafford there was an experiment with a Saturday start which was felt to be satisfactory in that 13,000 paid, with 22,000 turning up on the Monday. It was a match which season by season brought outstanding individual performances: Rhodes's 2,094 runs and 241 wickets against the old enemy, with 13 for 108 at Bradford in 1909, Brearley nine for 80 at Old Trafford in 1909; Hirst nine for 23 at Headingley in 1910; Spooner, twice missed before he had reached 14, 200 not out at Old Trafford in the same year against an attack consisting of Hirst, Rhodes, Haigh, Booth and Drake. And county rivals often found themselves in the same Gentlemen v Players dressing rooms or enjoying success at Test level such as the Peel-Briggs filleting of Australia at Sydney and the match-winning partnership between Brown and Ward at Melbourne in 1894-95.

The Golden Age began with the holiday Roses in bud. It ended with them approaching full bloom but for all the supreme artistry of the Golden Age, their richest flowering was yet to come.

Chapter Nine
WG in Holiday Mood

For all the burgeoning ferocity of the Roses encounters and the Trent Bridge-Oval duels, WG Grace remained the principal attraction of the early Golden Age holiday games.

He had come early to such matches, as far back as 1867 when he played for England against Middlesex for the benefit of the Marylebone Professionals' Fund, the subsequent South-North fixtures for the same cause at Lord's and his deeds during Canterbury Week. As county cricket expanded, WG's holiday appearances were made on behalf of Gloucestershire, who undertook traditional fixtures with Sussex. It was not long before the Whitsuntide crowds were royally entertained. At Hove in 1888, 1,117 runs were scored in three days, the match being drawn. By the end of Whit Monday – the first day – Gloucestershire were 361 for six with WG, who had gone in first, 188 not out. "There was a large crowd on the ground, the weather being beautifully fine, and the wicket was in that almost perfect condition in which we generally see the turf at Hove," said *Wisden*. On the second day Grace carried his score to 215 before hitting his own wicket playing at a lob from Walter Humphreys. "He had been in nearly seven hours," reported *The Times*, "and there was no falling-off from the masterly batting for which he is so famous, while he exhibited quite his old self in placing the ball."

He was now almost 40 and it was the eighth double century of his career. It was merely the prelude. A string of half-centuries followed in the matches and some useful bowling, too, although he was the junior partner in an innings victory at Ashley Down in 1889 when Bill Woof's left-arm spin exploited a helpful pitch. In 1894 his average declined to 29 before another of those remarkable summers which gave the lie to fears that the Old Man's skills had deserted him. He might have felt he owed the Bristol crowd a performance. August Bank Holiday 1894 had been wet and the announcement that no play would be possible was made at 3pm. WG organised an impromptu football match on the practice ground but the spectators were in no mood to be placated and demanded their money back. Haughty behaviour by CB Fry did not help and some of the players were jostled as they left the ground. Fry rubbed salt into the wound by making a century next day, Fred Parris's off breaks and clever variations of pace claiming 15-98 in the day, including the wicket of Grace twice. Sussex won that game by an innings and Parris followed it with five for 14 (20 Gloucestershire wickets for 112 in three consecutive innings) before a Whit Monday crowd of 10,000 at Hove in 1895. Grace, his thousand runs in May and his 100th hundred already banked, scored 91 in the first innings but Sussex again won comfortably. Gloucestershire broke the spell after a blank August Bank Holiday Monday, when the 18-year-old Charles Townsend, then in the midst of a purple patch, spun Sussex to defeat with his leg breaks.

Victory was sweet but Grace exacted full vengeance in 1896. During the Whitsuntide game at Hove he made 243 not out (226 on Monday), hitting 33 fours, but nearly finished on the losing side. Sussex, following on, declared at 420 for three with centuries from George Bean and Billy Marlow, who shared an opening partnership of 211, and from Ranjitsinhji. Gloucestershire, set 204 to win in 75 minutes, quickly lost WG and had to settle for a draw with only three wickets left.

The Champion, 48 years of age, grey of beard and edging towards corpulence, must have felt like settling Sussex's hash once and for all. Between 9,000 and 10,000 people packed the Ashley Down ground on a glorious August Monday in 1896 in anticipation of a feast: WG on the one hand, Ranjitsinhji, his successor as the finest batsman in the country, on the other. Things did not begin well for Gloucestershire. Grace opened with his bespectacled son WG junior, who was bowled for a single with only four scored. It was probably the worst move Sussex could have made. By the end of the day a jubilant crowd cheered the Old Man – 193 not out in a total of 341 for three – all the way back to the pavilion. Before a similar-sized crowd on the second day, Fred Tate and Parris struck back, capturing three wickets for the addition of only 14 in the first half hour. WG was then joined by the former Marlborough captain Sidney Kitcat and they raised the 400, Grace 228. The pair added 193 for the ninth wicket before Grace was bowled for 301, with 29 fours in eight hours at the crease.

"Probably Grace never played better cricket in his life," said *The Daily Telegraph*. "He made very few risky strokes, and absolutely gave nothing that could be called a chance." Kitcat remained undefeated with 77 – he was carried shoulder-high to the pavilion – and Sussex, responding to 551, were beaten by an innings with less than 15 minutes remaining. For good measure, Grace took three for 23 in the second innings. A hundred followed at Ashley Down in the 1897 August match and there should have been another one a year later. WG was now 50, still basking in the glory of his Gentlemen v Players birthday party at Lord's in July. The match against Sussex was meandering to a close when Grace, batting down the order and on 93, suddenly declared the innings closed. It appeared that 93 was the only score under 100 he had not made in first-class cricket until then.

Soon he was gone from Gloucestershire to his twilight years with London County. He was not yet finished with the holiday games. He was at Aylestone Road, Leicester at Whit in 1903 and with the remnants of London County under the guise of the Gentlemen of England against Surrey on Easter Monday 1905, the occasion of Jack Hobbs's debut. At Whit in 1906 he scored 64 and 44 not out at Fenner's against Cambridge University for the bare bones of London County, now aptly styled WG Grace's XI. Then, nearly half-a-century after his appearance for England against Middlesex in the Marylebone Professionals' Fund match, WG Grace attended a charity match on Whit Monday 1915 at Catford Bridge to raise money for Belgian refugees. This had been arranged by Archie MacLaren, who was stationed at Catford, and Alec Hearne, who lived there. Hearne invited him to play but he withdrew because he felt unwell on his arrival at the ground. Instead, he offered to take a collection box round and presented a bat to the man of the match, Captain Percy Burke. A photograph shows him putting a coin into the box. Within four months he was dead, at the age of 67.

WG was well aware of his obligations to the Bank Holiday crowds. Of his 13 double centuries, three were made at such times and, if the Canterbury Week 344 is included, two of his three triples delighted spectators spending precious days at a cricket match. His departure from Gloucestershire left a holiday void but it was quickly filled in that age of gold. Ranjitsinhji made 154 at Bristol in 1899 and the following season there was a match packed with drama at Hove. Sussex made 366 for seven before a large Whitsun attendance, Ranjitsinhji falling three short of his hundred. On the second day the innings closed for 391 and soon after the start of Gloucestershire's reply, Charles Fry was no balled by umpire Bill West for throwing. *Wisden* said that Fry – called on three previous occasions in 1898, once by West – bowled with a perfectly fair action when going on a second time. Gilbert Jessop then took centre stage with 179 made out of 257 in 105 minutes, including 34 fours. Gloucestershire amassed 496 and with Sussex 26 without loss at the close, 547 runs were scored during the day. Ranjitsinhji made a hundred on the Wednesday and he and Fry made centuries in a rain-affected return at Bristol.

By now the counties' fortunes were poles apart. Sussex were runners-up in 1902 and 1903 and Gloucestershire lingered in the bottom three. Whitsuntide at Hove in 1903 found a large crowd gathered in glorious weather, appetites whetted for more home success. They soon had plenty of cause for celebration as Gloucestershire, 94 for three when their captain Jessop came in, went into lunch at 129 for five. The mighty Jessop and the wicket-keeper Jack Board then turned the day on its head. Jessop made 286 in 175 minutes, hitting 42 fours before falling to a one-handed catch in the deep by Ranjitsinhji. His runs were made out of 355 and he reached 50 in half an hour, 100 in 75 minutes and 200 in two hours. He made only one mistake, surviving a sharp chance to mid-on when he had made 98. Gilbert Laird Jessop, at 29, was at the height of his powers, his sensational 104 against Australia in The Oval Test of 1902 still fresh in the mind. Although only 5ft 7in, he bent low as he shaped to play, a method which earned him the sobriquet of The Croucher. Extraordinarily quick on his feet, he possessed a wide range of shots played with immense power and timing. He was also a fine fast bowler and a superb fieldsman at cover and later at deep mid-off. Board, 71, helped his captain add 320 for the sixth wicket in 150 minutes, the Sussex attack including Albert Relf, Fred Tate, Cyril Bland, George Cox and Joe Vine. By the close Gloucestershire were 480 for nine and if the partisan home support left the ground in disappointment no better Whit Monday entertainment can be envisaged.

In an assessment of Jessop, Charles Fry, who fielded throughout the hurricane, said that Jessop's manner of batsmanship was altogether unique. "He crouched low over his bat as he grounded it, he dipped his head almost to his sloped bat handle as he sighted the flight, then he catapulted himself into a sort of rapid chasse towards the pitch of the ball and flung his bat at it with a long elastic sweep, arms at full length but with abruptly locked-back wrists which he unloosed into the stroke at the finish." He went on to say that he hit the ball "all round the clock from over cover-point's head to the ropes behind square-leg" as well as square cutting any short-pitched ball.

Throughout his career, 1894-1914, Jessop's runs were scored at an average of 80 per hour. Until 1910 six runs were awarded for a hit only if the ball went out of the ground and not just over the boundary line so many of his fours would have counted six if the regulations had been in force earlier. At Hove Sussex had to follow on but an unbeaten 162 from Ranjitsinhji saved the match.

The Gloucestershire-Sussex holiday fixtures had not long to run. From 1906 to 1908 Gloucestershire met Essex, a fixture which, win or lose, brought rich pickings for George Dennett, including all ten Essex wickets in an innings at Bristol in 1906. The last six seasons before the 1914-18 war saw the establishment of the West Country derby between Gloucestershire and Somerset. It was to prove a happy association for two struggling counties with a large amateur contingent descending on the games. Somerset had eight and Gloucestershire four at Whit in 1914 and that summer found both clubs battling to avoid the wooden spoon. Gloucestershire suffered this fate, despite a one-wicket victory over their rivals in a Bristol game dominated by the left-arm spin of Dennett and Somerset's Jack White. Jessop soon made an impact: 103 in 75 minutes at Bristol in August 1910 and an undefeated 81 to bring Gloucestershire a five-wicket victory at Taunton over the 1911 Whit period. And Charlie Parker gave a forewarning of things to come with a match analysis of 12-144 at Bristol in the following August. Parker's great days of devastation with his left-arm spin lay a decade hence but batsmen took due note.

As for Sussex they seldom found the subsequent holiday games of that period enjoyable. A mix of fixtures with Kent, Hampshire, Middlesex and then Kent again brought only three victories in 18 matches. There was victory by an innings at Southampton in the Whitsuntide game in 1910 and Ranjitsinhji returned to first-class cricket, each time after a four-year absence, in 1908 and 1912. But Sussex ended the Golden Age on a high note with a 34-run victory over Kent at Canterbury in 1914.

Chapter Ten
Lord's and the West Country

Rain affected the Whitsun fixtures in three consecutive years from 1897 to 1899 and again in 1902, 1909 and 1913. At what is usually a more settled period of the year the weather had also intervened in the August games of 1894 and 1895 and in 1902 when on the Tuesday and the Wednesday of the Canterbury fixture between Kent and Hampshire it was said to be the worst for a decade. The Whit weekend of 16-18 May 1891 saw snow fall to a depth of six to seven inches in Norfolk and there was a severe frost on both Sunday and Monday mornings.

The risks of such weather did not deter professionals seeking the grant of a holiday game for their benefits. They preferred to dwell on the record gates not just at the large arenas but from lesser venues such as Hove, Leyton and Bristol, where Whit Monday attendances of 10,000 were not unusual. Lord's, of course, was a popular ground for benefits. The North-South matches for the Marylebone Professional Cricketers' Fund gave way to matches between Middlesex and Somerset, which lasted as a holiday attraction for almost a couple of decades. The Lord's match was generally set aside as a benefit for long-standing members of the MCC ground staff, such as Mordecai Sherwin, Tom Mycroft, Wilfred Flowers, William Gunn, George Hay, William Attewell, Dick Pougher and so on. George Burton, a man of many parts, coachsmith, slow bowler, member of the groundstaff for 21 years, Middlesex scorer and secretary of the Cricketers' Fund Friendly Society, actually received two: Middlesex v Somerset as a player in 1892 and again when he was scorer in 1905.

Somerset were full of optimism when they made the journey to London in 1891. A year earlier the official Championship had begun, although the new era crept in almost unnoticed; in his research into the competition's history, Robert Brooke was unable to trace any mention of the opening fixture – Gloucestershire v Yorkshire at Bristol on 12-14 May 1890. The holiday fixtures also scarcely reflected the making of history. At Whitsuntide there were first-class matches involving Lancashire - Kent, Nottinghamshire - Surrey, Sussex -Gloucestershire and Yorkshire-Australians. Among the lower orders Essex met Derbyshire and there were a few local derbies: Glamorgan-Monmouthshire, Leicestershire-Warwickshire, Northamptonshire-Staffordshire and Northumberland-Durham. The programme was even smaller over the August Bank Holiday: Gloucestershire-Sussex, Surrey-Nottinghamshire and Kent v Australians. Interestingly the two Roses counties met second class opposition, Lancashire playing Warwickshire and Yorkshire entertaining Staffordshire.

The Second Class County Championship in 1890 was dominated by Somerset, who also flexed their muscles with two matches against Middlesex. They won at Lord's over Whitsuntide, after some fine bowling from Ted Tyler and George Nichols and an aggressive innings by their captain Herbert Hewett. Twelve victories and a tie – the return with Middlesex at Taunton - provided Somerset with a ticket into the first-class ranks and they were duly admitted for the 1891 season.

The opening fixture at Lord's was an anti-climax. Whit Monday and the final day were washed out, although more than 4,000 people attended on the second day. Soon it became an established holiday arrangement, with the Lord's fixture at Whit and the Taunton return in August. Beneficiaries prayed for fine weather. Sherwin was happy with a Whit Monday attendance of 11,914 in 1894 but Mycroft did even better a year later when 18,000 turned up on the Monday – they were rewarded by hundreds from the Palairet brothers, Lionel and Richard, who shared a second wicket partnership of 177 – and 7,961 on the second day. Others were less fortunate. George Hearne's match in 1898 saw the last two days rained off and then in 1899 MCC arranged with Middlesex for the match to be given to Flowers as an acknowledgement of his long and excellent service to the club. Not a ball was bowled on Whit Monday and on a drying pitch the next day, the game was over in three hours: Somerset 35 and 44, JT Hearne taking eight wickets and Albert Trott eleven. Middlesex's total of 86 was enough for victory by an innings. Five years later Nottinghamshire took pity on Flowers and granted him the proceeds of a match at Trent Bridge.

John Thomas Hearne was one of the great bowlers during the Golden Age. He stood 5ft 11 in and brought the ball down with a perfectly straight arm, his right-hand medium pace delivered accurately and with an appreciable off-break. Varying his pace cleverly, he used at times to send down a ball which swung with his arm and he was unplayable on a crumbling pitch. His benefit in 1900 attracted 16,000 on Monday and 10,000 on Tuesday. Middlesex were 69 behind on the first innings but Andrew Stoddart, in his final innings for the county, made the highest score of his first-class career: 221 with 36 fours in nearly five hours. Stoddart was accustomed to large scores and big occasions: 485 for Hampstead against Stoics two days after the 1886 August Bank Holiday, four visits to Australia, twice as captain, notably 1894/95 when he returned with the Ashes, and earlier holiday games, 150 and 121 at Lord's in 1895 and 1896 and 109 at Taunton in 1897. His massive effort at Lord's (he was stumped, as much through exhaustion as anything else) set up a Middlesex victory, Trott doing the rest with five for 102. It was a fitting swansong for Stoddart. He had declined the captaincy and virtually dropped out of first-class cricket, only turning out against Somerset as a favour to Hearne.

The ever-popular Australian Albert Trott joked that he had "bowled himself into the bloody workhouse" as a result of his exploits during his benefit match in 1907. 'Albatrott' made a sensational entrance to Test cricket against the English tourists in 1894/95 but he was inexplicably omitted from the 1896 Australian side captained by his brother Harry. Instead, he took the advice of the famous umpire Jim Phillips to settle in England and secure a residential qualification with Middlesex. He became a highly-successful all-rounder, hard-hitting batsman, brilliant field and a bowler with a rare skill for varying his pace, who formed a devastating combination with Hearne. As a batsman, Trott's most memorable feat was to hit a ball from Monty Noble over the pavilion at Lord's when playing for MCC against the 1899 Australians. The following year he took all ten Somerset wickets for 42 in an innings at Taunton on an August Bank Holiday Monday pitch drying under a hot sun. Play did not start until 3.15pm and nine of Trott's victims were unassisted. He bowled unchanged with JT Hearne, Trott delivering 14.2 overs, Hearne 15 without taking a wicket. Somerset, 50 behind on the first innings, set Middlesex 278 for victory and after Pelham Warner made 84, Trott, 34 not out, steered them home with one wicket and seven minutes remaining.

His career was in decline by the time of his benefit in 1907. More than 7,000 people turned up on Whit Monday, a fair crowd on a day of unpleasant weather, an indication that the 'workhouse' quip need not be taken too seriously. They saw Middlesex make 286, enough to earn them a lead of 50 as a result of some good left-arm bowling from Frank Tarrant. By the close of Tuesday's play Middlesex had been dismissed for 213, leaving Somerset with a target of 264 on the final day. A sparse crowd on Wednesday morning saw Somerset begin well, Lionel Palairet and Len Braund opening with 56 before Tarrant had Palairet caught. Trott caught Johnson in the slips off Tarrant at 74 and then came the drama.

Talbot Lewis was leg-before, Massey Poyntz deceived in flight and bowled, Sammy Woods suffered a similar fate when trying to chop the ball away and Ernie Robson clean bowled. Trott had taken four wickets in four balls and there was very nearly a fifth, Fred Lee missing a delivery which was said to have clipped a stump but failed to dislodge a bail. Gregor MacGregor, the wicket-keeper, evidently thought that Lee was out for he did not take the ball, which went for byes. Trott was not finished yet. In poor light he had Mordaunt caught by Mignon at mid-off and bowled Wickham first ball. He completed his hat trick and ended the match by dismissing Bailey, easily held by Mignon. Somerset were dismissed for 97, Trott taking seven for 20 – four in four and a hat trick in the same innings. Woods, his fellow-Australian, presented him with a straw hat. Hand-painted on the band were seven rabbits bolting into the pavilion and Trott wore it for the remainder of the season. The headlines belonged to Trott but Tarrant also played his part: 52 and 28, six for 47 and three for 35. Braund saw all ten wickets fall, carrying his bat for 28.

Stoddart and Trott shared a common fate, the former shooting himself in April 1915 in the face of financial problems and an unfortunate marriage, Trott having chosen a similar way out of his troubles, mainly caused by ill health, the previous year. Such was the darker side associated with two of the great figures from the series but there was another whose only legacy was pure charm and style. Lionel Palairet (Repton, Oxford University, Somerset, the Gentlemen and England) epitomised Golden Age grace, a batsman of whom HS Altham wrote: "A perfect stance, an absolutely orthodox method, power in driving that few have evoked and withal a classic grace and poise, unruffled even in adversity."

LCH Palairet introduced poetry to the games with hundreds at Lord's and Taunton in 1895 and several other notable performances during which he engaged in holiday duels with JT Hearne. Palairet brought a glimmer of light to Somerset, who were usually at the receiving end of trouncings from Middlesex. An exception was 1902 when Hay's benefit at Lord's saw some fine cricket. On a cold Monday Len Braund wrecked the Middlesex first innings only for Trott to respond in kind. Trott was then badly missed at slip by Braund when he had made five and he went on to 103, leaving Somerset 313 to win. The two Palairets and Braund were soon out towards the end of the second day before the captain, Woods started a recovery. That evening, at a dinner given by the Somerset London Society, Woods said: "Well, gentlemen, I hope you will come up to Lord's tomorrow and see us win." Robson made 76 and Lewis 63 but Somerset still needed 11 when the last man, the left-arm spinner Beaumont Cranfield arrived at the crease. Woods greeted him: "Keep your bat straight and still. Just stop 'em. I'll get the runs." 'Cranny' promptly managed a legside boundary from the first ball he received, which pitched outside the off stump. Woods uttered a few expletives and made it clear that Cranfield would not face another ball. He didn't and Sammy, aggressive batsman, a fast bowler in his youth and a bold, inspiring skipper, steered his team home with an unbeaten 88. Just for good measure Somerset completed the double that year with a seven-wicket win at Taunton after only two hours' play had been possible on August Bank Holiday Monday. The defeats were avenged by Middlesex in 1903 with victory by 112 runs at Lord's (Attewell's benefit) and registering 316 for eight to gain a two-wicket success at Taunton in August.

In 1908, the final year of the holiday series, Somerset's Randall Johnson, another great amateur stylist, both at the wicket and in his dress code, delighted the Taunton holiday crowds with two centuries in the match.

Chapter Eleven
Joining the Party

Nine counties contested the County Championship after Somerset's admission in 1891 and in May 1894 it was decided to introduce four more. Matches played by Derbyshire, Essex, Leicestershire and Warwickshire were declared first-class, although it was too late to include them in the competition that year. In October Hampshire were added to the list and the five newcomers joined in 1895.

They had no impact on the established holiday games, solving any perceived difficulties by, in the main, meeting each other. Since their relegation to second-class in 1888 Derbyshire's principal opponents had been Essex, although they had also faced Yorkshire and Leicestershire. Fred Spofforth, married to a Derbyshire girl and now living in the county, turned out against Yorkshire in the 1889 Whit match at Derby and returned a match analysis of 15 for 81, Bobby Peel's corresponding 15 for 67 failing to avert defeat by 54 runs. For the most part, Whitsuntide meant Essex at Leyton and the August return at Derby, with Charles Kortright's pace causing Derbyshire's batsmen to hop around. Levi Wright, the 'grand old man' of Derbyshire cricket, said Kortright became aware that William Chatterton, who had a good record against Essex in this period, thought that the fast bowler threw. In a subsequent confrontation Kortright sent two balls screaming past Chatterton's nose and yorked him with a third. Wright also tells the tale of the Derbyshire bowler GG (George) Walker, who had an unhappy introduction to Kortright at Leyton in 1893. "The first time we met Kortright, Walker was not playing so that when we began to talk about the wonderful pace of this new bowler GG would not believe it. Essex had a fast bowler named Harry Pickett and GG would not take it in that anything could be faster. However, when we got to Leyton, his impressions were soon upset. He watched Kortright from the pavilion and at last with doubt went in to face him. He had only three balls. As he said on his return, the first was coming back over his head from the wicket-keeper when he got his bat down, the second was in the 'keeper's hands when he made his stroke and the third, he found, had knocked one of his stumps as far back as the wicket-keeper before he knew what to do. Then he admitted that Kortright (who finished with seven for 39) was fast."

When the teams met at Derby in August 1893 Harry Bagshaw and William Storer helped their side to a total of 262 and some fine left-arm fast medium bowling from Joe Hulme left the home team 160 to make in less than three hours. Wright and the left-handed Bagshaw batted superbly and the runs were obtained in 95 minutes for the loss of one wicket. The amateurs shared the same dressing room and Wright overheard Hugh Owen whisper to the Essex captain AP (Bunny) Lucas that Kortright had a sore heel but that if only they could make him forget it for about six overs the match was as good as won. A small bottle of champagne was produced and Kortright unleashed. "As I was going in first with Bagshaw I thought it policy to put Baggy on his guard. So I told him what had happened and we agreed to stick it, patiently for those six overs, if we could, and take all the advantages afterwards. That first half hour I shall never forget, for the way

Bagshaw dodged the fast rising ball and ducked when they went over his head proved that things were very lively. How I went on I can't remember but we survived and then the fun began." Wright was run out for 57 at 144 and Bagshaw left undefeated with 90, Kortright's figures being 13-0-59-0.

The competitive nature of these matches, even though they did not rank as first-class, is self-evident and there was a rift between the counties after this game. Hulme had been absent owing to a league engagement when Derbyshire batted and his subsequent return to take ten wickets in the two innings left Essex so incensed that no fixtures were arranged between the counties in 1894. Hampshire became Derbyshire's holiday opponents, although the matches at Southampton and Derby that summer were not deemed first-class. Derbyshire had fallen out with Essex over the Hulme incident; now, in 1894, they started falling out amongst themselves. Wright recalled that George Porter, their fast-medium, bowler, suffered from problems with 'hot feet'. "At the end of the day's play he could always be seen emerging from the dressing room to change his boots in the open air." It was a reference to this misfortune that brought to a head a serious quarrel between Chatterton and Davidson. Practically throughout the whole of one season, although they were together, almost daily, either at Lord's or in county cricket, they did not speak to each other unless circumstances compelled them."

"We had concluded a game in London, prior to the Southampton match, in such good time that some of the players were able to get across to the Isle of Wight to enjoy the Sunday on the island. During dinner it seems Davidson made a remark across the table to Porter, who took it so much to heart that he burst into tears, got up and left the room. Then the dramatics took place. Chatterton, head of the table, rose and addressed Davidson, laying down the terms under which they were to meet on and off the field for the future unless one desired a severe thrashing." Nevertheless Porter's experiences of the Hampshire fixtures were not all unhappy. Tom Soar and Harry Baldwin bowled unchanged in Hampshire's victory by an innings at Southampton in 1895, Derbyshire reversing the result in August with Porter returning a match analysis of 14-100.

Derbyshire, with Wright, Bagshaw, Chatterton, Storer, Walter Sugg, Sydney Evershed, the captain and the allrounder George Davidson, were a powerful batting side at this time; had the great days of the later fast bowlers Arnold Warren and Bill Bestwick coincided with this array then the county would have been a force in the Championship. As it was the death of Davidson at the age of 32 in February 1899 was a grievous blow and fortunes slumped. Hampshire, too, had a useful team in the 1890s, strengthened periodically by the availability of army officers who were stationed nearby. Captain EG Wynard was the finest of their regular batsmen; Major (later Brigadier-General) Robert Poore the most sensational. Poore, an attacking player with a powerful off drive, made full use of his height, 6ft 4in, at the crease and had been a prolific batsman in Indian cricket. He was posted to South Africa and represented that country against England in 1895-96, with little success. Arriving in England, Poore made his Hampshire debut in 1898 and the following year – his only full season - averaged 91.23 before military duties restricted him to occasional appearances.

Poore was prominent in a run-feast at Derby over the 1898 August Bank Holiday but had to play second fiddle to the home batsmen. The weather was glorious, the pitch, prepared by the long-serving groundsman Albert Widdowson, perfect and a crowd of 2,300 ringed the playing area by one o'clock on the Monday.

Evershed won the toss and opened the innings with Wright. Runs came freely, although Wright was troubled by the lob bowling of Quinton, yet another army officer. By lunch the score was 186 for two, with Wright and Storer in the middle. Wright went on to 134, Storer 100 and by the close of play the score was 477 for four, with Chatterton and Davidson together on 103 and 34 respectively. Next morning, before another crowd of 2,500, runs came quickly and Derbyshire reached 645, which remained their highest total until 2005. Chatterton, 142, and Davidson 108, added 176 for the fifth wicket which must have allowed some common ground for conversation. Evershed had asked Davidson to get out as quickly as possible as he felt there were already sufficient runs on the board but instead of hitting out the batsman continued gradually towards his century. Quinton emerged from the carnage with five for 93 and then completed an undefeated hundred as Hampshire followed on. Davidson, six for 42, had made early inroads during the first innings before Poore's unbeaten 121 enabled them to reach 240 and they easily saved the match.

Poore shredded county bowlers in 1899 but Derbyshire got off relatively lightly: he did not play at Whit and made 79 and 53 not out in an easy Hampshire victory at Derby. More often than not the games became confrontations of the lowly. In 1903 and 1905, for example, the Whitsuntide match brought Hampshire their only victory of the season, Hesketh Hesketh-Prichard, traveller, writer and fast bowler, taking ten wickets in the first and thirteen for 78 in the second. The August Bank Holiday week of 1908 saw one the most significant developments in Derbyshire's history, when on the second day of the Hampshire match at Derby (Tuesday 4 August) Will Taylor was appointed as secretary - a post he was to hold for 51 years.

After 1908 Derbyshire's opponents until the outbreak of war were Essex, friendship and fixtures having been restored in 1895. Their bowlers, still with nightmares about Percy Perrin's unbeaten 343 at Chesterfield in July 1904 in a match Derbyshire won, suffered further torture at Leyton in 1912 when Essex declared at 609 for four. Perrin (245) and Charles McGahey (150) dominated Whit Monday with a partnership of 312 for the third wicket. Essex had the better of these encounters and the last holiday game before the war was barely a contest. Derbyshire made only 31 and 94, Bert Tremlin, who performed a hat trick, and Johnny Douglas bowling unchanged.

Bowlers had tended to dominate Essex's earlier holiday matches against Leicestershire from 1894 to1900, Walter Mead, Pickett (all ten at Leyton in 1895), Kortright and Leicestershire's Pougher taking plenty of wickets. Kent then provided more local opposition for Essex, Perrin making two hundreds in 1901 and Essex winning by an innings at Leyton in 1902. Hampshire engaged in derby games against Sussex in 1909 and 1910 and Kent in 1911-12 before meeting Middlesex in the last two pre-war seasons. There was time for Jack Hearne and Patsy Hendren to delight the Southampton crowd in August 1913, whilst the following year's Lord's fixture at Whitsuntide saw play start on the Saturday.

Chapter Twelve
Best of Enemies

Neighbourhood rivalry forms an ancient cricketing tradition almost as old as the game itself and such matches are often cornerstones of the county and club fixture list. It took time for these to become established over the holiday periods, although by the outbreak of the 1914-18 war a pattern was emerging.

A typical example was Leicestershire, who met Derbyshire on a few occasions before being upgraded to first-class in 1894. They then began a series of fixtures against Essex with a victory at Leyton, the game being a triumph for their allrounder Dick Pougher. He was a more than useful batsman but it was as a medium-paced bowler with a high delivery and wicked break back that he became best known. In the 1894 Whitsuntide game at Leyton he made an undefeated 109 and took six for 29 and eight for 60. A year later it was the turn of Arthur Woodcock, who, for a time, was considered to be the fastest bowler in the country after Kortright. This was the match in which Pickett took all ten in Leicestershire's first innings, earning himself a collection of £20 on Whit Monday. Leicestershire struggled from the start, Mat Chapman labouring for 70 minutes over 14 but Woodcock made 20 in boundary strokes and the total reached 111. Six of Pickett's victims were bowled, four caught and he operated unchanged to return 27-11-32-10, Mead conceding 50 runs in 21 overs and Kortright 24 in six. *Cricket*'s contemporary account recorded: "Essex supporters took advantage of the Bank Holiday on Monday to visit Leyton to the number of about 8,000. The feature of the day was the remarkable achievement of Pickett. Though helped by the ground, which was very fast and somewhat fiery, his success was due to grand bowling." Woodcock and Pougher struck back with five wickets apiece and although Kortright took eight for 63 in the second innings, Chapman made 56 to leave Essex 199 for victory. Woodcock's pace prevailed with seven for 62 and Leicestershire won by 75 runs. In 1896, Walter Mead's slow-medium off breaks brought him nine for 75 in Leicestershire's second innings and a match analysis of 14-132 at Leyton and it was Kortright's turn at Grace Road in 1897 with five for 58 and six for 86.

Kortright then demonstrated his skill with the bat in 1898. The Whitsun game was ruined by rain after a record attendance of 10,724 packed the Leyton ground on the Monday and during the August Bank Holiday match at Leicester Kortright (112) and Herbert Carpenter (133), helped Essex to a total of 515. Kortright was undefeated with 60 at the close of Monday's play, when Essex were 413 for seven, and he completed his hundred on the second day. His two wickets in the Leicestershire first innings cost 101, and it was the final day crowd which was treated to the full, explosive effect: six for 41 in the follow-on, five clean bowled, as Essex won by an innings.

The Grace Road spectators saw the developing power of the Essex batting in the August match of 1899. Frederick Fane (207) and Perrin (132) added 235 for the second wicket and McGahey weighed in with 99. Their total of 673 brought victory by an innings, despite a typically determined hundred from Albert

Knight. There was a similar margin of victory in 1900 at Leyton, when it was McGahey's turn to make hay with 184. After Essex moved on to matches against Kent, Leicestershire filled vacant dates with fixtures against the touring Philadelphians, the Australians (in 1902 at Aylestone Road the pace of Ernest Jones reduced them to 51 all out before lunch on Whit Monday), the South Africans and some games against London County. Leicestershire had moved from Grace Road to a new home at Aylestone Road in 1901. Grace Road, which was served only by horse trams, was too far from the centre of Leicester and the three mainline railway stations, Midland, Central and Belgrave Road. Aylestone Road was only half-a-mile from the centre and there was a healthy increase in attendances.

In 1905 Leicestershire found a soul mate in the newly promoted Northamptonshire and the gaps in their fixture list were now more or less filled permanently. These may have lacked the glamour of the Roses encounters or Nottinghamshire-Surrey but they provided some fine cricket. Aylestone Road on August Bank Holiday 1905 was an early example with three innings completed on the Monday, Leicestershire winning on the second day. The South African bowlers Schwarz and Vogler proved too much for the home batsmen in a Whitsun break from the Northamptonshire fixture during the googly summer of 1907 but there was a particularly good match at Aylestone Road in August. The home side needed 163 to win in the final innings and half the side were out for 112, George Thompson's sharp fast-medium bowling proving a handful. Two were needed when the ninth wicket fell and it took a leg bye to settle the issue. Leicestershire won by an innings at Northampton in 1908 after Jack King and the left-handed Sammy Coe had shared a fourth wicket partnership of 249, the Whit Monday score rising from 43 for three to 381-6. Northamptonshire won by a similar margin in 1909 and honours were generally even.

An exception was 1912 when Northamptonshire surprised the cricket world by finishing runners-up. They gained a comfortable win by nine wickets over Leicestershire at Whitsuntide, the first time they had beaten them at home, and were poised for victory in the return at Leicester. Sydney Smith performed a hat trick and took seven for 47 with his slow left-arm bowling, Leicestershire being dismissed for 96. Northamptonshire closed their innings 115 ahead and the home side had lost six wickets for 96 when the game ended. The wet August was crucial. Rain also deprived Lancashire of a win in the Roses match at Old Trafford: had both games finished as expected then Northamptonshire would have been champions and not Yorkshire. But the moment passed and the abiding memory of 1914 was Coe's unbeaten 252 in the Whitsuntide match at Aylestone Road. He batted only 240 minutes with a six, a five and 39 fours, Leicestershire reaching 453. George Geary took six for 75 in the first innings and the fast bowler Alec Skelding, of later thick-lensed umpiring fame, six for 85 in a 214-run victory. This was followed by a narrow Northamptonshire win in the August match. In this they were helped by Leicestershire batting a man short in the second innings, one of their amateurs, the solicitor-soldier Captain Aubrey Sharp, having been summoned to his regiment on the outbreak of war. The crowd seated on forms around the County Ground shouted: "You'll be back in a fortnight." He wasn't, although he survived the war. Sharp recalled: "We only wanted 84 to win so I left them it to them. Actually we lost by four runs. The point is I left my boots and bat behind. They were handed to me when we went back to Northampton in 1919." William Wilson, of Billing Road, Northampton, also left memories of this match. He recalled George Thompson's windmilling action, how his arm used to go over twice before he delivered the ball and that there was no food on the ground except for a wooden hut near the bowling green and an old man selling 'George Hirst' toffee. When Leicestershire played, there would be a special atmosphere of leg-pulling and banter, with the home crowd calling the visitors 'woolly backs' because they made vests in Leicester.

If Northamptonshire's admission to the Championship solved Leicestershire's holiday problems, the arrival of Worcestershire in 1899 filled a West Midlands' gap and provided another derby fixture. Warwickshire enjoyed a rich holiday list with matches against Kent, the 1896 and 1899 Australians and Yorkshire before meeting their neighbours. Rain restricted play to two hours before lunch on Whit Tuesday in 1899 but a series began in 1900 which was only ended by the war, with results more or less evenly balanced. There was an early controversy. In the August match at Edgbaston in 1901, the visiting wicket-keeper Tom Straw was given out for obstructing the field – two years after a similar dismissal at Worcester. On the first occasion – not a holiday game – Straw hit the ball into the air and started to run, bumping into Glover as he tried to catch the ball. The 1901 incident involved Dick Lilley, Warwickshire's wicket-keeper, who was at the crease.

Such contests between two unprepossessing sides which generally finished in mid-table did not set the blood racing. Indeed, the 1907 August fixture produced some dull cricket in showery weather. But there was much to commend: hundreds from the artisans such as Sep Kinneir, Willie Quaife, Dick Pearson and Fred Bowley (seven in all against Warwickshire) and glimpses of high quality from Lilley, RE Foster and Ted Arnold. At his best Arnold was one of the best allrounders in the country. In addition to making three hundreds against Warwickshire he virtually won the 1903 August game at Edgbaston single-handedly with a match analysis of 13-79. Six years later he followed an innings of 200 not out with seven for 44 to bowl his side to an innings victory at Edgbaston. Warwickshire were dismissed for 141 and Arnold and William Burns added 393 for the fifth wicket in four and a quarter hours of phenomenal scoring.

The Fosters were somewhat overshadowed, RE making a hundred at Edgbaston in 1901 and HK 215 in Worcestershire's total of 556 at New Road in August 1908 being notable exceptions. In the latter game Willie Quaife saved the day for Warwickshire with an undefeated 189 in the second innings, the three days producing 1,351 runs for the loss of 28 wickets. Reginald Erskine 'Tip' Foster, tall, slim and lithe, was one of the great stylists of the age of gold, alongside Palairet and Spooner. His triumphs graced stages far beyond New Road: 171 for Oxford in the 1900 Varsity match, two separate hundreds for the Gentlemen at Lord's ten days later and 287 for England against Australia at Sydney in December 1903. Business restricted his appearances after 1901, except when he captained England in the 1907 series against South Africa, and he could not afford the time away to lead the team in the 1907/08 Ashes games. Thus the appearances of this greatest of the Foster clan came to be cherished, such as 1906 when he could spare only the second week in August for cricket, the matches against Warwickshire at Worcester and Somerset at Taunton. He scored 35 in the first match and 198 and 10 in the second but his first appearance of the season inspired his colleagues. Worcestershire made 633 against their rivals, WB Burns 125, Harry Foster 124, and the wicket-keeper GF Wheldon 89 not out, the match being drawn.

The unrelated Frank Foster was appointed captain of Warwickshire in January 1911 at the age of 22. A fine left-arm fast medium bowler and a forcing right-hand batsman he emerged in 1908 and impressed in the Gentlemen-Players matches two years later. In 1911 he proved a match winner in Warwickshire's Championship summer, achieving the double and heading both sets of averages. Yet they looked nothing like title winners early in the season, defeat by Worcestershire at New Road leaving them ninth in the table. Here Pearson's 155 meant they needed 300 to win on a pitch helpful to bowlers and they went down by 116 runs. By the time of the August return at Edgbaston they were in contention and this was reflected by a Monday gate of nearly 19,000. Fast bowler Frank Field was forced to leave the field on Wednesday because of sunstroke, Arnold once again proving a thorn in Warwickshire's side with 87 ensuring a draw.

Frank Foster dominated the matches in the closing years of the Golden Age. Match figures of 11-131 helped bring victory at Dudley in the 1912 Whitsuntide game, a season when Worcestershire finished bottom of the table. Then at Dudley on Whit Tuesday 1914 he made an unbeaten 305 in some four and a half hours with a five and 44 fours, declaring Warwickshire's innings at 645 for seven. He came in at 197 for three with his side already nine runs in the lead, scoring his runs out of 448 made while he was at the crease. On the final day Maurice Foster – one of the seven brothers to play for Worcestershire – made 51. Frank Foster, wicketless in the match, turned to Frank Field with the score on 85 for four and he took six for two in 52 deliveries – three bowled, two caught and bowled and one leg before. It brought victory by an innings and 321 runs. A low scoring return at Edgbaston was left drawn, no play being possible until 4pm on the final day.

In the face of the developing county tradition, the tourists sometimes had to make do, to the delight of cricket followers away from the main centres. In 1902, for example, the Australians attracted an August holiday crowd of 10,000 when they met a combination of Glamorgan and Wiltshire at Cardiff, with similar attendances three years later for a game against South Wales. In 1907 the South Africans found themselves at Leicester and Dublin and in 1911 India spent their Bank Holidays at Cardiff and Perth.

The classic holiday fixtures for the tourists were in 1912 when the Triangular Tournament was held, with Australia and South Africa sending teams to England. Poor weather and a dispute which weakened the Australian side contributed to the tournament's lack of success but the first match at Old Trafford over Whitsuntide left its mark on Test history. Kelleway and Bardsley made hundreds for Australia and Faulkner an unbeaten 122 for South Africa. With three wickets remaining the Springboks needed only 34 runs to avoid the follow on but the leg spinner Tom Matthews finished off the innings with a hat trick. South Africa had made 70 for three in their second innings when Matthews struck again with a second hat trick. Curiously they were the only wickets he took in the match – two bowled, two leg before and two caught and bowled.

When the teams met again during August Bank Holiday the match at Trent Bridge was ruined by the weather. South Africa made 266 for eight on the Monday but only 2,365 paid for admission, most people feeling the charges were too high. The South Africans then had their best day of the tournament, carrying their total to 329 and dismissing Australia for 219 but continuous rain ruled out play on the final day.

Chapter Thirteen
End of the Golden Era

No county epitomised the spirit in which cricket was played during the second period of the Golden Age more than Kent. Attractive and enterprising, they were champions in 1906, 1909, 1910 and 1913 and runners-up in 1908 and 1911.

For a decade it was a team of superb balance but it took time to rise from the bottom of the table in 1895 to its strongest position since the days of Mynn, Felix and Hillyer. A great deal of credit went to Captain William McCanlis, coach at the Tonbridge Nursery which produced Colin Blythe, James Seymour, Edward 'Punter' Humphreys, Wally Hardinge, Jack Hubble and Frank Woolley. Early in Canterbury Week 1896, the Kent committee met in Lord Harris's tent and Frank Marchant, the county captain, proposed they should negotiate with Tonbridge Cricket Club for some young players to take part in matches at the Angel Ground. Thus the nursery was born. Seven players, Blythe, Arthur Fielder, William Fairservice, Seymour, Humphreys, Woolley and the wicket-keeper Fred Huish were regular members of the four Championship-winning teams and Jack Mason, Kenneth Hutchings and Edward Dillon played in three of them. Skippered in turn by Cloudesley Marsham, Dillon and Lionel Troughton, Kent were more than a match for the best with Fielder's pace, the left-arm spin of Blythe and Woolley and a blend of amateur style from Cuthbert Burnup and Hutchings allied to steady professionalism from Seymour, Humphreys and Hardinge coming to the fore at various periods.

Such a team attracted the holiday crowds but Kent had gone through a lean period, despite the presence of the three Hearne brothers, George, a left-arm bowler and left-handed batsman, Frank, a right-handed batsman and useful round-arm bowler and Alec, who developed from a leg break and, later off break bowler into a sound batsman. The Hearnes' father, 'old George Hearne', had been groundsman at Catford Bridge where Kent played their early home matches but it was Canterbury which provided the sons with one of their greatest triumphs. They were all in the Kent side which was the only county to defeat the 1884 Australians. Kent were dismissed for 169 but Alec Hearne struck back with five for 36 and after Lord Harris (60) and Frank Hearne (45) steered the home side to a total of 213, the tourists were dismissed for 109, James Wootton taking three for 21 and Alec Hearne two for 30. The Australians returned to Canterbury during the August Bank Holiday of 1886 (they lost by ten wickets after George Hearne made an unbeaten 53 and Wootton took ten for 100 in the match), in 1888 and 1890, Kent succumbing each time to the bowling of Turner and Ferris, and 1893, when Alec Hearne, five for 35, reduced them to an all out total of 60 in their second innings, Kent winning by 36 runs.

Kent spent their Whitsuntides at Bramall Lane from 1884 to 1887. Alec Hearne, then only 21, took five for 13 and eight for 35 as they cruised to an eight-wicket victory in two days in 1885, only for Bobby Peel and Tom Emmett to avenge the defeat two years later. A crowd of 6,000 watched the second day's play, when Yorkshire, needing 105 to win, lost five men for 42, the hard-hitting George

Ulyett being run out for 21. The Hon. MB Hawke then scored 36 not out, striking a six to end a game which Yorkshire won by four wickets. It was a summer of sunshine and hard pitches in 1887 and at Canterbury Yorkshire ended Monday's play on 305 for one, Ulyett making 124. Louis Hall and Fred Lee also reached three figures and the innings closed at 559 in 610 minutes. Kent had to follow on but Frank Hearne, although in pain from an injury, sored 144 and saved the game.

Walter Wright's left-arm swerve came to the fore in Kent victories at Old Trafford in 1888 and against Middlesex at Canterbury in 1889 but Lancashire took their revenge with an innings victory in two days in 1890. It was now that another Hearne, Walter, entered the Kent lists. He was a cousin of the trio and the brother of Jack Hearne, the great Middlesex and England bowler. Walter Hearne's career as a medium paced bowler was to be cut short through injury but he enjoyed a remarkable match at Manchester in 1893. Although William Patterson was unbeaten with 82, Kent could only reach 191, Briggs taking eight for 87. He then hit 66 in Lancashire's reply of 166, Hearne 7 for 74. Mold struck back and Lancashire were left 195 for victory but Hearne, eight for 40 and 15 for 114 in the match, bowled his side to an 80-run victory. After Walter Hearne's career finished in 1896 he became Kent's scorer until his death in 1925 at the age of 61.

Warwickshire provided Kent with holiday opposition for a couple of seasons before they settled down to a home and away series with Lancashire from 1896 to 1900. These were unhappy days for Kent and they failed to win any of the ten matches, although eight were left unfinished. Jack Mason and the future Canon William Rashleigh made hundreds at Canterbury in 1896 but MacLaren saved the day with his unbeaten 226. A year later, 20,000 people watched Whit Monday's play at Old Trafford but it rained for the next two days. Lancashire rubbed it in with an innings victory at Canterbury, when MacLaren made 244 and Briggs returned 13-135. There was more Manchester misery in 1898 when 6,000 turned up on Whit Monday, play being restricted to 25 minutes and little more on the remaining two days. At least Alec Hearne enjoyed better weather for his benefit at Canterbury, making 80 not out and 74 not out, Johnny Tyldesley charming the crowd with 127. But Kent seemed cursed by the Lancashire weather, no play being possible at all over the 1899 Whitsuntide. They gave Lancashire a fright at Canterbury, Mason and Burnup making runs in a total of 305. A declaration left Lancashire needing 318 but Ward dropped anchor for four hours and the match was drawn. At last the Old Trafford weather relented for a late Whitsuntide in 1900, although Mason must have had doubts about his decision to bat first when three wickets were down for 13. Burnup and Mason (68) then added 110 before an old Cambridge Blue Thomas Perkins came to the middle. The holiday crowd of 17,000 were treated to a partnership of 221 for the fifth wicket in 110 minutes before Perkins was caught off Briggs for 88. By the close Kent were 401 for six, Burnup having hit 28 fours in making 200 out of 390. The match was drawn.

Rain restricted Monday's play to 50 minutes when the teams met at Canterbury but during the next couple of days Blythe made his first impact on Canterbury Week. The professionals found it difficult to get into the Kent side in those days; for example nine amateurs took the field against Lancashire in 1899, Alec Hearne and Huish being the exceptions. But Blythe was exceptional. He took 114 wickets in 1900, his breakthrough season, as Kent rose to third. Arguments would rage as to who was the better slow left-arm bowler, Rhodes or Blythe – or

Peate, Peel and Briggs, for that matter - and they were generally inconclusive. 'Charlie' Blythe loved playing his violin and his artistic, imaginative temperament meant that he ultimately found cricket a strain at the highest level but more than 2,500 first-class wickets at 16.80, 100 in Tests, are telling statistics. At Canterbury in 1900 he took six for 40 and five for 32 in Lancashire's innings of 152 and 82 for eight, numbering Ward, Johnny Tyldesley and MacLaren among his victims. Kent had discovered a gem and Blythe would enjoy many more days of success at the St Lawrence ground, notably nine for 67 in the Essex first innings on August Bank Holiday Monday 1903. Johnny Douglas hit back for Essex with five for 63 but Kent won by ten wickets. By now Kent had appointed a manager, Tom Pawley, who, under the jurisdiction of the Canterbury Week sub-committee, was responsible for organising the Week.

Canterbury was the perfect setting for Kent's charge to the title in 1906. The weather was almost perfect and there were record attendances on four of the days. Burnup, Blaker and Marsham made hundreds in a total of 568 against Sussex and the rate of 100 runs an hour was maintained in the second match of the Week against Lancashire, both games being won by an innings. A year later Kent won by an innings at Hove, running up a big score and then turning Fielder and Blythe loose on a rain-affected pitch. They fielded nine amateurs at Canterbury in 1907 but it was a Sussex pro Robert Relf who had most cause to remember the match. He was unbeaten with 67 in the first innings and made 210 in his team's second attempt.

Kent were outstanding in 1909, winning 18, ten by an innings, of their 30 matches and losing only two. Middlesex, their latest holiday opponents, were caught in the whirlwind. They were routed at Canterbury in 1909 and at Lord's in the Whitsun game of 1910, Dillon, Woolley and Day made hundreds. Kent needed only 40 minutes on Wednesday morning to complete an innings victory. Fortune favoured them at Canterbury: 393 for seven on the Monday and then rain in the night altering the nature of the pitch to such an extent that another innings success was recorded, en route to another title. Kent then took part in a remarkable match at Southampton in the 1911 Whitsun. Hardinge made two hundreds and Kent, who did not enforce the follow on, set Hampshire an unlikely 567 to win. Charles Fry, now playing for Hampshire after taking over the training ship *Mercury* at Hamble on Southampton Water, made 104, Philip Mead got 73 and Hampshire finished on 463 for eight, Remnant and Newman sharing an unbroken partnership of 105 for the ninth wicket. The three days produced 1,446 runs. Fry's appearances for Hampshire may have been spasmodic but he entertained the holiday crowds: 123 and 112 in the Canterbury heat of 1911 were followed by 143 at Southampton in 1912 when he shared a partnership of 246 for the third wicket with Mead, who made 106. Only the two wicket-keepers did not bowl in another high-scoring game. Fry, however, was not particularly popular at Canterbury. During Hampshire's second innings of the 1911 game he showed his displeasure when Blythe, with Kent badly needing a breakthrough, tossed the ball up to him. Fry effectively accused him of cheating by throwing the ball up into the sun. The crowd booed and Lord Harris had to get involved before the row fizzled out.

Kent treated their followers to a variety of holiday opponents between 1894 and 1914 - Warwickshire 1894 and 1895, Lancashire 1896 to 1900, Essex 1901 to 1905, Sussex 1906 to 1908, Middlesex 1909 and 1910 and Hampshire 1911 and 1912. They performed a double over Sussex in 1913 but had to be satisfied with a draw in the 1914 Whitsun fixture at Hove. That took place early in June and by the time of the return at Canterbury war clouds were placing cricket in perspective.

The heir to the throne of Austria-Hungary, Franz Ferdinand, was assassinated at Sarajevo on 28 June and a month later Austria declared war on Serbia. By noon on Bank Holiday Saturday 1 August Germany and Russia were at war. The Germans, who next declared war on France, demanded free passage through Belgium. The Belgians refused and this brought a change of mood in London. People had not wanted the country involved in a Continental war; indeed an antiwar demonstration was planned for Sunday in Trafalgar Square. After the news from Belgium, the demonstration faded away and on Sunday afternoon crowds in Downing Street, called for war. The next day, August Bank Holiday Monday, was, in most places, a beautiful, cloudless, summer's day and cricket followers made their way to Old Trafford and The Oval, to Canterbury and Southampton, Edgbaston, Northampton, Derby and Bristol.

On Tuesday morning the Germans crossed the Belgian border. The British Cabinet met at 11am and sent the Germans an ultimatum which would expire at midnight. At Derby, an army officer, Captain Richard Baggallay, led Derbyshire against Essex and was at the crease when a telegraph boy brought out a message ordering him to mobilise. "I showed the telegram to the Essex captain, JWHT Douglas, and we agreed that we must abandon the match unless it ended that day." By 5.30pm Essex had completed an innings victory and at nine o'clock, the nation's leaders assembled in the Cabinet Room. Midnight came and went and, with no word from Berlin, Great Britain was at war with Germany.

Cricket continued. Yorkshire won at Old Trafford, the match ending early on Wednesday. There were close finishes at Bristol and Northampton, with narrow wins for the home teams and the games at The Oval and Worcester were draws. At Canterbury, Vine made 140 and Blythe took six for 107 in the Sussex first innings of 384. A declaration left Kent 130 minutes to make 172 and at 105 for four they needed 67 in an hour but although Seymour batted well they lost by 34 runs, George Cox taking six for 45. Kent gained an innings victory over Northamptonshire in the second Canterbury match but, shorn of most of its social functions, the Week was a financial disaster. Attendances were meagre and the Old Stagers' performances and the two balls were cancelled.

So the August Bank Holiday matches which began in the shadow of conflict ended with the nation at war. The season dragged on, until WG Grace published a letter in *The Sportsman* of 27 August urging closure. In England there would be no first-class cricket for four seasons. The game flourished in the leagues and there was an occasional holiday fixture: Hobbs making 126 for Army Service Corps at Catford on Whit Monday 1915, for example, and there was an England-Dominions fixture at The Oval in 1918. But for many – and these included 34 county cricketers – who never returned from the killing fields, 1914 was the last cricket they would ever see. RE Foster had already succumbed to diabetes in May 1914 and he was followed by WG and Victor Trumper the following year. Among the war dead were Kenneth Hutchings, Major Booth, WB Burns, the South African googly bowlers GC White and RO Schwarz and, at Ypres in November 1917, Colin Blythe.

Some found solace in the memories of the holiday games, none more so than the Canterbury Weeks. Here a memorial to Blythe was unveiled in August 1919 during a match between the Band of Brothers and Kent Club & Ground. The inscription read: "He was unsurpassed among the famous bowlers of the period and beloved by his fellow cricketers."

Chapter Fourteen
Cornerstones of the Season

Golden Age euphoria had masked an unpalatable truth. Amidst the style and glamour which attracted huge attendances on summer days some counties, such as Gloucestershire and Worcestershire, faced a continual battle for survival.

Their cause was not helped by the power of the Big Six – Yorkshire, Lancashire, Nottinghamshire, Middlesex, Surrey and Kent. The Championship was their playground. During the first 42 seasons of the official competition from 1890 to 1935, Yorkshire won 18 titles, Lancashire and Surrey each won seven, Kent four, Middlesex three and Nottinghamshire two. The exception was Warwickshire in 1911. Derbyshire won in 1936 but the status quo was restored until Glamorgan upset the apple cart in 1948. Of the smaller fry, Worcestershire were bottom four times in the 1920s, Glamorgan thrice, Derbyshire twice and Northamptonshire once. Leicestershire, Warwickshire and Somerset were seldom far away.

Increasingly, the poorer counties turned to amateurs, many of indifferent quality. The holiday fixtures took place when amateurs, some of them schoolmasters, were available. In 1919 Somerset and Gloucestershire each fielded six amateurs in the Whit fixture at Taunton and there were 13 in the return at Bristol, seven of them in the Somerset team. A Hampshire side at Lord's contained seven amateurs, including three army captains, a major and a reverend. At Leyton in the Whitsuntide match Essex and Kent fielded 12 amateurs. Such combinations were far from unusual during the period, Somerset and Gloucestershire pushing the total up to 15 at Bristol in August 1921. Ernie Robson and Archie Young were the only professionals in the Somerset team.

Random amateurs with fancy, coloured headgear but little ability (although Kent and Middlesex offered exceptions in quality) cut no ice with pros who had to give up places and match money to accommodate them. Conversely, for some amateurs who were genuinely first-class, it was, perhaps, no more than a single, full season, a break between public school and university and a teaching career. Others found it a pleasant diversion, not dissimilar to country house cricket as the sons of the wealthy followed their pre-ordained path as heirs to the estate, the church or the army according to seniority. The policy saved money but the lack of continuity often upset the balance of the team. As time passed, the selection of an amateur became more a question of merit than cost-cutting and it should be recognised that, between the wars, the breed produced some the finest captains in the history of the Championship. GR Jackson, JWHT Douglas, BH Lyon, Lord Tennyson, APF Chapman, FT Mann, AW Carr, J Daniell, PGH Fender, AER Gilligan, MK Foster, MFS Jewell – the initials are evocative of a long-ago era but synonymous with positive and sometimes innovative cricket.

Playing hours in 1919 were longer as the counties experimented with two-day matches. The joy of a return to normality on the cricket field after the years of conflict was tempered by a feeling of dissatisfaction over the new arrangements. The day's play went on until 7.30pm, by which time the cricketers were weary and many spectators had headed for home and the evening meal. At least it got the domestic season going, the weather was generally fine and Yorkshire won a Championship that was open until the final day.

Worcestershire's absence - beset by financial problems they arranged only nine first-class friendly matches before returning to the competition in 1920 - meant a change to the holiday programme, Derbyshire meeting Warwickshire and coming from behind to win at Edgbaston after some fine bowling by Bill Bestwick. The defeat was avenged by Warwickshire at Derby in August despite another prodigious effort from Bestwick, countered by a century by Len Bates. "The old cricket feud between Lancashire and Yorkshire broke out again at Old Trafford yesterday in a contest that went on through the long day with unfailing keenness," wrote Neville Cardus at Whitsuntide. Lancashire won at Manchester and the return at Bramall Lane was drawn. Names which would dominate the titanic Roses struggles of the 1920s rang out; hundreds for Harry Makepeace and Charlie Hallows and for Yorkshire's Herbert Sutcliffe and Percy Holmes, who shared an opening partnership of 253 in the August match. Cecil Parkin took 14 for 123 at Manchester and Ernest Tyldesley made two half-centuries at Sheffield.

The war delayed the 24-year-old Sutcliffe's entry into county cricket, when, after demobilisation from a commission in the Green Howards, he was given a place in the Yorkshire side. Possessing courage, concentration and a flawless technique, his defensive mastery became a byword but he could score quickly when required and was a fine hooker of fast bowling. Sutcliffe, who was to form England's best-ever opening partnership with Jack Hobbs, had a rare temperament which allowed him to focus on one problem at a time and while he might not have the artistry and elegance of Hobbs or the majesty of Hammond he was among the finest of batsmen. By contrast Percy Holmes was 31 when his association with Sutcliffe began, his career having begun, albeit with little success, in 1913. Holmes possessed a wider range of strokes and was a more carefree batsman than his partner yet he was the perfect foil as 69 opening partnership of more than a century testify. At Sheffield they had a hundred up by the end of the first day in reply to Lancashire's 124, continuing on Monday to 253, made in three hours.

There was heavy scoring, too, in the other great holiday fixture between Nottinghamshire and Surrey. George Gunn made 169 and 185 not out at Trent Bridge, sharing an unbroken stand of 233 in the second innings with his brother John, who made 62 and 111 not out. Hobbs was in the runs at Nottingham and The Oval, both matches being drawn. The 14-year-old Harold Larwood walked to Trent Bridge – a round trip of 24 miles – especially to see Hobbs bat and the future Derbyshire and England all rounder Leslie Townsend, then just 16, saw his first county game. "George Gunn was my hero that day and has been ever since. What a glorious start for my first view of county cricket – a lovely sunny day on the beautiful Trent Bridge ground, and to see George walking down the wicket to fast bowler Bill Hitch."

No county enjoyed the first post-Great War holiday fixture more than Middlesex. During the Whitsun match against Hampshire at Lord's, Greville Stevens, 18 and still at University College School, took seven for 104 in the first innings and had a match analysis of 10-136 with his leg breaks and googlies on his debut. He was to recall that if Harry Lee had not grassed a sitter he would have had eight for 80. Middlesex amassed 608 for seven declared, Jack Hearne 218 not out and Patsy Hendren 201 adding 325 in 175 minutes for the fourth wicket. 'Young Jack'

Hearne was a cousin of JT, an impeccable and stylish right-hand batsman who demonstrated artistry in placing the ball and combined this with a sound defence. Ill health turned him into a more cautious batsman than he might have been but he bowled leg breaks and googlies off a very short run with sufficient success to record five doubles of 1,000 runs and 100 wickets. His great friend Elias Hendren – Patsy because of his Irish ancestry – was a short and stocky right-hand batsman who drove and cut powerfully and showed great courage in hooking fast bowling. They began their partnership on Whit Monday, Hearne ending the day on 53 and Hendren 62. Alec Kennedy toiled away for 55 overs, emerging from the carnage with seven for 202, but it was Middlesex's match. Hampshire regained some self-respect at Southampton, Mead, Brown and Hill getting into the nineties as the home side established a first-innings lead of 151. Harry Lee, one of three cricketing brothers (Frank and Jack each played for Middlesex and Somerset) posted an unbeaten hundred as the game meandered to a draw.

In the West Country Somerset defeated Gloucestershire at Taunton during Whitsun, albeit not without baffling some absent followers. The Rippon twins, Sydney and Dudley, both played for the county with reasonable success as solid openers, although Dudley finished soon after the war because of ill health. Sydney was on sick leave from the Civil Service, where he was employed by the Inland Revenue, and consequently was unavailable for selection – or, at least, he should have been. When a player withdrew, he was replaced by one S Trimmell, who made 92 and 58 not out. People following the match in the newspapers were baffled because nobody seemed to have heard of Trimmell. *The Western Daily Press* correspondent was not fooled: "S Trimmell, who is far better known facially to Somerset cricketers and supporters than he is to the general public, played in capital style. Although his name is new, he is by no means a stranger to county cricket." Trimmel was none other than Sydney Rippon, as his son the Rt Hon Geoffrey Rippon QC, MP explained to David Foot: "The fact is that my father was on sick leave from the Civil Service at the time and shouldn't have been playing. He was needed by the county, so he appeared on the scorecard and in the press under his grandmother's name. Everyone treated it as a huge joke when it emerged what had happened. I suppose today there'd be an absolute furore."

The Bristol return was drawn while Leicestershire, boosted by hundreds from Aubrey Sharp and Arthur Mounteney, drew with Northamptonshire at the County Ground. The visiting batsmen piled up the runs when the teams reconvened at Aylestone Road, Hawtin making 129 not out in a total of 407 for five declared, although Leicestershire survived. Rawlins Hawtin, a sound right-hand batsman, could find time for only 85 first-class matches between 1908 and 1930, mainly because of business commitments, but, as a staunch committee member, he more or less kept the club going single-handedly during the Second World War. Kent's matches against Essex produced plenty of runs: two hundreds for Perrin and one for Jack Russell at Leyton and another for Russell and an undefeated 172 for Wally Hardinge, who carried his bat in the face of some fine seam bowling from Douglas at Canterbury. The matches, like so many in 1919, were drawn. Sussex, the odd one out among the counties, met the Australian Imperial Forces at Hove, coming close to victory at Whitsuntide but suffering a beating in August, largely as a result of the bowling of Gregory and Collins.

With the Championship restored to three day matches in 1920 the holiday fixtures approached perpetuity. Nottinghamshire-Surrey, Lancashire-Yorkshire,

Leicestershire-Northamptonshire and Gloucestershire-Somerset had become established before the 1914-18 war. Now they were joined by Derbyshire-Warwickshire, Essex-Worcestershire, Hampshire-Kent and Middlesex-Sussex in what would become cornerstones of the season. There were to be occasional variations. Combinations of Gloucestershire, Hampshire, Kent and Somerset changed the menu in half-a-dozen years between the wars and the old Warwickshire-Worcestershire rivalry was restored in 1936 and 1937 when Derbyshire met Essex for a couple of years. Such anomalies were generally isolated and did not last.

Chapter Fifteen
Lord's and the Seaside

Around 14,000 people made the journey to Lord's on Whit Monday with more than the usual degree of anticipation in 1920. Middlesex had started their Championship programme with a resounding victory over Warwickshire. Sussex had done even better, winning their opening three games to arrive at headquarters brimming with confidence.

Although this was to prove something of a false dawn they were a strong and attractive side and to add piquancy to the fixture Monday was the second day. Rowland Ryder, the secretary of Warwickshire, had proposed that the starting days for all county matches should be changed from Mondays and Thursdays to Saturdays and Wednesdays. The benefits were becoming apparent. Many people, otherwise deprived by the Monday beginnings, were now able to see all or part of the first two days of the Bank Holiday fixtures. Thus on Whit Saturday, Sussex were bowled out for 232 by four o'clock, chiefly through the seemingly innocuous slow medium off breaks of Harry Lee, who took five for 21 in 11 overs. Lee then ventured out with his captain Pelham Warner to begin the Middlesex innings.

In 1920 Plum Warner was in his 47th year. Middlesex had had a poor time of it in 1919 and he had considered stepping down but was persuaded to give it another summer, although he announced that this would be the last one. The team had developed into a powerful batting side, with Warner, Lee, Hearne and Hendren and the amateurs Nigel Haig and Frank Mann capable of making big scores. Hearne, now relying mainly on off breaks and an occasional cutter after a finger injury in 1919, and the new, giant fast bowler Jack Durston were the mainstays of the attack but Lee, Greville Stevens and the fast medium Haig added support. There was usually a sprinkling of amateurs to add colour in more ways than one, as Ronald Mason wrote: "…the slight, spare figure of Warner leading the half-dozen amateurs down the pavilion steps, Harlequin, Free Forester, I Zingari caps abounding, the little animated knot of professionals fanning out obediently from the gate of the rabbit hutch."

By the close of Saturday's play Warner and Lee were still together with the score on 156 and Sussex found no respite on the second day. Lee made a century before departing at 241, Warner going on to 139 before edging Arthur Gilligan to the wicket-keeper 43 runs later. Haig, in his first innings of the season, struck 20 fours in a dazzling 131 in 110 minutes, overshadowing Hearne, who was still there on 116 as the fourth century maker of the innings when Warner declared at 543 for four. A demoralised Sussex were then bowled out by Lee, six for 47 and 11 for 68 in the match, Middlesex winning by an innings and 130 runs at 6.45pm on Whit Monday.

Such fixtures between Middlesex and Sussex saw a lasting relationship developing out of an earlier flirtation. Hendren's first big match hundred had been made on a similar occasion at Lord's in 1911 when Middlesex won a game set aside for JT Rawlin's benefit. They repeated this success at Hove but only after a desperate struggle. Needing 184, John Douglas and Frank Tarrant led off with 54 in 40 minutes but by the close of Tuesday's play, seven wickets were down for 157. Warner was still there, however, and on the final day his undefeated 71 got his side home without further loss. Warner was back with a century at Lord's in 1912, Middlesex winning by an innings, and the Hove return was ruined by rain, no play being possible on the second day.

Middlesex's visit to Hove in 1920 came at the end of a spell of wet weather which left the skies overcast and the pitch soft and puddingy. Apart from the obvious holiday attraction, the match appeared to have little significance. Yorkshire, Surrey, Kent and Lancashire had set the pace in the Championship, Middlesex and Sussex enjoying respectable seasons without having anything other than an outside chance of mounting a bid for the title. Surrey headed the table in the week prior to August Bank Holiday but suffered a devastating defeat by Kent at Blackheath and were surprisingly beaten by Nottinghamshire in the holiday fixture. Middlesex were sixth in the table going into the Hove match, having lost narrowly at Leyton and nobody in the side held any serious hopes of winning the competition. Warner lost the toss and Herbert Wilson, a popular and successful captain between 1919 and 1921, decided to bat, mainly on the basis that there might be runs to be had on an unresponsive pitch. At first Vallance Jupp and the experienced Joe Vine encountered few difficulties but things changed when the sun broke through. Stevens fully exploited what became a vicious, drying turf, taking seven for 17 in 47 balls. By mid-afternoon Sussex were all out for 92 and although Arthur Gilligan bowled Warner for a duck, Lee and Hearne dug in. The Sussex attack looks strong on paper but Gilligan and Maurice Tate were not what they would become four years hence and Albert Relf and George Cox were well into the veteran stage. Lee and Hearne added 144 in two hours and on the Monday Lee carried his score to 132, Hendren made 88, Mann hit three consecutive sixes off Tate and Warner was able to declare at 369 for nine, a lead of 277 with a day and a half to spare.

Only the half was needed as Sussex were all out in two hours, Durston taking three relatively expensive wickets with Stevens cleaning up to the extent of six for 43 in 13 overs: match figures of 20.5- 5- 60-13. Modestly he was to say 50 years later that even if he hadn't bowled a single ball, Middlesex would still have won. As it was, their victory by an innings and 123 runs was the launch pad for nine consecutive victories. They scraped home against Kent in the second match of Canterbury Week, the closing run culminating in a memorable win over Surrey at Lord's which brought them the Championship.

Middlesex were champions again under Frank Mann in 1921, attendances of 10,701 on the Saturday and 18,275 on Whit Monday seeing them gain a comfortable victory over Sussex. Lee and Hendren each made hundreds in adding 210 for the third wicket in two hours during the second innings. These were heady days for the county and it was reflected in crowds such as 21,057 on Whit Monday 1922. They enjoyed a run of seven consecutive victories over Sussex but, as Tate and Gilligan approached their best seasons, the gap narrowed. The margin was only three wickets at Lord's in 1923, Hearne standing firm against some fine bowling from the Sussex pair, and the home side won emphatically at Hove in August. Middlesex made another strong bid for the title in 1924. Tate and Gilligan bowled them to defeat at Lord's (41 all out in the second innings, Gilligan eight for 25) but they won at Hove and seemed certain to head the table before a poor finish let in Yorkshire. For the remainder of the decade, both teams descended to mid-table ordinariness, their clashes memorable only for notable individual achievements. Tate took eight for 105 in 54 overs at Lord's in 1925, Hearne making a century, and there was a close finish at Hove that year.

This game produced one of those fascinating 'matches within a match' which occur when players of the highest quality who are at the peak of their careers are in opposition. On this occasion Sussex were dismissed for 117 but Tate hit back with six for 72. By now he had developed from a run-of-the-mill medium slow bowler into the fast-medium genius who obtained such deceptive swerve and pace off the pitch. At Hove the only batsman to face him with confidence was Hendren, who was unbeaten with 82. "As a bowler he made the batsman play at five balls out of six. He was the finest fast-medium bowler I ever played with or against," said Hendren. Middlesex required only 92 to win on the last day but they were forced to work hard by Tate and the medium pace of Bert Wensley. Seven wickets were down for 74 and two more fell at the same total before Mann's unbeaten 17 and a single from Durston got them home.

Middlesex found little respite from Tate. He performed a hat trick in taking nine for 71 at Lord's in 1926, although Hendren tamed him with a second innings hundred as Middlesex made 366 for five – another example of the awesome batting power which brought an astonishing victory after they had been second-best for most of the game. Hearne and Lee chipped in but the turning point was a fourth wicket partnership of 121 between Hendren and Hon CN Bruce, later Lord Aberdare, who made 73.But some of the cricket during the 1920s was turgid, the Hove game of 1927 being an example. Sussex piled up a huge total and Middlesex spent 117 overs in making 305 for six. They had some excuse, Hendren (118) and Stevens (81) having to consolidate in a third wicket partnership of 140 after two wickets had fallen for eight, but it was poor holiday fare. Things grew worse a year later, although there was, at least, a decision on the first innings. The August crowds saw hundreds from Ted Bowley, KS Duleepsinhji and Tate in a total of 496, accrued in 148.3 overs. Middlesex responded with 497 for seven in 184 overs, ET Killick and Hendren adding 301 for the third wicket.

Ranji's nephew, Prince Kumar Shri Duleepsinhji, 'Smith' to the Hove faithful, averaged nearly 50 during his first-class career but never quite realised his full potential owing to ill health. His connections with Sussex provide another example of the type of meeting which often took place during the Bank Holiday weekends. After close of play on Whit Saturday 1924, Ranji came into the Sussex dressing room and invited Arthur and Harold Gilligan to a lunch party at his home, Jamnagar House in Staines. Here, in his study, Ranji discussed the possibility of his nephew playing first-class cricket. "He has acquitted himself quite creditably at Cheltenham and he is a very fair bat." Such was the beginning of an illustrious career, among the gardens, putting green and bowls lawn of a big house in Staines.

Sussex were developing into a fine side. Bowley, Tom Cook, the Parks brothers Jim and Harry and the Langridges James and John, Wensley, Walter 'Tich' Cornford, the diminutive wicket-keeper who stood up to Tate, and the added polish of Duleepsinhji, who came down from Cambridge and then captained the team in succession to Harold Gilligan in 1931 and 1932. RSG Scott followed him as captain and when business called he passed the reins to the South African Alan

Melville. From 1932 to 1934 Sussex were runners-up and they looked certain to take the title in the final year before blowing up towards the end. The Whitsun crowd saw Duleep at his best in 1930 when he made hundreds in each innings at Lord's, Harry Enthoven achieving a similar feat. Two more Middlesex amateurs, the fast bowling all rounder Gubby Allen and the leg spinner Ian Peebles routed the Sussex batsmen at Hove that year but the southern county's high placings in the table were reflected by decisive victories at Hove in 1931 and 1932, Tate having a match analysis of 13-58 and making 50 in the latter game.

All of this was to pale before Sussex's performance at Hove during the August Bank Holiday match of 1933. Middlesex had won the Whitsuntide game by an innings after some fine all-round cricket from Allen. But, despite the quality of the amateurs who flitted in and out and the continuing success of Hendren and Hearne, they were now the poor relations in such fixtures. Both Bank Holidays enjoyed scorching weather in 1933 and batsmen took full advantage. The Sussex innings at Hove was opened by Bowley, who was in his 44th year and his final full season. His partner was John Langridge, younger of the two brothers, and the Middlesex bowling was mastered from the start, with Bowley scoring at a rapid rate. He reached 50 out of 82 in the first hour, passing his century 15 minutes after the lunch interval. "All the bowling, on a wicket that seemed cruelly insensitive, was uniformly innocuous," reported *The Daily Telegraph*. "Nevinson, in between some rather expensive intervals, gave moments of discomfort and Haig slaved with great industry for long profitless periods. Allen, who owing to injured ribs, had been rested, was conscripted at 98, but neither his fiery onslaught nor the new ball brought any relief."

By teatime Bowley and Langridge had taken the total to 355. The 400 went up after five hours and speculation began about the possibility of a new record exceeding the 555 posted by Holmes and Sutcliffe at Leyton a year earlier. Close of play was normally at 6.30pm but it had been arranged to continue until 7pm. Three minutes after half-past six, the leg spinner Jim Sims trapped Langridge lbw for 195 (16 fours), with the total on 490. Sussex lost two more wickets in the extra half-hour and closed at 512 for three. Bowley was caught by Joe Hulme for 283, having struck two sixes, a five and 23 fours. *The Daily Telegraph* described Hulme's fielding on the boundary as absolutely tireless, saying he must have saved 40 runs.

Scott declared on August Bank Holiday Monday and Middlesex had a disappointing day. Hendren made 79, Haig a rapid 41 and the tail wagged but they had to follow-on 222 behind. With his second ball, Tate shattered Lee's wicket and had Hearne leg-before first ball. Only five runs were on the board when Tate bowled Fred Price. The Sussex bowler, now in the veteran stage and forced to yield the stage to Larwood, Voce, Allen and Bowes on the recent Bodyline tour, had taken three wickets for one run. Hendren and Allen steadied the ship but Hendren fell at 45 and Middlesex closed on 92 for four. Ninety minutes sufficed on the final day to give Sussex their 14th victory of the season, although Allen resisted for two and half hours for 80. James Langridge, with cleverly flighted slow left-arm assisted by a couple of stumpings from Cornford, polished off the innings, Sussex winning by an innings and 65 runs. Gubby Allen did not forget the humiliation. A year later he wrecked the Sussex batting at Hove with eight for 58 and five for 90 although Middlesex had to hang on at the end for a draw.

Allen was at the crease in the Whitsuntide fixture of 1936 when the youthful Denis Compton joined him at No 11 with Middlesex seeking a first innings lead in response to Sussex's 185. "Gubby was determined to get them," said Compton. "Maurice Tate was bowling and Gubby came up to me and told me to play forward to him. 'Play forward,' he said, 'and stick there'. For some reason I played back twice and was nearly out." Eventually Compton (14) was given out lbw by Bill Bestwick, the former Derbyshire fast bowler who, like several of his kind and generation, had enjoyed a pint throughout his career. Allen remonstrated with Bestwick. "Bill, you're a so-and-so cheat. Young Compton wasn't out and well you know it." Bestwick replied: "I know he wasn't sir. But you had your first innings lead and I was dying to spend a penny so I gave him out." Rain on Tuesday when the match was delicately poised put paid to the fun after 15,000 people had seen some magnificent bowling from Tate on Whit Monday.

Middlesex had now entered on a period of success in which they finished third in 1935 and runners-up in the four seasons before the 1939-45 war and again in 1946. Allen, the leg spinning all-rounder Walter Robins, the big-hitting fast bowler Jim Smith and Sims were the most successful bowlers and Compton, Bill Edrich and Jack Robertson emerged to maintain the tradition of Hendren, Hearne and Lee. Their batting was once again as powerful and attractive as any in the country. At Hove in 1937 they piled up 632 for eight declared, Hendren, at the age of 48 and in his final season, 187, Hulme 125 and Compton 61. The old and the new in Hendren and Compton added 158 for the fourth wicket. Sussex collapsed twice before Owen-Smith's well-flighted leg breaks and Middlesex had the match won by Monday evening, the margin being an innings and 351 runs. The following Whitsuntide saw 30,000 pass through the turnstiles as a benefit match for Fred Price produced 1,157 runs and a Middlesex victory. Price, who later became a notable umpire after his days as Middlesex's wicket-keeper were over, played a central role at Hove in 1938. After a first innings' deficit of 118 Middlesex hit back through some fine pace bowling from Laurie Gray. This left them needing 300 in the fourth innings and although Edrich made 95 it took some aggressive hitting from Smith and an unbeaten 52 from Price to secure a three wicket victory. This avenged a rare success by Sussex at Lord's in 1937, when they won by 210 runs. They had only two victories at headquarters between the wars, in 1924 and 1937, and won seven of the 40 holiday contests against 22 by Middlesex. This was mainly due to a 15-2 margin in Middlesex's favour between 1920 and 1929, matters being more even during the 1930s.

Sussex ended the period with a strong batting side – John and James Langridge, Jim and Harry Parks, George Cox and Hugh Bartlett each exceeded 1,000 runs in the 1939 Championship – but were short on bowling, where Jack Nye, James Langridge, Jim Cornford and Jim Parks had to shoulder the burden. Nevertheless the two decades had provided some eventful cricket and it was a pity that the final holiday match of the 1930s should end in anti-climax. Only three and a quarter hours play was possible on the first two days in August 1939 at Hove, Jack Holmes winning the toss and sending Middlesex in. Edrich (161) and George Mann (88) put on 221 in less than three hours after three wickets had fallen for 32. The innings closed at 328 and when Sussex had lost seven men for 143, Ian Peebles, Middlesex's captain, faced a dilemma. The title was decided by the total of points divided by matches played. A lead on the first innings brought four points but matches were ignored in the calculations if there was no decision. Therefore a win on the first innings in a match which was obviously going to be drawn would have meant a drop in Middlesex's Championship average. The regular bowlers were rested and the game fizzled out with Sussex on 253 for nine. It was all very low key.

Chapter Sixteen
Roses in Bloom

In the 21 seasons between the wars only five clubs won the Championship: Yorkshire 12 times, Lancashire five, Middlesex twice and Nottinghamshire and Derbyshire once each. The Roses stranglehold can be carried a stage further. In only two seasons, 1921 and 1936, were neither of these counties in first or second place – but in both campaigns Yorkshire finished third. During the seven seasons from 1922 to 1928, Yorkshire won the title in the first four and Lancashire the last three.

Such dominance was reflected in the power struggles which took place annually at Whitsuntide and August Bank Holiday, in particular those of the 1920s. They represented county cricket at its highest technical peak – and sometimes, from the entertainment point of view, at its worst. In those 21 summers, 42 matches were played, Yorkshire winning 13, Lancashire five and 24 being drawn, nine of them consecutively from 1927 to 1931. All of Lancashire's home games were at Old Trafford, alternating each season between the two holidays. Bradford's Park Avenue ground, Headingley and Bramall Lane at Sheffield, allocated on a rota system, were the Yorkshire venues.

Each county produced immensely strong teams. Lancashire in 1926 could field Harry Makepeace, Charlie Hallows, Ernest Tyldesley, Frank Watson, Jack Iddon, the emerging Len Hopwood, the captain Major Leonard Green, Frank Sibbles, Richard Tyldesley, Ted McDonald and the wicket-keeper George Duckworth. Eight of them played Test cricket; during inter-war Roses games Ernest Tyldesley made four hundreds, Hallows three, Makepeace and Watson two apiece. The bowlers' equivalent, five wickets in an innings, was performed by McDonald (five), Richard Tyldesley (four) and Sibbles (three). The Makepeace-Hallows opening combination (Makepeace and Watson exchanged places in 1927) came third among all county teams in the period, behind Hobbs and Sandham and Holmes and Sutcliffe.

A year earlier, in 1925, Yorkshire had won their fourth consecutive title with a team of awesome power: Percy Holmes, Herbert Sutcliffe, Edgar Oldroyd, Morris Leyland, Wilfred Rhodes, Roy Kilner, Emmott Robinson, the captain Major Arthur Lupton, George Macaulay, the wicket-keeper Arthur Dolphin and Abe Waddington. Again there were eight Test cricketers. The Roses centurions during the inter-war period were Sutcliffe (nine), Holmes (six) and Leyland (two). Rhodes, Robinson and Macaulay each had three five-fors and Kilner two. Sutcliffe played in 41 of the 42 matches, scoring 3,006 runs, average 52.74.

Cardus revelled in it all. From the artisans – Rhodes and Robinson disagreeing over a rain-affected pitch at Bradford, Rhodes predicting it would take spin at four o'clock and Robinson saying 'Nay Wilfred, quarter past' – to the lyrical: "The old occasion comes again – Lancashire and Yorkshire at Old Trafford, the game spiky with antagonism, the crowd now shouting joy to the sky and now tasting bitter ashes in the mouth" – he told the tale through rainy days and sunny days.

The professionals, with a no-fours-before-lunch philosophy resulting in a scoring rate of below 2.5 runs per over, put it differently: "What we want in Yorkshire and Lancashire matches is fair do's – no umpires and fair cheating all round," Kilner is alleged to have said. And the crowds, vast numbers packing the grounds so that on August Bank Holiday Monday 1926 at Old Trafford 38,600 people paid, the total number being estimated at 45,000. Bramall Lane, too, attracted its hordes. Leyland found the barrackers on the Sydney Hill small beer compared to the Roses. "They should come to Sheffield on Bank Holiday and hear t' crowd there. Why, compared to them, those folks on t'hill sounded to me as harmonious as Huddersfield Choral Society." The attendances beggar belief: 67,000 over three days at Old Trafford in August 1920, 20,000 on the August Saturday at Old Trafford in 1921 when rain prevented play on the Monday, 26,000 on August Monday at Bradford in 1923, 20,000 on the Saturday and 30,000 on Whit Monday at Headingley in 1924 with 36,000 on the Monday of the Old Trafford return, 36,000 on Whit Monday 1925 and 25,000 on the Bramall Lane Saturday in 1925. More than 30,000 at Old Trafford on August Monday 1928, 25,000 on Whit Monday 1933 at Old Trafford, 20,000 at Bradford on August Monday 1935 and 30,000 on August Monday 1938 at Old Trafford.

From the resumption after the war, the clashes rang with outstanding individual performances. Robinson took nine for 36 at Bradford in 1920 and Holmes made two centuries in the return at Manchester when Spooner provided a glimpse of the Golden Age with 62 and 63. Encounters were tense. Never more so than the final day of the August match at Old Trafford in 1922. AA Thomson found it "a perfect example of the Yorkshire and Lancashire struggle so tightly locked in a wrestler's grip that neither side could move and often did not seem even to try." Richard Binns thought it "the queerest Lancashire v Yorkshire match I ever personally saw. To this day I have not been able to arrive at a wholly satisfactory opinion of the incidents that marked the closing stages of it." Binns held that some hateful goblin of uneasiness presided over the game and must have grinned with unholy glee at the strange and malodorous twist that he gave to the affair.

It was a low scoring match with the bowlers generally in command. The second day, Monday, was lost to rain and on the final afternoon Yorkshire needed 132 for victory. They were without their captain Geoffrey Wilson, who had been staying at the home of Myles Kenyon, his Lancashire counterpart and had fallen ill with appendicitis. The match swung Lancashire's way. By 6.30pm Yorkshire had slumped to 98 for eight: 34 still required with one wicket left. Kenyon requested the extra half hour, surely ample time to take one wicket. But Wilfred Rhodes, who had come in at the fall of the third wicket, was batting well and he was partnered by Rockley Wilson, master-in-charge of cricket at Winchester, who played for his county during the August holidays. Rhodes was aged 44 and Wilson 43, past their best perhaps but still possessing immense character and experience. Rhodes was no stranger to last wicket tension, having partnered Fred Tate and George Hirst in losing and winning causes in the 1902 Ashes. Time moved inexorably on and the total crept up but still that vital wicket did not fall. Now it was Yorkshire scenting victory but then only three runs came in five overs as they clung on, desperate to avoid defeat.

When Cecil Parkin prepared to bowl the last over of the match, Yorkshire, 127 for eight, needed five runs with Rhodes on strike. Parkin's first four deliveries were played back to him, the batsman making no attempt to score. Then a no ball added a run to the score, 128 and just four to win. Again Rhodes showed no aggressive intent, although he claimed afterwards that the umpire's call had been late. Parkin's fifth legitimate delivery was again met with solid defence. The last produced a single to third man. Yorkshire 129 for eight, Rhodes 48 not out, took two points for their first innings lead of four runs in a drawn match. "The issue of it," wrote Cardus, "was unresolved – Lancashire frustrated, Yorkshire frustrated, the multitude frustrated."

It was a multitude which needed nerves of steel. At Headingley in 1924 Yorkshire needed 58 to win the Whitsun match. They were bowled out for 33 by Parkin's off breaks and Richard Tyldesley's leg spin. The pitch suited the bowlers but nobody who turned up on Whit Tuesday morning anticipated such an outcome. The crowd was in a relaxed mood, laughing as Holmes and Sutcliffe were followed by a small dog as they walked to the middle to begin the quest. Soon Yorkshire were three for three; ten were added before Rhodes was deceived by Tyldesley and Oldroyd clean bowled by Parkin. Only Kilner resisted and the match was over by 12.40pm.: Tyldesley six for 18, Parkin three for 15. Eager to get home to Manchester, Neville Cardus caught a tram from Headingley. The guard asked him about the margin of Yorkshire's victory. "I said, 'They haven't won; they've lost.' He replied, 'Ah mean t' cricket match – did they lose any wickets?' When I assured him I had referred to t' cricket match, and that Yorkshire really had been defeated he suspended business on the spot; he did not give me a ticket, but turned his back on me and walked to the front of the tram, where he opened the door and told the driver. Then the tram proceeded a mile or so into Leeds by its own volition."

The 1926 match in August was the 100th between the counties. Yorkshire, champions for the past four years but dislodged that year by their rivals, had won the Whitsun match at Bradford by an innings. By the time August came around the pair were locked at the top of the table, Yorkshire having a slender lead. Hot, sunny weather ensured a big attendance. "Never has Old Trafford made a handsomer sight than yesterday (Monday): 45,000 sat (or stood) there rank on rank, happy as sandboys, happy in their applause, happy in their grumblings," Cardus wrote. The total attendance, 76,617, was the third highest-ever at a county match. Only Surrey-Yorkshire at The Oval, 80,000 in 1906 and the Headingley Roses match, 78,792 for George Hirst's benefit in 1904 surpassed it. They watched a three-day struggle for first innings lead. On Saturday Lancashire ended at 297 for two, declaring at 509 for nine on Monday. Makepeace and Ernest Tyldesley made hundreds and Rhodes took seven for 116 in 42 overs. By the close, Yorkshire were 183 without loss and on Tuesday Holmes (143) and Sutcliffe (89) took their partnership to 199. Yorkshire battled on. Matches with no result on the first innings were not counted and with the ranking based on the percentage of points to points possible, no results had obvious advantages. Rhodes stonewalled but fell trying to cut. "After tea the struggle was tense – a tug-of-war, both sides at an intolerable strain, the rope taut, with no man giving ground at this end or that," Cardus wrote. Watson's leg spin proved decisive and the last wicket fell at 352.

McDonald's pace brought him wickets at Old Trafford in the 1927 Whitsun game as he dismissed Sutcliffe and Leyland for ducks in a comfortable Lancashire victory. Such contests between the Australian fast bowler and the England opener were rich holiday fare. Sutcliffe avenged his failure with 95 and 136 in the

Headingley return and 140 and 126 in the two 1928 matches. Leyland, superb middle-order left-hand batsman and more than useful slow left-arm bowler, was undefeated with 211 at Headingley in the 1930 Whit match after taking seven for 52 the previous August at Bradford. Moments of sadness enveloped the 1930 matches, the Leeds fixture being marred by the death of Sir Frederick Toone, Yorkshire's secretary and Rhodes making his final Roses appearance at Old Trafford. Hedley Verity succeeded to the mantle of slow left arm, albeit in a different style from Rhodes, promptly taking five for 54 in 1931 at Old Trafford.

August Bank Holiday Saturday 1931 found Lancashire's bowlers impotent against Holmes and Sutcliffe. McDonald, admittedly now past his best, was hit for five fours by Sutcliffe in two overs just before lunch, which came at 123, Sutcliffe 80 Holmes 38. Runs flowed; 280 for none at tea, Sutcliffe 171 Holmes 95, 300 at five o'clock until, at 323, Sutcliffe (195) pulled a ball from Hopwood towards deep mid-on, a yard from the boundary. Paynter, dashing forward, took a diving catch – according to Cardus the catch of the season - a yard from the boundary. Holmes went on to 125, Yorkshire declared on Monday at 484 for seven and enforced the follow on but the match was drawn.

Now there were fresh duels, Verity eight for 107 as the Lancashire and England left-hander Eddie Paynter hit 152 (five sixes and 17 fours) at Bradford in the 1932 Whit game. The holiday Monday was early, 16 May, and the pitch belonged to the bowlers. Cardus felt that Paynter played "the most original, the most imaginative, the most courageous and the most belligerent innings seen in a Lancashire and Yorkshire match since the war." They were both overshadowed by Sibbles on Whit Monday. A sodden ground prevented play until 2.30pm and the first ball of the day, an outswinging half volley from Sibbles, accounted for Holmes, who chopped the ball to backward point. Sutcliffe battled away but Yorkshire, 38 for four, crashed to 46 all out, Sibbles 20.4-13-10-7. Sutcliffe (27) was the only batsman to reach double figures. Seam and cut did the damage and Yorkshire fared little better in their second attempt: 167 all out, Sutcliffe 61, Leyland 43, Sibbles five for 58 and match figures of 47-21-68-12, Lancashire winning by an innings and 50 runs. It should surprise nobody that Yorkshire exacted revenge with an innings to spare at Old Trafford in August.

As old gave way to new there was a slight Yorkshire decline in the late 1920s, when the main challenge to Lancashire came from Nottinghamshire and Kent. But the broad acres were full of talent. Sutcliffe, Holmes and Leyland were joined by Wilf Barber, Arthur Mitchell and later, the young Len Hutton. The skipper Brian Sellers, left-handers Frank Smailes and Cyril Turner and the wicket-keeper Arthur Wood added beef to the middle order. The attack contained two bowlers of Test quality in Verity and Bill Bowes, at his best as a fast medium bowler, delivering a nasty outswinger from a great height off a short run. They were supported by the right arm medium pace of Smailes and Ellis Robinson's off spin. Generally the 1930s saw the pendulum swing Yorkshire's way. Mitchell made 123 in a Yorkshire total of 341 at Old Trafford in 1933 and on Whit Monday Lancashire collapsed twice in the face of George Macaulay's medium paced off breaks. They were all out for 93 and 92, Macaulay taking seven for 28 and five for 21.

Then, after winning three consecutive Championships, Yorkshire had to give second best to Lancashire in 1934; indeed they finished sixth, their lowest position since 1911. Lancashire, too, had a new team: Watson, Hopwood, Ernest Tyldesley, Paynter, Iddon, Horrocks or Halliday, the captain Peter Eckersley, who sometimes flew to matches in his own plane, Richard Tyldesley, Duckworth, and the opening bowlers Frank Booth and Dick Pollard. Yorkshire never led the Championship that summer but at Bramall Lane over Whitsuntide they gave their old rivals a severe mauling. In gloomy weather with cold, wintry blasts which caused many people to think twice about going and then decide against it, Sutcliffe and Mitchell began with 143 for the first wicket, Mitchell reaching his hundred before rain brought a merciful end to the day. Play did not start until after lunch on Monday and after Yorkshire declared at 346 for five, Lancashire struggled against Verity on a pitch drying under the hot sun. They were 93 for seven by the close and followed on 235 behind, going in again soon after noon. Iddon battled for 62 as 10,000 Yorkshiremen held their breaths but they got home at 5.35pm by an innings and three runs, Verity returning a match analysis of 60.3-37-53-8. Meanwhile, at Lord's Sussex hung on for a draw with nine wickets down, Melville having made a century, and headed the table after the Whitsun games on May 22, staying there until August 14 when Lancashire took over. By then the loss of August Bank Holiday Monday to the weather had turned the Roses match into a battle for first innings lead, which was won by the White Rose despite 142 not out from Iddon.

So Yorkshire could still claim some bragging rights in 1934 and although Derbyshire were champions in 1936 they dominated the remainder of the decade. The powerhouse worked to a simple formula: a big score and then roll over the opposition twice.

Lancashire were fourth in 1935 but declined to eleventh and ninth before a partial recovery took them to fourth and sixth in 1938 and 1939. As far as the outcome of the Championship was concerned the matches between Derbyshire and Nottinghamshire were of greater importance in 1935 and 1936 but the Roses games remained an attraction, notably at Bradford in 1935 where nearly 20,000 howled for blood as Bowes (six for 16) caught the visiting batsmen on a green August Bank Holiday Monday pitch and reduced them to an all out total of 53. Watson led a recovery with 141 in the follow-on but after Bowes had taken six for 83, Yorkshire got home by seven wickets.

In 1937 Lancashire sprung a surprise. They had been heavily defeated at Old Trafford during a gloomy Whitsuntide but positions in the Championship were rendered meaningless at a Bramall Lane basking in hot August weather. After the early loss of Hutton, Sutcliffe (122) and Mitchell (71) took the score to 145 before Mitchell was bowled by Pollard, who then got among the rest, the innings closing for 246. Consistent batting earned Lancashire a useful lead. Iddon's hard hitting right-hand batting had been a thorough nuisance to Yorkshire in recent matches and he was also a slow left-arm bowler fully capable of exploiting a wearing pitch. He dismissed Sutcliffe late on the second day and then on Tuesday he had a field day. Yorkshire felt that if they could set Lancashire 150 they could win the match but Iddon, with nine for 42, restricted the target to 91. Some brilliant cutting and driving by Cyril Washbrook took them to 70 without loss by 3.30pm but they had to struggle to make the remaining 21, losing five wickets in the process. It was Lancashire's first victory at Bramall Lane since 1899 and it was thoroughly deserved in what was one of the finest Roses matches of all time. Full value for money but not everybody was happy. It was here that Cardus found a Sheffield man deep in dejection. "His wife was with him and I heard her say: 'Well, you *would* come, wouldn't you?'"

Revenge was swift and savage. Yorkshire won the 1938 games at Bradford and at Old Trafford, where they amassed 453, thirty thousand watching the carnage on Monday. They surpassed this during the 1939 Whitsuntide, when, after Lancashire's 300 and Hutton's failure left the home Saturday crowd pleasantly satisfied, the juggernaut took over. On Whit Monday Sutcliffe (165) and Mitchell (136) took their second wicket partnership to 288. Sellers and Wood piled on the pressure and the declaration came at 528 for eight. Paynter and Norman Oldfield batted well but Bowes (six for 43) brought about a collapse and Yorkshire won by an innings and 43 runs. Sutcliffe was missing for the August Bank Holiday game but his heir, Len Hutton, treated the Headingley faithful to a full display of the qualities which had produced his 364 against Australia at The Oval a year earlier. Hutton had been ready for first-class cricket when he was only 17 in 1934, George Hirst saying there was nothing to teach him and Sutcliffe predicting a golden future. With a superb technique, a sound defence and a fluent and graceful strokemaker, Hutton became one of the greats, linked with Hobbs as England's finest opening batsman. But his innings at Headingley was not before time. In eight Roses matches he had never got beyond 46 and was averaging a mere 22.60.

On that final afternoon, after Ellis Robinson had taken eight for 35 and 13-115 in the match, Yorkshire set out on their quest to make 147 for victory. The sun came out, the pitch was difficult and four wickets were down for 83; 64 needed but Hutton was still there with 59. Yardley fell at 106 but with Sellers hanging on and Hutton farming the strike, the runs came. At 130, Hutton was 91 and rain was in the air. He reached his century just as the umbrellas were opening and then lifted the ball over cover where Washbrook – his post-war opening partner with England - chased it and just failed to hold a very hard chance. It took Hutton to 105 and proved to be the winning hit, just as the rain came down in torrents.

A great innings and a great match was a fitting way for Cardus's 21 years of rare sport to reach a temporary halt.

Chapter Seventeen
Hatching Bodyline

For the first part of the period between the wars matches between Nottinghamshire and Surrey retained much of their 19th century aura. Nottinghamshire were champions in 1929 and runners-up in 1922, 1923 and 1927. Surrey's highest placing was second in 1921 and 1925.

The spectators still passed through the gates at Trent Bridge and The Oval regardless of the Championship tables. After all, these were clashes between two of the Big Six counties and people were attracted by batsmen of quality: George Gunn, Joe Hardstaff junior, Walter Keeton, Charlie Harris, Jack Hobbs, Andrew Sandham and Laurie Fishlock. These were opposed by high calibre bowlers such as Harold Larwood, Bill Voce, Harold Butler and Alf Gover. But it was the leadership which added lustre to the earlier part of the period. Teams captained by Arthur Carr, Percy Fender and Douglas Jardine were incapable of playing anything other than positive cricket for very long.

Carr, ironically, was born in Surrey, at Mickleham. An attacking batsman who drove powerfully he scored heavily at Sherborne and demonstrated great promise for Notts before the war. Appointed captain in 1919, he added improved judgement to his aggressive style and became a consistent runmaker. Carr played in 11 Tests, captaining England in the first four against Australia in 1926 and in two against South Africa in 1929. He enjoyed a pint, visits to the racecourse and in contrast to some of his fellow amateurs, he was very close to the professionals. A drinking culture developed, with Carr, who had a private income, in the chair and the professionals hard-pressed to keep up. He was a spirited defender of Larwood and Voce over the Bodyline issue in 1934 and this led to his dismissal by Nottinghamshire in December. An Extraordinary General Meeting demanded his reinstatement but subtle manoeuvring at the club's AGM reversed the decision and this ended his career with the county.

Percy George Herbert Fender was an even more colourful character. A controversial and shrewd captain of Surrey from 1921 to 1931 his leadership somehow contrived to keep a team deficient in bowling high in the table. Fender, a hard-hitting batsman and leg break and googly bowler, had a sharp eye for a batsman's weak spot which he fully exploited. Raymond Robertson-Glasgow wrote: "He hated the dull finish, the formal declaration, the expected stroke, the workaday over. He rescued treasures of cricket from dust and oblivion, snatched off the covering and showed them to an astonished and delighted public." Fender's long sweaters and spectacles became rich sources of material for the cartoonist Tom Webster and the Surrey fast bowler Alf Gover recalled that he had the finest cricket brain he ever come across in over 50 years in cricket, going on to say that Fender was "a fine player and the greatest of captains, of course, but pitches, people's techniques, the lot: he knew it all."

He never captained England – Carr believed Fender rather than Percy Chapman should have succeeded him in 1926 – and many found this an injustice. Others, however, pointed to his moderate performances in 13 Tests. John Gunn said that life was never commonplace when Carr and Fender got together and a story from Gover illustrates this. Carr was batting in the Whitsuntide match at Trent Bridge and Fender decided to bait him with a tempting leg side ball. Gover was at forward short leg and Fender warned him to fling himself flat when he tugged at his shirt collar before bowling. "After an over or two Percy George tugged at his collar, I ducked as Carr swung wildly at the full toss which came along. It was still high in the air as Fender called out 'Carr caught Gregory bowled Fender', and so it was. Harold Larwood also recalled that Carr always tried to hit Fender out of the ground with almost every stroke.

Fender and Carr were colleagues on several occasions for Gentlemen v Players and during the MCC tour of South Africa in 1922-23 captained by Frank Mann. They spent a lot of time together, Fender trying to help his friend overcome the problems he was experiencing on the matting pitches. "Arthur could drive like a team of runaway horses but he couldn't cut and I was always on to him to improve his cutting. He never did learn to cut properly, to my mind."

It was typical of Fender that he offered to stand down as captain early in the 1931 season when it became apparent that Douglas Jardine was likely to lead England in Australia in 1932-33 and needed experience. The change was eventually made in March 1932. Jardine's reign as a county captain was brief, although not without success. His fame – and notoriety – was destined for other arenas.

There was early evidence of the Carr-Fender rivalry. At Trent Bridge in 1920, Surrey won easily, Fender taking eight for 66 in the second innings, Carr alone of the batsmen remaining long with 56. In August Surrey badly needed a win to resurrect their title ambitions following defeat by Kent at Blackheath. They led by 64 on the first innings and set Nottinghamshire 272. The visitors obtained the runs for the loss of seven wickets, Carr being undefeated with 105. The two counties, incidentally, were among the last to embrace Saturday starts, the 1920 and 1921 matches beginning on Mondays, 24,197 attending on the August Monday of the latter year. By and large, the era belonged to Hobbs: 151 not out at Trent Bridge in 1922, 105 in The Oval game a year later, 203 not out at Whitsun and 105 at The Oval in 1924, 189 at Trent Bridge in 1925, a hundred before lunch in the 1927 August match and so on.

Hobbs and Sandham enjoyed their share of three-figure openings against Nottinghamshire but a new threat was on the horizon. Hobbs had predicted that the 21-year-old Harold Larwood would have a bright future and the fast bowler proved the point by twice dismissing The Master cheaply in the 1926 Whitsun match. Larwood was to find Surrey's batsmen to his liking, with 87 wickets in 21 matches at 15.68, including that of Sandham on 13 occasions and Hobbs nine. His best performance was seven for 35 at Trent Bridge in 1927, match figures of 11-106 helping his side to a nine wicket victory. Throughout the summer Nottinghamshire ran neck and neck with Lancashire before they met problems at The Oval. There was no Larwood and Hobbs and Sandham took full advantage with an opening partnership of 203. Surrey declared at 522 for seven and Nottinghamshire then spent 114 overs in making 259. Nevertheless they made the journey to Swansea in the knowledge that only defeat by lowly Glamorgan would cost them the title. They went down by an innings – Glamorgan's only Championship victory that season – and a planned civic reception in Nottingham had to be cancelled.

Nottinghamshire were runners up again in 1928 but suffered embarrassment against Surrey at Trent Bridge. George Gunn made 122 but the batting failed until Arthur Staples and Fred Barratt came together at 238 for seven. Barratt hit 96 in 85 minutes, including a six which bounced on the top step leading to the pavilion. Staples made 94, the pair adding 167 for the eighth wicket and the total reaching 457. Hobbs made 122 but Nottinghamshire had a lead of 169. Carr then made a crucial error in deciding against enforcing the follow on. In poor light Nottinghamshire lost four wickets for 15 in 30 minutes before the close of Whit Monday's play and they were all out for 50 against Fender and Peach. Carr did his best with 22 and Larwood removed Hobbs with his second ball before a run had been scored but Sandham batted sensibly and Surrey won by seven wickets.

When Nottinghamshire won the Championship in 1929 the pace of Fred Barratt and Larwood was reinforced by the burly figure of Bill Voce, with his mixture of left-arm swing and spin, and the Staples brothers Sam and Arthur. The batting was sound: Whysall, George Gunn, Walker, Carr and Payton, although their average age was 42. Lancashire and Yorkshire were Nottinghamshire's chief rivals but Surrey were now confined to the lower half of the table. Nottinghamshire won the Whitsun game but there was a high scoring draw at The Oval. Whysall and Carr made hundreds in a total of 409 and at the Monday's close Surrey were 411 for six, with Sandham and Tom Shepherd passing three figures. Rain on the final day made it all academic. When the duel was resumed at Trent Bridge in 1930, Larwood removed Hobbs for five but Andrew Ducat (218) and Sandham (152) shared a huge stand as Surrey piled up 501, the match being drawn.

As far as the Championship was concerned there was nothing significant about the 1931 matches but Nottinghamshire won a particularly fine game by nine wickets at The Oval. Surrey gained a first innings lead of 64 before Larwood and Voce routed them for 82 in their second innings, Hobbs getting 43 of these before he was bowled by Larwood. By 1932 Carr possessed the most lethal pair of fast bowlers in the country. It was a combination made all the more potent by their contrasting styles, high pace from Larwood and left arm in-swing which could be extremely nasty, from Voce. It was not lost on Jardine, the new Surrey and England captain but it was Nottinghamshire who were on the receiving end in the Whitsun game. In poor light George Gunn and Walter Keeton opened the innings after Surrey had been dismissed or 108. The first ball appeared to slip out of Gover's hand and hit the 53-year-old Gunn full pitch on the right side of his face, just against the eye, as he tried to turn the ball to leg. The ball rebounded onto the wicket. Gunn staggered away and after being laid on the grass he was attended by a doctor and taken to hospital with severe concussion. He was allowed home and told to rest for a few days. Effectively his career was over and Charlie Harris took his place as Keeton's partner. It was an association which lasted until 1949 and produced 45 three-figure opening stands – Harris the anchor man and Keeton providing the flourish. The match was drawn, George's son George Vernon Gunn making an unbeaten 89.

By the time of the August game most of the team to tour Australia had been announced. Larwood and Voce were included and England's hope of limiting Bradman's phenomenal run scoring was obviously being placed in fast bowling. Jardine had first been impressed by Larwood on August Bank Holiday Monday in 1925 when 34,000 people packed The Oval. Percy Fender was aware of Larwood's pace and Jardine asked him: "Is this chap as fast as they say he is?"

Fender replied: "Yes." Jardine watched as Hobbs and Sandham played three overs from Larwood when the Surrey innings began shortly after lunch. "He does not look so fast to me," Jardine said. The innings was well established when Jardine faced Larwood who was brought back for his second spell. The first two balls beat Jardine for pace before he managed to make contact with the third. "He immediately turned to the pavilion and raised his cap to me," said Fender. Jardine (53) was last out, his stumps shattered by Larwood. It is also worth pointing out that Jardine made 64 for the Gentlemen at Lord's in July 1932 against a Players' attack including Larwood, Voce and Tate.

In the final Test at The Oval in 1930, Bradman had given hints of discomfort when facing Larwood on a pitch freshened by rain, sparring dangerously at rising balls, although it did not stop him making 232. Jardine had spotted this when watching a film of the innings. An idea grew. Frank Foster was consulted about his 1911-12 series field-settings for sharp, left-arm in swing and talks took place with Fender and others. During the August Bank Holiday Oval fixture of 1932, Carr invited Larwood and Voce for a meal. Larwood felt there was nothing unusual in this - "we were always going out with the skipper" – but this time was different. Carr said Fender had told him Jardine wanted to learn more about Larwood and Voce "and proposed to ask the two bowlers and myself out to dinner to discuss things. We all went to the grill room at the Piccadilly Hotel."

Larwood's biographer Duncan Hamilton described the grill room as having a white, high ceiling, ornate coving, Corinthian columns inlaid with gold, chandeliers that cast a tallow light and white tablecloths laid with silver and cut glass. Larwood said: "Leg theory was mentioned. I could see what they had in mind. Bradman was the big problem. He was the key man in Australia and Jardine wanted to curb his rungetting." Jardine asked him if he could bowl at the leg stump, making the ball come up into the body all the time so that Bradman had to play his shots to leg. Larwood replied that he thought that he could and that it was better to rely on speed and accuracy when bowling to Bradman because he murdered anything loose. Larwood went along with the idea as he felt that it was the best chance of dominating Bradman. Walter Hammond also left an account in which he visualised Carr demonstrating field placings with bread rolls, pepper pots and silver coins on the white tablecloth. As the group broke up, Carr is said to have taken Jardine to one side and said quietly: "If any of them are hard to move, tell Lol that they have been saying he is not so fast as he used to be. Then he'll show them what pace on the leg stick really is." The county match, influenced by the weather, was drawn. Nottinghamshire made 267, with Keeton and Carr among the runs and Maurice Allom taking five for 69. They gained a lead of 90, Voce four for 50, Larwood two for 44. The pair appeared to have experimented with a form of leg theory. *The Times* reported that they bowled to 'many short legs,' Surrey's wicket-keeper Ted Brooks –unbeaten with 37 on a rain-affected Monday when Surrey reached 130 for eight - being 'hit on almost every part of his body.' England won the 1932-33 series 4-1, Larwood taking 33 wickets at 19.51, Voce 15 at 27.13 and Bradman averaging 56.57 in four Tests.

After the winter of controversy there was an echo in the 1933 Whitsun match. The local newspaper had organised a shilling fund for Larwood and Voce which produced £388. A presentation was made to the two bowlers by Douglas Jardine on the upper deck of the West Wing stand at Trent Bridge on Monday evening. Silver salvers were also presented from the county club. Larwood also treasured a silver ash tray from Jardine, inscribed: "To Harold for the Ashes 1932-33. From a grateful skipper." In a drawn match, Jardine was caught Larwood bowled Voce for 67 and Fender made 106, hitting a five and 16 fours.

Voce gave Surrey a taste of fast leg theory at The Oval in 1933. He took two early wickets and struck the 50-year-old Hobbs several times on the hip and thigh, the large holiday crowd hooting its disapproval. As Voce tired, he was punished by Hobbs and Fender, who both made hundreds, although in his final over of the day he delivered what Fender said was the fastest ball he faced in his career. It rose sharply off a length at him. Fender never saw it – "the only time in my life, I think, that I was ever frightened at cricket," – but instinctively held his bat in front of his face. The ball struck the bat handle and flew over the wicket-keeper's head for four.

Carr, Fender, Jardine and Bodyline passed into history and if Larwood lost some of his high pace in subsequent seasons he continued to give Surrey's batsmen little peace, four consecutive innings in 1936-37 bringing him 21 wickets at 8.57. Voce, too, had his success and there was a poignant moment in the 1937 Whitsun game. It was to be Larwood's last appearance in the series, his emerging successor Harold Butler destroying Surrey's second innings with eight for 15 including a hat trick. Butler's pace also routed Surrey at Trent Bridge a year later but the southerners had the last laugh. A century from Fishlock helped Surrey set a target of 275 but although Keeton made 95, Nottinghamshire could manage only 263, Gover taking five for 69.

After the high drama of the early 1930s the decade ended quietly. The immediate memories as war closed in were of batsmen indulging themselves on perfect Oval pitches – Surrey 447, Nottinghamshire 443 in 1938 – rather than struggling against extreme and hostile pace. Harris (179) was the only centurion in this match and *Wisden* reflected ruefully: "Compared with those great struggles of bygone days between these two clubs, the cricket in this match was very disappointing." Wisden had a point, for a curiosity of these fixtures – despite much positive cricket - is that between the wars 27 matches were left unfinished, more than the Roses encounters. Nottinghamshire had nine wins and Surrey six. Some honour was restored at Trent Bridge in 1939 when Nottinghamshire made 264 for three to win by seven wickets, Hardstaff (114 not out) and Gunn (92 not out), sons of famous fathers, sharing an unbroken partnership of 216. Hardstaff gave an elegant display of forcing strokes in this innings. At the age of 28, this most stylish of batsman had established himself in the England side but the war interrupted a Test career which might have been on the threshold of greatness. With Keeton, he made attractive runs at The Oval on a rain-interrupted August Bank Holiday Saturday but there was no play on Monday and none after 3.30pm on Tuesday – a miserable end to the inter-war series.

Chapter Eighteen
Breaching the Big Six

Warwickshire finished bottom of the Championship table in 1919; their new holiday opponents Derbyshire were to do so in 1920 when they endured the worst season in their history. It was not an encouraging start but better times were ahead with the appointments of Freddie Calthorpe as captain of Warwickshire and Guy Jackson as his Derbyshire equivalent.

Both counties also had the benefit of strong administration. Rowland Ryder was associated with Warwickshire for nearly 50 years, beginning as assistant secretary in 1895 before succeeding William Ansell as secretary, a post he held until his retirement in 1944. Will Taylor served as secretary of Derbyshire from 4 August 1908 until 31 December 1959, a period of 51 years and 149 days which exceeded that of the previous longest-serving secretary AJ Lancaster of Kent by 17 months.

Taylor and Ryder could appreciate the financial benefits from alternating holiday matches at Derby and Edgbaston, each ground handily situated for away support. The problem was the contrasting nature of the venues. Edgbaston had already been recognised as a ground fit to stage a Test match and would soon do so again. But the County Ground at Nottingham Road, Derby, was another story. Facilities were basic, to say the least.

In 1920, Warwickshire won both matches with ease, Harry Howell's pace proving too much, with Calthorpe also joining in the fun at Edgbaston. Howell took eight for 69 in the second innings as Derbyshire succumbed again at Edgbaston in 1921 but he was upstaged by Bill Bestwick, who returned to Derbyshire at the age of 46 to take 147 wickets at 16.72 each. Derbyshire had been dismissed for 181 but Bestwick returned figures of 31-10-65-9 to bowl his side into a 40-run lead. Warwickshire won easily enough in the end but Bestwick was again among the wickets when the teams met at Derby in August, when Len Oliver scored 151 and Harry Storer registered his maiden century for the home side. This set up what could have been an interesting finish before rain restricted play to 25 minutes on the final day.

Bestwick was at the centre of a celebrated occasion in the 1922 Whitsuntide match at Derby. Warwickshire won by 10 wickets after more devastation from Howell but during their first innings Bill Bestwick and his son Robert bowled to Willie Quaife and his son Bernard – the only time in first-class cricket that father and son have bowled to father and son. Six overs were delivered from opposite ends on Whit Monday but it was one of the fathers, WG Quaife, who came out best with 107 before he was bowled by Bob Bestwick. In addition to two fathers and sons in the match there were brothers Cyril and John Smart and the cousins Guy and Anthony Jackson for Warwickshire and Derbyshire respectively – quite a family affair.

Both counties had been hovering around the lower reaches of the table but Derbyshire were improving and they hammered the point home at Edgbaston in the Whitsuntide fixture of 1923. Jim Horsley and Bestwick bowled Warwickshire out for 122 and then Storer and Sam Cadman steered them to a lead of 111. Needing 132 for victory, Derbyshire struggled but Guy Jackson held firm. He was missed at long leg when he was 12 and again at slip on 13 but his innings of 82 not out got Derbyshire home by four wickets. Jackson went a stage further in the return at Derby with an unbeaten 109 but the match was drawn.

The series entered a period of eight consecutive drawn games between 1923 and 1927, with only a few individual performances of note. George Stephens and Arthur Croom shared a ninth wicket partnership of 154 for Warwickshire at Edgbaston in 1925; Bill Bestwick made the final appearance of his career on August Bank Holiday Saturday in 1925 at Derby; Len Bates and the young Bob Wyatt made big hundreds at Derby in 1926, Tiger Smith caught four batsmen and stumped three in the first innings at Birmingham the following August and followed this with 177 when opening the innings at Whitsuntide in 1927. There was a close finish to this match. No play was possible on Whit Monday and on the last day Derbyshire, 244 behind on the first innings, had lost eight wickets for 200 when bad light halted play at ten minutes to five. After a 35-minute delay the game resumed and Archie Slater was brilliantly caught at point by Partridge off Calthorpe for 105 after a stay lasting three hours and 10 minutes. Derbyshire hung on, closing at 242 for nine.

In 1927 Derbyshire selected their side mainly from twelve players: Storer, Joe Bowden, Slater, Guy Jackson, Garnet Lee, Jim Hutchinson, Stan Worthington, Les Townsend, the long-serving wicket-keeper Harry Elliott and Wilf Shardlow, with the final place going to Anthony Jackson or another amateur Escott Loney. By the first week in August they were third, behind Nottinghamshire and Lancashire, with Yorkshire fourth. The August Bank Holiday match provided the County Ground faithful with some excellent cricket, Derbyshire needing 231 on the final day. Major Llewellyn Eardley-Simpson, a club official for 47 years and a noted historian, described it as one of the finest he ever watched. "On the first innings our visitors led by 60, and at the end of the second day they were 213 ahead with three wickets in hand. On the last morning these three soon fell and, with 231 to win we had 72 for the loss of Joe Bowden by lunch – quite a fair appetiser! But things soon began to go wrong, and with six down for 147 it was a fight. There was soon another victim and I shall never forget how I marked off the last 50 runs on the back of a score card, which is still a treasured possession. Fortunately, Anthony Jackson and Les Townsend were full of confidence, and when the latter, in trying to drive Howell out of the ground, was caught by Willie Quaife at cover, the game was a tie. It was left to Harry Elliott – not for the only time – to win the game; he scored a single, and we took the points with two wickets to spare." Anthony Jackson was unbeaten with 34 and Derbyshire finished fifth in the table.

Eardley-Simpson also recalled the 1928 Whitsun match at Derby. Derbyshire made 295, Hutchinson hitting 111 and Arthur Richardson 49. Derbyshire were doing well but Wyatt made a hundred and Reg Santall and Danny Mayer added 104 in 55 minutes for the ninth wicket, enabling them to lead by 62. Richardson made an unbeaten 70 and, after some hesitation, Jackson decided to declare, leaving Warwickshire to score 176 in 115 minutes. "Two full pitches in the first over were eagerly accepted, and Tiger Smith helped Norman Kilner to rush up

150 in 80 minutes and the game was lost by six wickets with five minutes to spare."

When Jim Hutchinson died on November 7 2000 he was 22 days short of his 104th birthday. He remained lucid to the end, a treasure house of information about those distant days, related from the comfort of his armchair at his home in Thurnscoe, between Barnsley and Rotherham. He had fond memories of the Bank Holiday matches. "I enjoyed making a hundred at the County Ground but I sometimes wondered what the Warwickshire players and supporters felt about coming to Derby," he said. "But they had a good team, with Willie Quaife and Bob Wyatt scoring plenty of runs against us. Harry Howell had a bit of pace and Danny Mayer was a real pro – a tireless fast medium bowler who had a lot of work to do. Both teams got on well and one or two of them enjoyed the get-togethers over the holidays. There was always a bit of banter between the spectators and in the field at Derby you could sometimes pick up the Brummie accents in the crowd."

At least Hutchinson was soon to see the last of Quaife. In 1928 he was allowed to pick his retirement match for his only appearance of the summer and he chose Derbyshire at Edgbaston on 4, 6 and 7 August. Parsons made 114 for Warwickshire but it was Quaife's day; 115 made in 260 minutes at the age of 56 years 140 days. Warwickshire declared at 564 for seven but although the follow-on was enforced, the match was drawn. In 60 matches against Derbyshire, Quaife scored 3,161 runs, average 44.52, with six hundreds.

By now another rivalry was beginning to develop. Derbyshire won at Edgbaston over Whitsun in 1929 despite an unbeaten hundred from Wyatt. The mercurial Tommy Mitchell baffled most of the other Warwickshire batsmen with his leg breaks, to which he would soon add the googly. Beginning with 1929 he was to take a hundred wickets in ten consecutive seasons, 104 of them at 19.02 in 22 matches against Warwickshire. As Wyatt averaged nearly 45 against Derbyshire the pair soon became worthy adversaries and they toured Australia in 1932-33, when Wyatt was Jardine's vice-captain. Mitchell played under Wyatt's captaincy against New Zealand at Auckland in 1933 and Australia at Headingley when Bradman made 304 in 1934. Mitchell, an outspoken, bespectacled character, enjoyed his best season in 1935 and was controversially selected for the second Test against South Africa. Leather-jackets, the larvae of the daddy-long-legs, had been at the Lord's pitches and Wyatt had been impressed by Mitchell's bowling at Edgbaston that season. He felt he could win the match for England but the selectors wanted an allrounder, Walter Robins. After a long meeting Wyatt got his way but the outcome was disastrous. South Africa won by 157 runs, Mitchell's three wickets in the match costing 164 runs. Pelham Warner, the chairman of the selectors, felt that Wyatt relied too heavily on Mitchell and seemed obsessed by him. Wyatt told a different story, challenging the unanimity of the opposition to him and saying he had particularly outspoken support from Percy Perrin, another selector. Wyatt believed that with the match lost, Warner tried to lay the blame on his captain by not accepting any corporate responsibility of selection.

The frustration spilled out on to the field. Mitchell said Wyatt wanted him to bowl at the leg stump from the pavilion end. "I refused," said Mitchell. "He was telling me how to bowl and I didn't like it. So I turned to him and said, 'You couldn't captain a box of bloody lead soldiers." Mitchell had just bowled Siedle, who tried to hook a googly and missed. One of the umpires, Tiger Smith, said

Wyatt moved from gully to mid-on to coach Mitchell. "Tommy got so fed up with Wyatt telling him what to send down that he told him to go on himself – with a few colourful adjectives thrown in – and he was taken off." He never played for England again, although he was honest enough to acknowledge that his form had not been good enough.

Wyatt had been the undoubted victor when the pair were on opposite sides in the 1930 Whitsun game at Derby. Townsend and Storer made hundreds, enabling a declaration at 448 for seven and Warwickshire then lost two wickets for 28. Croom (110) helped Wyatt add 173 for the third wicket, Wyatt going on to 145 in six and a half hours, an innings which included 79 singles. Mitchell had to be content with two for 79. A spectator recalled that the players lunched in a marquee at the back of the pavilion, leaving them with a short walk back to the enclosure. Wyatt and Rev JH Parsons came out and were waylaid by autograph hunters. Wyatt, with an innings to resume, signed only a couple but Jack Parsons satisfied everybody. A year later, in the August Bank Holiday game at Derby, Warwickshire won by nine wickets after Partridge and Mayer reduced the home side to 93 all out. At lunch on Saturday they were 56 for nine but Mitchell laid about him for 29. There was no way back for Derbyshire, particularly as George Paine, the tall slow left-arm bowler, had a five-wicket haul in their second innings. Spin again played a decisive part when Derbyshire won at the County Ground in May 1932, Mitchell and the slow left-hander Tommy Armstrong accounting for 18 of the 20 Warwickshire wickets. Warwickshire just failed to win at Edgbaston in August, Elliott and Mitchell hanging on desperately at the close with eight wickets down.

Challenges were now being issued to the Big Six and in 1933 Derbyshire and Warwickshire emerged as contenders. The holiday encounters were bitterly fought. At Birmingham in June, Paine and a leg spinner Harold Jarrett had Derbyshire out for 226, Storer making 94. Wyatt, who succeeded Calthorpe as Warwickshire's captain, hit 166 and Derbyshire began the last day 107 behind with all their wickets in hand. Lee and Storer shared an opening partnership of 131 but the innings faded and Warwickshire had little difficulty in winning by eight wickets. Ample revenge was gained in glorious August weather at the County Ground. Townsend top scored with 172 not out in a total of 448 for eight before Jackson declared and although Wyatt made an unbeaten hundred the lead was 251. In view of the heat and its effect on his weary bowlers, Jackson did not enforce the follow-on and Derbyshire scored quickly to set a target of 410. The pitch started to deteriorate and Warwickshire, collapsing against Bill Copson and Mitchell, went down to a 317-run defeat.

Derbyshire finished sixth in 1933, with Warwickshire a place below them and the following season brought more improvement. Warwickshire had undergone some criticism for playing 'safe' cricket but in 1934 victory became the aim. The Ashes series claimed Wyatt for a good part of the summer but in his absence the county found able qualities of leadership in Rev JH Parsons, George Kemp-Welch, Norman Partridge and Len Bates. There were runs from Wyatt, Croom, Kilner, Bates, Santall and a new wicket-keeper-batsman Jack Buckingham. Paine also made useful runs and had a phenomenal season with the ball. Mayer and Eric Hollies, emerging as a leg-break and googly bowler, lent support: indeed Paine and Hollies toured the West Indies under Wyatt's captaincy in 1934-35.

It was a fine team but it had to give best to Derbyshire over Whitsun at the County Ground. It was cut and thrust throughout; Warwickshire, 267, gaining a first innings lead of four which could have been more but for Harry Elliott's unbeaten 72. Copson then dismissed Kilner and Bates before retiring with a strain but Worthington and Mitchell rose to the occasion and Derbyshire needed 179. Storer (79) and Denis Smith (45) set them on the way with a third-wicket stand of 98 and although the middle order faded, they got home by two wickets. There was another evenly-balanced return at Edgbaston, where Derbyshire led by 21 on the first innings before rain intervened.

The 1934 season found Derbyshire in third place and Warwickshire fourth but that was as high as Warwickshire got, eighth in 1935 being followed by lower-half positions for the rest of the decade. Instead it was Derbyshire who continued a rise which is without parallel in the history of the Championship. Almost on the point of going out of the competition in 1920 and last again in 1924 when they failed to win a match, their home-grown team finished second in 1935, first in 1936 and third again in 1937. It was a remarkable side, forged under Cadman's coaching and the captaincy of Jackson and his successor Arthur Richardson, with Harry Elliott as senior pro. The batting, with Smith, Stan Worthington and Les Townsend, was more than adequate and the variety of the bowling, pace from Copson, incisive fast-medium from the Pope brothers George and Alfred who could also make runs, sorcery from Mitchell and medium-paced off spin from Townsend, formed the best-balanced attack in the club's history. Yet they yielded to Warwickshire at Edgbaston in 1935, defeated by six wickets after Mayer, Paine and Hollies had wrecked the first innings and Wyatt's medium pace claimed five for 30 in the second. At Derby in August Townsend and Santall made hundreds and there was some good bowling from Hollies and Mitchell before Derbyshire sealed victory by 77 runs.

In 1936, Derbyshire's Championship season, the holiday fixtures reverted to the pre-war pattern with Warwickshire meeting Worcestershire and Derbyshire facing Essex. Rain marred the Whitsun games; a crowd of 5,000 turned up at Derby on Whit Monday but the Worcester match was a financial loss. The weather also intervened at Edgbaston but Derbyshire had better luck at Chelmsford. They had led the table since defeating Warwickshire during Chesterfield's first-ever cricket week in July but tension was mounting. An added ingredient was the strength of the Essex pace attack. Nichols, Farnes and Stephenson were all of international quality and they lost no time in making an impact. Five Derbyshire wickets were down for 29 and the whole side out for 80, Farnes taking five for 20. Copson and Alf Pope hit back but the close of August Bank Holiday Monday found Derbyshire on 195 for seven, only 56 ahead. They were all out on the final morning for 240, leaving Essex 102 to win. At 57 for three they were cruising but Mitchell changed the course of the match. Using the googly to full advantage he took six for 25 in five overs. Essex lost their last seven wickets for 24 and Derbyshire won by 20 runs.

In 1937 they returned to Chelmsford at Whitsun, the game ending on the Monday in Derbyshire's favour although Peter Smith took 11-121 for Essex. Smith was again among the wickets at Ilkeston during the August holiday, Essex winning by six wickets despite 151 from George Pope in the second innings. As for Warwickshire, they were defeated by Worcestershire at Edgbaston, despite promising performances from two future stalwarts Tom Dollery and Jimmy Ord.

The return at New Road was inconclusive, although Worcestershire's Bernard Quaife made 89 against his old county, for whom Len Croom scored 81 and 115.

During this interregnum there were some notable performances in the Derbyshire-Warwickshire matches outside the Bank Holidays in 1937. Wyatt (232) and Dollery (128) shared a fourth wicket partnership of 253 at Edgbaston, Wyatt declaring at 523 for seven. Derbyshire followed on but saved the game and then a fortnight later at Derby, Copson took eight for 11, including four wickets in four balls, as Warwickshire were sent packing for 28. He extended this to five in six when the second innings started, Derbyshire winning by five wickets. It was soon avenged when the holiday fixtures were resumed in 1938, when the 21-year-old Peter Cranmer was appointed as Warwickshire's captain in succession to the deposed Wyatt. At the County Ground over Whitsun, Warwickshire, set 311 for victory, lost half their wickets for 39 and the plight seemed hopeless. Dollery (134 not out) and Buckingham (124) then completely altered the course of the match with a partnership of 220 for the sixth wicket, Warwickshire winning by six wickets. Dollery made another hundred in Paine's benefit at Birmingham but Alf Pope (103), Smith, Worthington and the captain Robin Buckston helped build a lead of 190. Copson (six for 36) did the rest and Derbyshire won by an innings and 28 runs.

Inevitably Dollery was among the runs again over the 1939 Whitsun, with 177 in a Warwickshire victory at Edgbaston, Hollies taking 11-127, and there was an interesting switch of venue for the August match. In 1938 Derbyshire had used a ground belonging to Ind Coope & Allsopp Breweries at Burton-on-Trent in Staffordshire, which attracted a Saturday gate of 5,350 for a match against Gloucestershire. Consequently, the 1939 August Bank Holiday fixture was allocated to Burton but the game was dogged by bad weather. Rain restricted play to less than seven hours on the first two days and the final day was blank. It was frustrating for Derbyshire, who had a lead of 142 with all their second innings wickets in hand.

It was a miserable end to an even series which produced much fine cricket between the wars. The rivals remained the only counties to have broken the stranglehold of the Big Six and for a time in the mid-1930s it looked a toss-up which club would do so again.

Chapter Nineteen
The Record Holders

With Woolley in full flow and Freeman's sorcery baffling all but the very best of batsmen, Kent's holiday cricket offered a vivid contrast to the grim encounters between York and Lancaster and the fast bowling confrontations at Trent Bridge and The Oval. They never won the Championship between the wars, being runners-up in 1919 and 1928 and finishing in the first five 16 times, yet undisputedly remained in the Big Six.

Dudley Carew, who so evocatively captured the spirit of the game in the 1930s, said that nowhere in the country – Yorkshire and Lancashire certainly not excepted – did partisanship run as high as in Kent. "The game is even more talked of and the day's play more disputed in Kentish pubs than in the pubs of Bradford or Nottingham," he wrote.

There was plenty to discuss. Frank Woolley, tall, stately, the supremely graceful left-handed batsman. Alfred Percy 'Tich' Freeman, a stocky little chain-smoking gnome of a man, who first played in 1914 and was 31 when cricket resumed after the war. Wonderfully controlled leg breaks, with a well-disguised googly or top spinner, perfect length and cunning flight, brought Freeman remarkable success, a peak of 304 wickets in 1928 part of a sequence in which he snared 2,090 victims in eight English seasons. Later Leslie Ames would emerge as one of the greatest wicket-keeper-batsmen of all time, forging from 1927 a famous partnership with Freeman, victims succumbing, caught or stumped by Ames or gobbled up by Woolley at slip.

Kent's holiday opponents were usually Hampshire and here was Philip Mead, a tall, solidly built left-handed batsman of the highest class. For 30 years, he excelled in the slips and was the mainstay of Hampshire's batting, imperturbable, sound in defence, adept at taking singles, strong on the leg side and driving on either side of the wicket. Kent knew him well; during his career, including matches outside the holiday periods, he took 4,486 runs off their bowlers, with 15 hundreds and an average of 52.77. In the Championship nobody made more runs than Mead's 46,268 or took more wickets than Freeman's 3,151, of which 226 were in matches against Hampshire.

The versatile George Brown, left-handed batsman, right-arm medium paced bowler and occasional wicket-keeper, Walter Livsey, the wicket-keeper, Alec Kennedy who bowled medium paced inswingers and leg cutters and Jack Newman, who opened with the new ball and then turned to off breaks, were other stalwarts in the Hampshire team. They were led by Lionel Tennyson, another of those colourful, charismatic characters who enriched the game in the 1920s. Grandson of the poet, Tennyson, who became the third Baron in 1928, was associated with Hampshire cricket from 1913 to 1936, captaining the side for 14 years from 1919 onwards. A hard-hitting batsman, his courage knew no bounds – there was the famous occasion when he made 63 and 36 against Gregory and McDonald with a basket guard on his injured left hand when leading England in

1921 – and he skippered Hampshire to their 155-run victory at Edgbaston after they had been dismissed for 15 in their first innings in June 1922. Livsey was his valet, laying out his clothes, running his bath and, occasionally, lending him money for pavilion card games. Hampshire were never higher than sixth in the Championship, usually ending just below mid-table, but they were popular opponents for most counties.

Canterbury might have been the epitome of festival cricket but the games lacked for nothing in intensity. Such matches were a popular choice for benefits – Woolley had his in the 1922 Hampshire fixture (£2,550) and Freeman's (£2,381) was held in 1929 when Gloucestershire were the visitors – but it was that of James Seymour's in 1920 which made history. Kent won at Southampton, where Woolley made 158 and they repeated the feat at Canterbury, Seymour making 74 in the second innings. Although he scored more than 27,000 runs in first-class cricket it was the litigation subsequent to his benefit which was of greater value to the professional side of the game.

Seymour received a demand for income tax on the gate money which was included in his benefit receipts. He appealed to the Income Tax Commissioners, who found in his favour. The Crown then took the case to the High Court, which upheld the Commissioners' decision. Not satisfied with this, the Crown turned to the Court of Appeal and was successful. Seymour's final victory came in the House of Lords, which established the right of the cricket benefit, unless guaranteed by contract, to be free of tax. Seymour was backed by Kent throughout the proceedings.

The County Ground at Southampton enjoyed record attendances at Whitsun when Hampshire won in 1921 but cricket was soon put in perspective. Tennyson made 98 with two sixes and 12 fours in 105 minutes and Fry 96 but this was overshadowed by events at lunch on the first day. Each side included one of the Cornwallis brothers, Oswald, a Royal Naval lieutenant who was making his Hampshire debut and Wykeham, an Army officer who opened the bowling for Kent. They received news that their older brother, Fiennes, an Army captain, had been murdered by the IRA while leaving a country-house tennis party in Northern Ireland. Tennyson and the Kent captain Lionel Troughton promptly allowed the brothers to leave the match.

More big crowds saw some fine cricket the following season. There was little in it at Whitsun after the first innings but Woolley made 188 and Hardinge 139 in Kent's second attempt, leaving Hampshire a target of 444. Led by Mead (152) they made a brave attempt after five wickets had fallen for 135. Mead and the rugby international Harold Day (91) added 219 to carry the score to 354 for five but the last five wickets went down for 38. Mead made another hundred at Canterbury, where the new Saturday start was held to be "not to the advantage of Canterbury Week but it was impossible to go back to the old system." This notwithstanding, there were few causes for complaint when Kent won the 1923 match. The highlight was an innings of 236 by the left-handed Jack Bryan. He drove one ball into the pavilion, where it became so heavily embedded in the glass of the picture of the 1877 Canterbury Week that a new ball had to be obtained. The actual ball, still bearing its scars of embedded glass, was suitably mounted and presented to the club.

Such was Kent's dominance that they won four consecutive matches by an innings but Hampshire turned the tables with a seven wicket victory at

Southampton in 1925. This marked the start of a period of superb matches. The 1926 Whitsuntide found Wally Hardinge joined by a new star in APF Chapman in a partnership of 297 for the fourth wicket. Percy Chapman had a brilliant career at Uppingham and Cambridge University and played for Berkshire in the Minor Counties before qualifying by residence for Kent, where he entered the brewery business. A former director of the brewery had bet Chapman 50 cigars that he wouldn't score a century and offered him two bottles of port for each fifty. An unbeaten 159 led to the director receiving a telegram: "Six Cockburn 1896: 2 large Coronas, Percy." A tall, polished, left-handed batsman who excelled in the off drive, Chapman was an attacking player who captained England in 17 of his 26 Tests and led Kent from 1931 to 1936.

Hampshire staged a remarkable fight back in the 1926 Canterbury game. Centuries from Hardinge and Chapman placed Kent in a strong position and at tea on the second day Hampshire, 268 behind on the first innings, were 57 for six. Most people thought it would be all over within half-an-hour on the final morning but Mead and John Parker, a young amateur, added 194 before the close. When Parker was out for 156 on the third day, the pair had taken their seventh wicket stand to 270 in 170 minutes. Livsey then helped Mead put on 84 for the ninth wicket, Mead carrying his bat for 175 in a total of 439. It left Kent just over two hours to make 172, a stand of 135 in little more than an hour by Woolley and Chapman bringing victory by nine wickets.

The following year, 1927, saw Hampshire pull off a remarkable win at Southampton. Newman took 12-176 but Hampshire needed 375 in the fourth innings. Brown, Newman and Day made runs but inevitably it was Mead who saw them home by four wickets. He was still there at the end on 108, winning this particular battle with Freeman who finished with an analysis of 29.2-4-115-0. Honours were usually even in such duels; so it proved at Canterbury in August 1927. Hampshire, following on 326 behind after Freeman had taken six for 38, made a better fist of it in the second innings although everybody bar Mead struggled against the leg spinner. His effort to save the match spanned four hours and with the last man Boyes as his partner Mead prepared to face Freeman for the final over. By the time the last ball was due to be bowled most of the crowd had accepted what appeared to be the inevitable and began heading home. Mead played for the ball to come straight on but it was a googly which went off the edge to slip. Mead caught Woolley bowled Freeman 128; Freeman eight for 91, 14-129 in the match, Kent beat Hampshire by an innings and 92 runs. Neither Mead (40) nor Freeman (39) could be described as being in the first flush of youth but the individual battles of 1927 between the Championship's record-holders represent a high water mark in county cricket.

The holiday fixtures changed in 1928 and hereabouts it might be useful to explain the pattern. Hampshire and Kent met from 1920 to 1927, in 1930 and 1933 and from 1936 to 1939. Kent faced Gloucestershire in 1929, 1932 and 1935 and Somerset in 1928, 1931 and 1934. Hampshire's opponents were Gloucestershire in 1928, 1931 and 1934 and Somerset in 1929, 1932 and 1935. There were fresh highlights. In 1928 Kent visited Taunton at Whitsuntide, Chapman and Ames adding 237 for the fourth wicket in an innings victory over Somerset. It was back to normal for 1930, Kent winning at Southampton but rain washing out the last two days of the Canterbury fixture. In the meantime, Mead soldiered on. At Bristol in 1931 Johnnie Arnold made a century as Hampshire defeated Gloucestershire by 66 runs and then at Southampton Mead battled away for an undefeated 72 out of a second innings 172 only to see his colleagues succumb to Tom Goddard and Charlie Parker as Gloucestershire challenged for the title.

At Bristol in 1932, Chapman defied Goddard and Parker in making 76 out of a total of 167 but Freeman struck back with seven for 37, earning his side a lead of 73. Whit Monday was lost to the weather and on the final day, Kent, seeking runs quickly, lost two wickets for 55 before Woolley and Ames joined forces for a decisive partnership, adding 153 before the declaration at 208 for two. Gloucestershire, set 272, could do little against Freeman (six for 59) and Kent got home in style. The match was also notable for a double failure by Hammond, who was dismissed for 8 and 17. Revenge was inevitable. In August, the Canterbury fixture ended on the second day after Hammond, 136 in 95 minutes had inflicted severe punishment on Freeman: 18-0-135-3, Parker, Goddard and Reg Sinfield wreaking havoc among the Kent batsmen. The crowd thirsted for entertainment and those enterprising captains Percy Chapman and Bev Lyon arranged an extra game which was a forerunner of limited overs cricket. Gloucestershire made 194 and Kent 201 for five, Woolley scoring 86 in half-an-hour.

By the dry summer of 1933 Mead was 46 but he showed no sign of letting up. Hampshire ended the season with three counties below them, Kent with only two above them but form counted for nothing at Southampton when the counties resumed their holiday fixtures for the first time since 1930. Kent were dismissed for 299, Ames retiring hurt on 69 after sharing a partnership of 123 for the fourth wicket with Bryan Valentine. Mead then dominated Whit Monday. He gave a faultless display for just over five hours, hitting a five and 23 fours in 198. Hampshire made 468 and then some fine pace bowling by the tall Oswald 'Lofty' Herman (10-199 in the match) left Hampshire needing only ten runs to win. Neil McCorkell, a wicket-keeper-batsman unlucky to be in competition with Ames, held six catches in the game.

The days of the musical chairs nature of the holiday fixtures were numbered. Kent faced Gloucestershire in 1935, Charlie Barnett's hundred at Bristol being emulated by Ames and Woolley, Kent winning by six wickets. They also won at Canterbury in a game played during a very hot spell. Hammond made 163 and Goddard took ten wickets for the visitors but they collapsed in their second innings and Kent got home by 60 runs. Hampshire drew both their matches against Gloucestershire in 1934 and had the worst of a rain-affected draw at Taunton in 1935. The return at Southampton was also inconclusive, although Mead, after an unbeaten 94 in the first innings, registered his 150th hundred in the second.

Freeman and Woolley remained prominent in the series until the ends of their careers, in 1936 and 1938 respectively. Woolley and Mead made hundreds in the Whitsun fixture of 1936, when Fagg scored 257 (39 fours) in a match which produced 1,108 runs for three completed innings. Kent, the Championship leaders at that stage, made 502, Fagg, first in and last out after being missed when eleven, sharing a second wicket partnership of 211 with Woolley. Hampshire got away to a flyer in reply, Dick Moore and McCorkell beginning with 126 in 90 minutes before Moore left for 67. McCorkell was trapped in front by Freeman for 99 but Mead went on to 126. Herman, with seven for 59, bowled Kent out for 137 on the final day but there was not enough time for Hampshire to go in again.

Ames was granted the Canterbury game in 1937 for his benefit and a year later, following a Hampshire victory at Southampton, a collection was made as part of a testimonial for Woolley. Kent won by an innings, 12,000 watching the finish at 4pm on Monday after another huge crowd had basked in blazing sunshine on the first day. A big score by Fagg enabled Kent to repeat their success at Whitsun in 1939 but Hampshire avenged this defeat with a seven-wicket win at Canterbury. It was their seventh holiday success in the inter-war years, Kent having 16 with only five matches drawn. Kent had the better of the fixtures played outside the holidays, winning five and losing one of the 12.

Chapter Twenty
In the West

There is a lovely story relating to the credentials which enabled Raymond Robertson-Glasgow to qualify for Somerset. A tall, fast medium bowler able to swing the ball appreciably, he did well at Charterhouse and played for Oxford against Cambridge for four years. Popular and with a rich sense of humour, Robertson-Glasgow became a distinguished writer on the game, a correspondent with national newspapers and an author of charm and style. Crusoe, his nickname, owed its origin to a match against Essex during which he yorked Charlie McGahey. The Essex captain, Johnny Douglas, had not seen the dismissal and when McGahey came into the pavilion, he asked him how he was out. McGahey replied: "I was bowled by an old so-and-so I thought was dead, called Robinson Crusoe."

In June 1920, Oxford gained a two-wicket victory over Somerset at The Parks, Robertson-Glasgow taking five for 20 in the second innings. John Daniell, the Somerset captain, asked him if he would like to play for the county. Robertson-Glasgow had no qualifications for Somerset, having been born in Edinburgh, but he had relatives at Hinton Charterhouse in the county, one of whom was MP for Bath. Typically, Daniell, a forthright character with a splendid disregard for bureaucracy, decided that was good enough.

Daniell was one of the great men of Somerset cricket. He was only an average batsman, although he could hit hard, but he was a brilliant fieldsman at silly point and a strong and resourceful leader. A rugby international who captained England, he was later president of the Rugby Football Union and an England cricket selector. Daniel, who had spells as a schoolmaster and a tea planter, captained Somerset from 1908 to 1912 and 1919 to 1926 – a keen, popular, scrupulously fair leader with a colourful vocabulary if things went wrong and an intolerance of slackers.

In 1920, his crew sometimes consisted of ten amateurs and Len Braund, who was in his final season. Such was the case at Taunton, where Gloucestershire won the Whitsuntide encounter by one wicket after Charlie Parker had taken eight for 45 in the first innings. Parker started his career as a medium paced left-arm bowler, George Dennett being established as the county's slow left-arm spinner. In 1919, with Dennett still serving as a commissioned officer in India, Parker switched to slow left-arm with devastating effect. He spun the ball fiercely at a pace a little quicker than usual with bowlers of this type and although he was 36 when cricket resumed after the 1914-18 war, he continued playing until 1935.

Gloucestershire also had to economise. In 1915 they sold their Ashley Down ground at Bristol to the local company JS Fry and Sons. For 17 years the ground bore the company's name and was used by their employees. Under the conditions of sale, Gloucestershire retained the right to buy it back for the same price and the repurchase was completed in April 1933 after a fundraising appeal. Most of the August Bank Holiday fixtures were held at Bristol.

For the 1920 August Bank Holiday return at Bristol, Somerset fielded another veteran all rounder Ernest Robson as their solitary professional but it was an amateur, John Cornish White, who stole the headlines. Jack 'Farmer' White, son of a cricket-loving farmer, first appeared in 1909 when he was 17 but it was four years before he gained a regular place. He was, like Parker, one of the best slow left-arm bowlers in the country but there the comparison ends. White, also a useful lower-order right-hand batsman, relied on flight, accuracy and changes of pace more than spin and he was a tireless bowler who could keep going for long spells. Unlike Parker, who appeared in only a single Test, White played in 15, touring Australia with great success in 1928-29. He captained Somerset from 1927 to 1931 and led England in four Tests. Taciturn, as befits a lover of a game of poker, White's reserved manner meant that he was not the most popular of men but nobody doubted his talent. Parker and Dennett each took four wickets in the dismissal of Somerset for 169 but Gloucestershire (who fielded six amateurs to make 16 in the match) collapsed in astonishing fashion for a total of 22. White took seven for 10 in nine overs, Robson claiming the other three for 12. Daniell's declaration left Gloucestershire a target of 274, albeit with plenty of time, and some fine batting by Charles Townsend and Alf Dipper changed the course of the game. Dipper, a solid, opening right-hand batsman who gave his county 24 years of service, made 48 and Townsend a brilliant 84 out of 119 in 75 minutes. Others chipped in and Gloucestershire got home with four wickets to spare.

White, Dennett and Parker all had a field day when Gloucestershire won the 1921 match at Taunton and then there was another remarkable finish in the August Bank Holiday game at Bristol. On Saturday Somerset were dismissed for 212, Parker taking all ten to return figures of 40.3-13-79-10. Percy Mills, for so many years an effective medium pacer and off spinner, conceded 116 runs in 38 wicketless overs. He fared better in the second innings with five for 92, leaving Gloucestershire to make 205. Five men were out for 65 before the captain Foster Robinson and the wicket-keeper, the little left-handed Harry Smith, added 74. Smith was still there at the end, with 62 in two hours as his side scraped home by one wicket. Already Somerset must have been getting fed up with Parker and he was at it again at Taunton in 1922, with 11-139 in the match and 77 in Gloucestershire's first innings.

The counties were there or thereabouts in mid-table but Somerset delighted their followers in 1923 with two resounding holiday victories; by 343 runs at Taunton (Rippon and Dar Lyon made hundreds and White and Jim Bridges, an in swing bowler who started as a professional but finished as an amateur, took the wickets) and at Bristol by an innings after centuries from Lyon and Guy Earle (a maiden one which took only 70 minutes) and some excellent bowling by Robertson-Glasgow. Gloucestershire's supporters had to live with the humiliation for the whole winter but the dark days were to be illuminated in the most brilliant fashion. They had fought well at Bristol in 1923, not least through a last wicket partnership of 131 between William Gouldsworthy and John Bessant, but of far greater significance was an innings of 47 by the young opening batman Walter Hammond. Hammond was born at Dover, the son of an Army NCO. During his father's absence in the war Walter's mother decided to send him to Cirencester Grammar School, where he arrived in April 1918. Within three weeks his father was killed in action. Hammond's schoolboy exploits attracted Gloucestershire's attention and he played his first games as an amateur shortly after his 17th birthday. He became a professional in 1921 but Lord Harris discovered that he had no birth qualification for Gloucestershire and he was forced into the sidelines for two years. Hammond's first full season was 1923 and thus began the career of one of the greatest batsmen in world cricket. He possessed all the strokes, although later on he eschewed the hook, and the power and grace of his cover driving has never been surpassed. A genuine allrounder, he could bowl anything from fast to fast-medium swing and as a slip fieldsman he was peerless.

Two other notable names, one on either side, emerged around this time – the brothers Malcolm Douglas 'Dar' Lyon of Somerset and Beverley Hamilton Lyon of Gloucestershire, the West Country clashes often leading to ferocious sibling rivalry. They were born at Caterham in Surrey and attended Rugby School. From here, MD went up to Cambridge, earning Blues in 1921 and 1922 and making his debut for Somerset in 1920. A wicket-keeper and forcing right-hand batsman in the middle order, he was regarded as one of the best never to be capped by England. Lyon was called to the Bar in 1925 and an appointment as a magistrate in Gambia spelled the virtual end of his cricket career. Bev was also a hard-hitting batsman who gained a Blue at Oxford in 1922 and 1923 and played for Gloucestershire from 1921 to 1947. An apostle of positive cricket, Bev Lyon, who was captain from 1929 to 1934, originated a scheme in 1931 of counties declaring their innings closed after a nominal single ball in an attempt to gain a result in a rain-affected match. He also advocated county cricket on Sundays, an idea which took 36 years for the authorities to adopt.

The batting of Hammond and Dipper and, inevitably, the bowling of Parker began to dominate the matches although Somerset ended a mini-drought of five games without a win with a 21-run success at the Fry's Ground in 1926, a season when Gloucestershire were without Hammond, laid low after a tour of the West Indies. He returned in style at Taunton in 1927, reaching 197 before he was bowled by White. Somerset had made 427, with White and Cecil Charles Coles 'Box' Case making hundreds in sharing a fifth wicket partnership of 240 but the match was drawn. So, too, was the return at Bristol but through no fault of Parker. Reg Sinfield, whose all-round ability as a middle-order batsman and slow right-arm bowler earned him an England cap in 1938, took the first wicket when he bowled Jack MacBryan and then Parker took over. Somerset were all out for 201, Parker returning 57.5-20-103-9. Going in again 54 ahead, Somerset declared with nine wickets down for 101: Parker 34-15-51-7, but the match fizzled out. Even by Parker's standards, match figures of 91.5-35-154-16 are exceptional, although they rank as only the third best of his career.

Holiday fixture switches found Gloucestershire meeting Kent in 1929, 1932 and 1935, in which they won one and lost four of the six matches. Hampshire were their opponents in 1928, 1931 and 1934, these six bringing two victories and a defeat. Somerset failed to win any of their six games against Kent in 1928, 1931 and 1934, suffering five defeats. They were more successful against Hampshire (1929, 1932 and 1935), remaining undefeated in the six matches, with three victories.

By 1930, Gloucestershire had emerged as one of the outstanding teams in the country. The signs had appeared in 1929, when Tom Goddard astonished everybody by taking 184 wickets. Goddard had been an ordinary fast bowler before Bev Lyon persuaded him to spend a season in the Lord's nets with a view to converting him into an off spinner. Goddard's height and long, powerful fingers were ideal physical attributes and he never looked back. For a time, Gloucestershire headed the table and were neck and neck with five matches left but finished fourth. They were runners-up to Lancashire in 1930, despite winning 15 of their 28 matches to Lancashire's ten.

A double over Somerset helped their cause, although they had to work hard at Taunton. Dar Lyon made 210 (he was dropped by Goddard at mid-off when he was two) in a Somerset total of 372 but Bev Lyon and Sinfield responded with hundreds and Gloucestershire ended Whit Monday on 385 for six. "Forget the holiday crowd – just stay there," Bev Lyon told Sinfield, who went out and told the umpire: "Sorry about this but I'm here until half-past six." He added: "I simply nailed my studs to the ground. The Bank Holiday crowd hated me for it. When they barracked me, I shouted back at them. I'd been told what I had to do." Stay he did for six hours 20 minutes. Gloucestershire gained a lead of 69 on Tuesday and after bowling Somerset out for 144, got home by eight wickets. Dar Lyon was furious with his brother. "If I'd been watching that rubbish, I would have wanted my money back. And you call yourself an advocate of brighter cricket? That was disgraceful, Beverley." The younger brother responded: "You took too much for granted. In the end we outmanoeuvred you." The return took place on the Clifton College ground, Parker having another of those matches in which he carried all before him. In his 48th year, he took seven for 44 and six for 29 and with Hammond making an unbeaten 100, Gloucestershire won by nine wickets. Three seasons on, the topsy-turvy nature of these holiday fixtures was reflected in victory by an innings for Somerset, Gloucestershire promptly avenging this defeat at Bristol in August.

In later years, neither side could mount a challenge for the title, although Gloucestershire were fourth in 1936 and 1937 and third in 1939 but some fine players took the stage as the older ones departed. There was aggression at the top of both orders. Charlie Barnett's discipline and variety of strokes earned him 20 Test caps between 1933 and 1948 and a couple of centuries against Australia. With Hammond, who changed status from professional to amateur in November 1937 and captained his country and his county, Barnett helped give Gloucestershire formidable batting power. His opposite number as a destroyer of attacks in the Somerset team was Harold Gimblett.

Goddard had a match to remember at Taunton in 1937 when he took six for 65 in the first innings and then made an unbeaten 61, Basil Allen scoring a century and Hammond taking six wickets in Somerset's second innings as Gloucestershire cruised home. They completed the double at Bristol, in a match which produced some splendid holiday cricket. Barnett (85) and Hammond (110) shared a third wicket partnership of 162 after Arthur Wellard had captured two early wickets. Bev Lyon then made a hundred as the total reached 452, Wellard – an opening bowler of England quality but better-known for his feats of rapid scoring – taking six for 126. Gimblett, partnered by Frank Lee, responded with a savage assault on the bowlers which brought him 100 in 95 minutes, including five sixes and ten fours. Goddard and Sinfield recovered from the mauling to dismiss Somerset for 264 but Allen, probably to rest Goddard, did not enforce the follow-on, leaving his rivals 376 in five hours. Lee made 48 and at four o'clock on Tuesday, at 159 for three, Somerset were still in the game. Then an astonishing spell from Billy Neale's rarely used leg breaks brought him six for nine in 25 balls and Gloucestershire won by 198 runs.

This was a period of rich entertainment for the West Country holiday crowds and at Whitsuntide in 1938 they enjoyed one of the most thrilling finishes Taunton had seen in years. With half their wickets down in the second innings,

Gloucestershire's lead was only 64 but a masterly innings by Hammond (140 not out), aided by Lyon (88) enabled Allen to leave Somerset 283. When their seventh wicket fell they still needed 112 but Bertie Buse stayed three hours for 79, Wellard lashed 68 in 40 minutes (six sixes and five fours) and the wicket-keeper Wally Luckes hit two fours in the last over of the day, bowled by Sinfield, to get his side home by one wicket. Somerset's followers who made the journey to Bristol for the August return were given another treat. Frank Lee and Gimblett gave them a good start but Sinfield took three wickets without conceding a run before Bunty Longrigg stopped the rot. Longrigg, a solicitor, was a hard-hitting left-hand batsman who succeeded Reggie Ingle as captain in 1938. In partnerships with Dickie Burrough and Bill Andrews, he saw the total ascend to 358 for seven, at which point he was joined by an old Reptonian John Barnwell. They flayed the bowling to the tune of 143 in 90 minutes, the last 50 in 12 minutes. Longrigg, who was on 189, then suddenly told Barnwell he was going to declare at the end of the over. Barnwell (45) wanted to reach his half-century and asked Sinfield for a half-volley. "My smite landed a foot inside the boundary. Four instead of six – and I finished on 49," said Barnwell, the declaration coming at 501 for seven. Wellard's pace then troubled everybody except Hammond and Allen and his seven for 80 enabled Longrigg to enforce the follow-on. Somerset tried hard to force a victory but Hammond made an unbeaten hundred, Barnett got 55 and the young left-hander Jack Crapp stayed while 103 were added.

Gimblett made a hundred in an inconclusive match at Taunton in 1939 but Goddard dominated the return at Bristol. Gloucestershire now had a side of perfect balance, with Hammond and Barnett joined by a younger generation of George Emmett, Crapp and Neale. Andy Wilson was a useful wicket-keeper-batsman, Sinfield one of the best allrounders in the country and in George Lambert and Colin Scott the county discovered a pair of 20-year-old opening bowlers who were rich in promise. Above all, however, there was the Bristol pitch which turned almost from the start and was fully exploited by Goddard. Gloucestershire mounted a strong challenge for the title in 1939, twice defeating Yorkshire, but they faded in the closing stages. In the August Bank Holiday game, Emmett made 96 but nine wickets were down for 228 when Goddard joined Wilson. They added 101 for the last wicket in 70 minutes before Wilson was out for 64, Goddard remaining undefeated with 56. Somerset were then caught on a drying pitch and went down by an innings and 109 runs, Goddard taking five for 15 and nine for 44 to return a match analysis of 14-59.

This was Gloucestershire's 13th victory in the holiday matches, Somerset winning six with 11 drawn. Of the 12 games played outside the holidays, Gloucestershire had a 4-2 advantage including a victory at Bristol during the second half of the 1935 Whit week when Hammond scored his 100th hundred.

Chapter Twenty-One
Wallflowers

Like wallflowers without a partner at an old-fashioned dance, Essex and Worcestershire faced Hobson's choice when the holiday fixtures were drawn up for the 1920 season. In 1919 Worcestershire's absence from the Championship halted their matches with Warwickshire, who arranged to play Derbyshire instead. Essex had met Kent in 1919 but the Kent-Hampshire fixtures of 1920 left the returning Worcestershire as the alternative.

Otherwise there was no reason, traditional or geographical, for Essex and Worcestershire to play each other at such times. They had met on only six previous occasions, in 1910, 1911 and 1914, with Essex winning three of the games and Worcestershire one. Furthermore, Worcestershire's disastrous record in 1920 meant they were hardly the most sought-after of holiday opponents. It was an unpromising start to a new relationship but a long and fruitful association developed, initially centring on Leyton at Whitsun and Worcester in August.

Unsurprisingly, Essex won both the 1920 encounters with ease, although Worcestershire made them fight hard for a time at Leyton. On Whit Monday, Bowley, now well into the veteran stage, made 131, full of stylish drives and cuts, Pearson got 87 and although Perrin made 72, Essex, at 305 for seven, were still 26 behind on the second day. But Douglas scored 128, McGahey and Reeves added 121 in 80 minutes for the ninth wicket and the total reached 501. Douglas and Reeves then bowled Worcestershire out for 119, Essex winning by an innings and 51 runs. At Worcester, the margin increased to an innings and 242 runs in the August Bank Holiday match after Essex made 500, Douglas, en route to a double and the captaincy of MCC in Australia, getting 147. Poor Worcestershire had no luck; Essex ended Saturday on 405 for three and then the home side had to contend with stoppages for rain on Monday. Joseph Dixon, an amateur all-rounder who had been at Felsted before the war, took five for 53 and six for 47 with his fast medium bowling.

Essex generally fared better than Worcestershire during the inter-war period. Their lowest placing was 16th in 1928, with a highest of fourth in 1933 and 1939. The pitch at Leyton usually ensured stacks of runs but the county relinquished their lease on the ground at the end of the 1933 season and became a wandering club. There were mixed feelings. They had played there since leaving Brentwood in 1885 and Leyton, for all its trams and dinginess, had something about it. Charles Bray, who captained Essex on occasion but became better known as the cricket correspondent of *The Daily Herald*, wrote: "It was a bold move but one that proved to be successful. At the same time all those who had played on the old Leyton ground left it with regret. It certainly did not have beauty or charm, its wickets over a long period were far too much in favour of the batsmen and on a cheerless day it looked, and indeed was, a miserable place. Yet it had a character of its own." The team, too, had character. Douglas was, for some years, the best allrounder in the country and the batting was usually strong, with Jack Russell, Jack O'Connor, a fine wicket-keeper batsman in Jack Freeman and, later on, allrounders such as Laurie Eastman and Stan Nichols. Tom Pearce and Denis Wilcox shared the captaincy for most of the 1930s and they often had a fine hand of pace, with Kenneth Farnes, Nichols, John Stephenson and Hopper Read feared on the county circuit.

For Worcestershire defeats such as those in 1920 became an all-too familiar tale. Maurice Foster captained the side from 1923 to 1925 and also had to make most of the runs after Bowley finished. Maurice Jewell, who led the team back into the Championship, took over in 1926 and in 1928-29. A shrewd captain and a strong disciplinarian, MFS Jewell was a useful, attacking batsman who gave his county unstinting service. It is easy at this distance to disparage some of the amateurs of the 1920s and 1930s but *Wisden*, in Jewell's obituary after his death at 92, paid tribute to the devoted labours of men who gave up their summers to somehow get a side together, captain it, and keep the county going. Jewell extended this to the winter, even organising concert parties to raise funds.

Pearson soldiered on; Fred Root emerged as a devastating exponent of sharply delivered in swing bowled to a strong leg-side field and Reg Perks, Dick Howorth, the South African allrounder Sid Martin and Peter Jackson developed into a balanced and long-serving attack. Cyril Walters, the Nawab of Pataudi and the stylish and consistent Harold 'Doc' Gibbons, gave the batting power and depth but Worcestershire never rose higher than tenth between the wars until 1939 when they finished seventh. There had been continuing improvement by a happy side skippered by Hon Charles Lyttelton, later Lord Cobham, and the memories of the miserable 1920s (last place in 1922 and again from 1926 to 1928, with only a solitary victory in 57 completed Championship matches in the last two of these seasons) began to fade. Even then there were occasional golden moments. Charles Preece, a medium pace bowler, had such a day at Leyton in 1921 when he took seven for 35 as Essex were dismissed for 90. Worcestershire were strongly place at 237 for five but Douglas struck with four wickets for no runs, finishing with seven for 91 as the lead was restricted to 155. Essex then gave a demonstration of their batting power: 560 for five (Russell 151) when Douglas, who was 123 not out, declared, leaving the visitors 406 to win. Harry Higgins, who had been severely injured during the war, made a great effort with 133 after the start was delayed but nine wickets fell in three and a half hours. Douglas took his match analysis to 14-156, the last wicket falling at 273, 15 minutes from the close. Honours were shared at Worcester, when 13 amateurs took part, and the home side had the last laugh by finishing above Essex in the Championship table. But they were embarrassed beyond measure at Leyton in 1922 when George Louden and Douglas put them out for 49 and hundreds from Dixon and Freeman helped Essex to 521. Higgins battled away again with an undefeated 66 but the rest could do little against the leg breaks of Philip Morris (seven for 43) and Essex's winning margin was an innings and 297 runs.

The tide turned at Leyton in the Whitsun match of 1923 – the first of Root's years of success with his new style. Essex were dismissed for 97, Pearson taking six for 52 and Root four for 32, and Root went on to make an unbeaten 53 in the face of some good bowling from Douglas and Louden as Worcestershire led by 162. Although Perrin stayed until the end for 55, Root took six for 63 as Essex succumbed by an innings and 11 runs. They avenged this setback at Worcester after Russell (147) and Perrin (122) shared a partnership of 256 for the fourth wicket. Root's match figures were 12-215 and Maurice Foster made 97 for the home side but Douglas was able to set a target of 423. Worcestershire made a brave stab at it, Foster (149) and the talented amateur Leonard Crawley (85) – who later played for Essex but was never able to spare much time for cricket – adding 155 for the second wicket, but they were all out for 319.

Root's method was not lost on Douglas, who altered his style in 1923. He adopted Root's field of six men on the leg-side, aiming at the leg stump with in swingers and this brought him much success in the closing years of his career. Meanwhile, Root was now proving a handful for everybody and after Essex won the 1924 Leyton game they felt the full force at Worcester over the August Bank Holiday. He took nine for 40 in an Essex total of 110, finishing with 13-108 in the match, which was won by Worcestershire. It would be five years before they tasted holiday success again, Essex winning four of the next eight matches in Worcestershire's lean years. But when victory came it had the stuff of fairy tales.

The season of 1929 began with Worcestershire entertaining the South Africans for the first match of their tour. None of the Big Six wanted the fixture at such an early stage of the season so Worcestershire seized the opportunity and began a popular tradition that endured, apart from an occasional summer, for many years. Then, on 18, 20 and 21 May the side was in Leyton for the Essex match, where despite 64 from Gibbons, they were soon struggling with eight wickets down for 206. At this point a wealthy, 43-year-old amateur, Albert Lane, joined Root. Lane, an off break bowler and useful middle-order batsman, was one of the best amateur cricketers in the Midlands. Known as Spinney, he appeared in 45 matches for Worcestershire between 1914 and 1932 and 12 for Warwickshire between 1919 and 1925 and also played for his native county Staffordshire. In 1936, when the county established a nursery to develop young talent, it was under Lane's guidance and he served on an emergency committee during the 1939-45 war. That Saturday at Leyton, he hit out from the start, striking seven fours in making 44 in 33 minutes while Root remained scoreless. Lane went on to 70 in 65 minutes, hitting 11 fours with bold drives and ferocious cuts and pulls. Worcestershire had a lead of 84 on the first innings and on Whit Monday Lane did it again. Going in at 127 for eight, he made an unbeaten 60 out of 70 in 50 minutes, leaving Essex 282 to win. Bray (73) and O'Connor (40) gave the innings substance but the batsmen struggled against Root and the 42-year-old Humphrey Gilbert. A barrister, Gilbert, who bowled medium paced off breaks, had won a blue at Oxford and appeared for the Gentlemen before the war.

Bray said that as the thrilling match drew to a close, Lane urged on the bowlers with offers of considerable sums of money for each wicket. "Fred Root bowled like a hero. He kept plugging away with his in swingers and at the other end HA Gilbert, the old Oxford bowler, tall and slim, already getting on in years, bowled himself to a standstill. We needed 282 to win and it was a hot day. Gilbert sent down 41 overs to take four for 73 and as each man got out Gilbert raced to the pavilion, poured a bowl of cold water down his back and raced out on to the field again to continue his bowling. Fred Root sent down 47 overs and took five wickets." Bray blamed himself for Essex's defeat by 42 runs. "I was well set and then got out when I should not have done. I saw Spinney Lane just before he died and he recalled with glee his own triumph."

Worcestershire's Maurice Nichol and his Essex near-namesake Stan Nichols made hundreds at Leyton in 1930 but were overshadowed by Jim Cutmore (180) and Peter Smith's emerging leg breaks and googlies as the matches now became more evenly balanced. Smith bowled his team to victory at Leyton in 1933 after Nicholls had made another century and Cutmore 98 in a total of 500 but

Worcestershire took partial revenge in August. Eastman (100) top scored in an Essex total of 477 and Farnes took five for 74 as the home side were made to follow-on 250 behind. Worcestershire then treated the New Road crowd to an exhibition of sheer quality. Walters and Gibbons opened with a stand of 100 before Gibbons left for 41 and on the last day Walters and Pataudi made the game safe with a partnership of 182, clearing off the arrears for the loss of only one wicket. Walters, batting stylishly, made 134 and Pataudi, combining superb defence with brilliant stroke play, hit a six and 27 fours in an unbeaten 231 as the game ended with Worcestershire 472 for two.

Sadly, however, the Essex-Worcestershire matches of the 1930s were overshadowed by events which put cricket in perspective. In 1934, on Whit Saturday, Essex were 367 for six at Chelmsford, with Pearce and Nichols making hundreds. The Worcestershire players relaxed on Sunday by playing golf. In the evening they took part in some light-hearted wrestling before going to bed around midnight. Among them was Maurice Nichol, one of their most consistent batsmen and a player who looked likely to play for England at one stage of his career. In 1933 the stylish Nichol finished the season with three consecutive hundreds, bringing his total to eight that season, when he made 2,085 runs. It was an encouraging return to form because he had been seriously ill with pneumonia in 1931-32 and during the 1933 Whitsuntide fixture at Leyton he was taken ill at Stratford Station and had to retire from the game. On Whit Sunday evening in 1934 he seemed quite well, smoking a pipe in the hotel and reading before retiring. On the Monday a large holiday crowd learned that Nichol had died in his sleep from what turned out to be an enlarged heart. He was 29. A few minutes before 11.30am, Walters led out the Worcestershire side, followed by the not out batsmen, Eastman and Bray. All were wearing black arm bands and the spectators and the rest of the Essex team stood for two minutes' silence before play resumed. The circumstances masked some entertaining cricket, Essex making 469 and Worcestershire, 444 for three by Monday's close, responding with 515. Walters (178) and Gibbons (104) opened with 279, Pataudi made 97 and Martin 72. In August at New Road, Dudley Pope scored 129 for Essex, the match ending in a draw. A month later he was dead at the age of 27, his car being involved in a collision with a lorry at Writtle, near Chelmsford. Another car driven by Peter Smith, with whom Pope was going to Walton-on-the-Naze for the weekend, had passed a little way ahead. Smith heard the crash and when he came back found that Pope had been killed instantly.

Five years later, the hoodoo struck again. Worcestershire had made a good start to the 1939 season and a win over Hampshire at New Road sent them off to Chelmsford for the Whitsuntide match in high spirits. Essex made 271 on Saturday but on Sunday evening Charles Bull, the opener, and Syd Buller, the wicket-keeper, were involved in a road accident at Margaretting between Billericay and Chelmsford. Bull was killed and Buller, who would become one of the finest umpires in the game's history, was seriously injured. Deprived of two players – although the twelfth man Hugo Yarnold was allowed to keep wicket – Worcestershire were beaten by 295 runs.

Amidst all this, Essex performed a double over their rivals in 1935 and then the clock was turned back in a change of fixtures. Old rivals were faced in 1936 and 1937 as Essex met Derbyshire and Worcestershire faced Warwickshire. In 1938 Essex entertained the Australians at Southend over Whitsuntide. The tourists, without Bradman, won a low-scoring match inside two days but the match attracted 20,500 people, with 12,500 on Whit Monday. Glamorgan were the visitors to New Road that year but the Essex-Worcestershire fixture was restored over the August Bank Holiday, Farnes having match figures of 14-119 as Essex won by four wickets.

As far as results were concerned, the Bank Holidays were anything but fruitful for Worcestershire. They won only four matches, in 1923, 1924, 1929 and 1931, losing 16 with 15 left drawn. Of the five played outside the holiday periods in 1936-38, each side won twice but the lingering shadows of the 1930s were the tragic deaths of Maurice Nichol, Dudley Pope and Charles Bull.

Chapter Twenty-Two
Woolly Backs and Cobblers

It was business as usual for the Leicestershire-Northamptonshire holiday fixture, which had enjoyed a more or less unbroken run since 1905. Like many counties, Leicestershire found themselves with a mixture of ageing veterans – the captain Cecil Wood, King, Whitehead, Coe and Benskin were all on the wrong side of 40 – and untried youngsters when the Championship resumed in 1919.

In time, a useful side developed. George Geary became a fast medium bowler of Test match quality with a devastating leg cutter and Ewart Astill, the county's first professional captain in 1935, a tireless off spinner. Alec Skelding provided pace and character and Shipman, Snary, Bale and Haydon Smith were among other post-war bowlers. Tommy Sidwell, Paddy Corrall and George Dawkes kept wicket, Shipman, Eddie Dawson and Leslie Berry were the leading runmakers, with Geary and Astill more than useful with the bat. In the Championship their highest placing was sixth in 1935 and they finished last in 1933 and 1939. For Northamptonshire, the inter-war period was one of almost unqualified failure. They never got higher than 12th and that was in 1919, when only 15 counties competed, and they finished bottom of the table on eight occasions. Yet at times they possessed some fine individual players: Ben Bellamy, long-serving wicket-keeper and middle order batsman, Vallance Jupp, a colourful and convivial captain and off spinning all -rounder, batsmen such as Fanny Walden, Jack Timms and Fred Bakewell, Bill Merritt, the New Zealand leg spinner and Nobby Clark, the fast left-arm bowler who played for England.

For both sets of supporters the Bank Holiday fixtures alternating at Northampton and Aylestone Road were eagerly awaited. Brian Chapman told of boyhood memories of Leicestershire: "…the well-loved Aylestone Road pavilion, seen through the sunny haze of youth, with sandwiches and tea in a medicine bottle, the whole washed down with "giant" cherry ciders." But to others the adjacent power station was an unpopular and dominant factor, with clouds of fine ash descending on the ground, creeping into buildings, clothes and sandwiches. Dudley Carew wrote: "On one side it is bordered by broad, squat monstrosities which look like overgrown oast-houses and belong in spirit to the set of some futurist, nightmare film of industrialism." Carew said that those people who approached cricket in the hey-nonny-no, village greensward spirit should have been compelled to spend a week at Leicester as a corrective to their idealism. At least there may have been some respite from the ash and dust during the holidays. By contrast, the County Ground at Northampton, with its relative ease of access from the town centre, attracted no such complaints. It had been used by the county since 1886 and was shared with Northampton Town Football Club – the Cobblers, relating to the town's association with shoemaking - from the 1897-98 season until the end of October 1994, when the soccer club left for the Sixfields Stadium two miles away. Cricket had been restricted at the beginning and end of the football seasons when matches clashed but neither usage had much effect on the other since the overlap was only about 20 yards. In 1923 a prominent local agriculturist, Alfred Cockerill bought the ground for £10,000 and gave it to the club to be preserved for sport for ever. The maximum seating capacity at Northampton at this time was around 7,500.

More often than not, then, the counties were to be found in the lower half of the table; the annual matches of significance only to themselves and other counties fighting to avoid the wooden spoon. In 1920, when each won on its opponents' home ground, the matches were notable for some fine pace bowling from Northamptonshire's William 'Bumper' Wells, a Leicestershire hundred from Harry Whitehead and glimpses of past glory from Coe and King. Leicestershire won both of the 1921 holiday matches, Aubrey Sharp, no doubt still celebrating his return from hostilities, making a century at Leicester in August. He repeated this in a victory by an innings for Leicestershire over the following Whitsuntide when Geary and Astill proved too much for the Northamptonshire batsmen at Aylestone Road, rain ruining the return although not before Claude 'Dick' Woolley, elder brother of Frank, registered an unbeaten hundred. The one-sided nature of these fixtures continued in 1923 – when Leicestershire finished 14th and Northamptonshire 17th and last - with another Leicestershire double, marked by another hundred for Sharp, more success for Astill and Geary and a glimmer of hope for Northamptonshire as Albert 'Taffy' Thomas claimed eleven wickets in the match with his medium paced bowling.

The rot was stopped with a couple of draws in 1924. This coincided with the arrival of Jupp, who at 33 already had a fine career behind him. He began with Sussex as a professional but reappeared as an amateur after the war. At the end of the 1921 season, during which he scored 2,169 runs and took 121 wickets, he became secretary to Northamptonshire, qualifying as a player from 1924. Jupp was secretary for 11 years, captain for six and achieved six doubles for the county before he finished playing in 1938. In 1924, Northamptonshire won only one match, against Derbyshire, the only county to finish beneath them, but the following season brought nine victories and 11th place. Again, however, they had to yield to Leicestershire, who although ending one place below their neighbours, gained a comfortable win at Northampton at Whitsuntide. Skelding was the matchwinner with eight for 79 and six for 46 – 14-125 – and he took eight more in the return at Leicester. Charles Bray recalled opening at Aylestone Road for Essex in his first match. His partner Jack Russell passed on some advice: "Mr Bray, there are two bowlers you are just going to face. One runs a mile and bowls medium. The other takes six strides and lets her go. That's Skelding and he's almighty quick."

Northamptonshire fought fire with fire. Nobby Clark bowled fast left-arm with a high, immaculate action. He could be moody and difficult to handle but he produced some outstanding performances and played in eight Test matches between 1929 and 1934. Clark was prominent in Northamptonshire's victory by 58 runs over the August Bank Holiday at Aylestone Road in 1927 – their first over Leicestershire since 1920. They started badly, only Walden coping with the home team's bowlers in a total of 169. Jupp hit back with a seven-wicket haul but Northamptonshire faded after a good start, leaving Leicestershire to make 209, but Clark, Bill Wright and Jupp proved too much. It was all the more satisfying because Leicestershire had a fine season in 1927, finishing seventh. On June 8 they were second, with only the champions Lancashire above them. Northamptonshire had to settle for 16th, one place above Worcestershire. Such a home defeat had to be avenged and there was an early opportunity when the

Whitsun match of 1928 was scheduled for Aylestone Road. Leicestershire gained a lead of eight before Astill destroyed Northamptonshire's second innings. Wickets fell regularly against Thomas and Clark but Berry and Shipman steadied matters and Leicestershire got home by two wickets.

Relative parity was soon to end. Between 1930 and 1939, Northamptonshire played 250 Championship matches, losing 138 and winning just 18. Famously, between 14 May 1935 and 29 May 1939, they failed to win a solitary match – 99 Championship games without a single victory. They were bottom in the table seven years out of ten, 16th in two of the others (1932 and 1939) and 13th in 1933, when they won five matches. And yet bottom place in 1930 and 1931 was not reflected in the holiday fixtures, although Leicestershire won comfortably enough at Aylestone Road in the first of these summers at Whitsuntide. Geary was the catalyst with figures of 30-11-35-6 and 31-13-43-6, taking full advantage of a drying pitch, and then in a return ruined by the weather, 27.1-11-35-6. In both games he fought a rare duel with Bakewell, who was one of the most exciting batsmen of his generation. Comparisons were made with Bradman and Trumper and at one time he was felt to be Jack Hobbs's natural successor. A glorious strokeplayer and a fine fieldsman at short leg, Bakewell appeared in eight Tests and could have been on the verge of an Ashes tour down under when his career was ended at 27 by a car accident in 1936 which left him with a badly broken right arm. Some described Bakewell as being his own worst enemy but his former captain WC Brown paid eloquent tribute: "During an all-too-short first-class career his approach to life in general may have seemed somewhat lackadaisical. Out in the middle, though, he was a splendid chap to have on the side." Needless to say he was among the runs in the 1931 match at Leicester, with 84 in the face of some fine bowling from Astill, although he was overshadowed by Berry's 156. Both of the 1931 matches ended in draws but Leicestershire completely outclassed their neighbours in 1932 with two victories by an innings. At Leicester they closed Whit Saturday on 375 for six and took their total to 438 on Monday, Armstrong remaining undefeated with 152. Northamptonshire then collapsed against Geary and Astill and they must have been heartily sick of the sight of them by now. Geary was 38, Astill 44 and they would continue for several more seasons yet; due notice being served in the August return at the County Ground which resulted in another innings defeat. Geary took seven for 60 in 36.5 overs and followed this with four for 37. Jupp battled away for a hundred but Astill's six wicket bag in the second innings completed the rout.

Then, in 1933, the sun broke through, albeit briefly. In the scorching heat of Whitsuntide, Northamptonshire crushed their rivals by nine wickets at the County Ground. With Larwood injured, Clark was the fastest bowler in the country that year, and he wrecked Leicestershire's first innings on Saturday, taking seven for 36 in a total of 141. Only Dawson (75) offered any resistance. Timms consolidated Northamptonshire's position with 113, Jupp made 59 and the lead was 166. By the close on Whit Monday, Leicestershire were 170 for six and although Armstrong made 61, Reg Partridge and Clark each took four wickets and Bakewell then played an enterprising little cameo as Northamptonshire quickly scored the 48 required for victory. Then for a time over the August Bank Holiday, in more hot weather (temperatures reached 93F on Sunday), Northamptonshire looked set to repeat this achievement. On Saturday Bakewell gave a superb display, hitting three sixes and 22 fours before being last out for 192. Only two other batsmen reached double figures in a total of 299. After building on a first innings lead of 130, Jupp, who had taken four for 36, set Leicestershire 283 on the last day on a pitch which was showing signs of wear. Shipman and Berry began with an opening partnership of 141 and there was more good batting from Armstrong and Dawson. In the end Leicestershire got home by four wickets, with ten minutes of the extra half-hour remaining.

The fine weather hid the clouds. Clark left for the leagues following a row with the county in 1930 but returned after a couple of years. Jupp gave up the captaincy in 1931 and missed the whole of the 1934 season with rheumatism. He was missing again in 1935, serving nine months in prison for manslaughter after a motor-cyclist died following a collision with a car driven by Jupp in January that year. He returned to the side in 1936, a season when Northamptonshire had five different captains.

The decline now began in earnest for Northamptonshire and the holiday matches were no exception. Leicestershire won by an innings at Aylestone Road and by five wickets at Northampton in 1934. Then at the County Ground in 1935 Geary and Smith bowled unchanged throughout an innings' victory. The margin was closer at Leicester in August; by 25 runs with only 15 minutes of extra time remaining after Northamptonshire led on the first innings by 127, Smith having match figures of 10-147. It was in 1935 that the 47-year-old Astill took over the captaincy, sometimes leading an all-professional side. The furniture magnate and cricket enthusiast Sir Julian Cahn ran his own teams on private grounds near Trent Bridge and at Stanford Hall, his home on the Nottinghamshire-Leicestershire border. Nottinghamshire had been the first to benefit from his largesse but in 1933 he was elected as Leicestershire's representative on the Advisory Cricket Committee at Lord's. In 1935 he appointed the New Zealand batsman Stewart Dempster, who was qualifying for the county, as manager of one of his furniture stores in Leicester. Dempster, who was to take over as captain, would not be available until 1936, hence the appointment of Astill for a single summer. It proved a popular and successful choice, the county having its best season to date, winning 11 matches out of 24 and finishing sixth. Northamptonshire were last, a place they would occupy from 1934 to 1938, but for a couple of years, they managed to escape from the holiday matches with a series of drawn games. Bakewell showed just what he might have achieved had he gone to Australia in 1936-37, carrying his bat for a superb 120 in a total of 211 at Leicester in 1936, the evergreen Astill taking seven for 30. Rain ruined this encounter and the August match was also unfinished, Bakewell making 151 out of 297, Dempster responding with a century for the visitors. In 1937, Jupp was in form with bat and ball but hopes of victory at Leicester in August after Northamptonshire led by 33 were dashed by Berry (184 not out) and Armstrong (100 not out), who shared an unbroken partnership of 243 for the second wicket. A declaration left Northamptonshire fending off defeat.

New names were entering the lists. Frank Prentice, who made a big hundred and the Australian slow left-arm bowler Jack Walsh, who was to baffle hundreds of batsmen with his chinamen and googlies for years to come, were to the fore in Leicestershire's Whitsun victory by an innings at Aylestone Road in 1938. In August, Leicestershire made 352 at the County Ground, Armstrong scoring 125. Northamptonshire fell one run short, Timms making a hundred, and they also provided three substitutes for opponents who were delayed by railway holiday traffic. The match fizzled out, the only other point of note being Geary's last appearance in such games. At the end of the season he became coach at Charterhouse.

By now Northamptonshire were under the captaincy of a 26-year-old Cambridge Blue, Robert Nelson, a stylish left-handed batsman who had spent the winter gaining experience on the Stock Exchange but saw teaching as his future profession. Nelson led the team in their opening game of the 1939 season which brought victory over Cambridge University at Fenner's – ending a winless run, including non-Championship matches, of 101 games. Reality soon kicked in as the first four Championship games produced a draw followed by three defeats before the Whitsuntide fixture at Northampton. Years later, Dennis Brookes recalled Frank Prentice greeting him by saying that Jack Walsh would bowl Leicestershire to victory inside two days. When Dempster won the toss for Leicestershire and chose to bat, condemning the home side to a probable fourth innings against Walsh, the prophecy seemed to have substance.

Within 35 minutes, Leicestershire had lost half their side to the seamers Reg Partridge and Jack Buswell for eight runs. Two young batsmen, Maurice Tompkin and Gerry Lester, staged something of a recovery but they were all out for 134, Buswell and Partridge each taking three wickets and Nelson nipping out the last two. By the close the home side were 210 for two. Percy Davis made 84 before he was stumped off Walsh, sharing a second wicket partnership of 176 with Brookes, who was still there with 120 despite suffering from a sore throat and a boil on the neck which eased as the day went on. On a beautiful Whit Monday, 5,000 people turned up (attendance figures are always relative to a ground's capacity and 5,000 at the County Ground was equivalent to quadruple that number at one of the Test arenas) and they saw Brookes go on to 187, with 24 fours in just over four hours. At that point it was the highest score of what was to become an illustrious career and with Nelson making 44 and Ken James, the New Zealander wicket-keeper, 42 not out, the declaration came at 510 for eight. Walsh delivered 33 overs and took two for 157. By tea Leicestershire were 53 without loss but Bill Merritt's leg spin then took over. Merritt had been a colleague of James on New Zealand's tours of England in 1927 and 1931 and qualified for Northamptonshire that season. After tea he bowled Leicestershire out for 183, taking six for 56, the match ending at 6.40pm, ten minutes into the extra half-hour and with a day to spare. Northamptonshire had won their first Championship match since a victory at Taunton in 1935, by an innings and 193 runs. The crowd swarmed towards the pavilion, where Nelson gave a speech from the balcony: "I want to pay tribute to the team who have struggled through a trying period without losing heart, and who have kept cheerful in all circumstances. I feel we have welded ourselves into a good side and I do not think this should be our last victory." The 12th man, Vince Broderick, recalled manning the payphone next to the secretary's office and taking calls from people asking for the score. After the last wicket fell he saw a lady run on and make off with a stump.

It was their solitary Championship win of 1939 but it was sufficient to lift them away from the bottom, one place above Leicestershire, who also won only one game. The August Bank Holiday match ended in stalemate. There was no play on the Saturday and on Monday Northamptonshire made 300. More rain restricted play to 70 minutes on Tuesday, Leicestershire getting as far as 83 for three before the weather brought an end to the inter-war period. Just over a year later, 2nd Lieutenant RP Nelson died when a bomb hit the Royal Marines barracks at Deal.

Statistically the Leicestershire-Northamptonshire series from 1919 to 1939 was one-sided, with Northamptonshire winning only four – in 1920, 1927, 1933 and 1939 - of the 42 matches and being defeated on 17 occasions. But in several years there were dogfights, with the counties occupying the last two positions in the Championship in 1931, 1937 and 1939. It made for some absorbing and often entertaining cricket, with the matches alternating over the holidays between Whitsuntide and August.

Chapter Twenty-Three
Welsh Fervour

In a period between the wars which was besieged by economic hardship and clouded by political unrest, the holiday games provided a welcome break. From the Championship, through the Minor Counties – Northumberland v Durham, Cornwall against Devon or Dorset, Lincolnshire v Cambridgeshire – and down through the leagues to the village green, they pitted neighbour against neighbour, allowing easier journeys by train, tram, coach and, increasingly for those who could afford it, by car.

In 1921 Glamorgan, founded at Cardiff in 1888, joined the ranks of the first-class counties. They finished last in the 1921 Championship, suffering a similar fate in 1925 and 1929; indeed only on two occasions was their final placing in single figures, eighth in 1926 and seventh in 1937. A cumulative table for the period shows only Worcestershire and, inevitably, Northamptonshire, beneath them. Nevertheless they fielded some fine individuals: Maurice Turnbull, a batsman who became the first Glamorgan player to appear in a Test match, Johnnie Clay, who developed into a fine off spinner and useful batsman in a career which lasted from 1921 until 1949; batsmen such as Dai and Emrys Davies, Arnold Dyson, Eddie Bates and John Bell and the bowlers Frank Ryan and Jack Mercer.

County secretaries consulted the railway timetables for journeys to Cardiff and Swansea. Cardiff Arms Park, situated in the centre of the city on the banks of the River Taff, saw Glamorgan play there until 1966 when the ground was redeveloped as the Welsh National Rugby Stadium, the county then using Sophia Gardens. By contrast the St Helen's Ground at Swansea is a mile and a half west of the city centre, on the foreshore of Swansea Bay. As the 17th county, Glamorgan were left without holiday opponents. The problem was solved in what turned out to be the best possible way, by arranging matches against the tourists.

They faced a formidable task in the first of these when the 1921 Australians came to Swansea over the August Bank Holiday. The Australians had been at Portsmouth over Whitsuntide, where they easily defeated the Combined Services, with 132 from one of the greatest of all left-handers Warren Bardsley and seven for 52 from Jack Gregory among the best individual performances. Bardsley made another hundred at Swansea, where the Australians piled up 461 for eight declared in response to Glamorgan's 213, Riches and Bates each getting into the 70s. The game was unfinished but Glamorgan had not disgraced themselves and 1922 must have been something of an anti-climax. There was no touring team that season and August Bank Holiday was spent defeating a combined Oxford and Cambridge University.

Morale had been low in 1923 as the team suffered a number of setbacks but a victory over Gloucestershire at the end of July left them in good heart for the Bank Holiday match against the West Indies at Cardiff Arms Park. The tourists had not then been elevated to Test status but, under the captaincy of HBG Austin, they brought a strong side to South Wales, including George Challenor and Learie Constantine. Although he was still qualifying, Glamorgan were able to select Mercer, the former Sussex medium fast bowler, for this match. The tourists had plenty of pace in Francis, John and Constantine and it was George John who did the most damage with seven for 52 as the home side were dismissed for 115. Some fine seam bowling from Trevor Arnott (seven for 40) restricted the lead to 86 but a large holiday crowd saw Glamorgan subside to 128 for four in their second innings. At this point Jimmy Stone, a batsman who had spent 15 years with Hampshire, made 108, adding 137 in 90 minutes with Frank Pinch (55). The total reached 324, leaving West Indies with a target of 239. They started well and at 185 for five were in sight of victory but Mercer trapped Challenor lbw for 105 and the innings subsided for 195, Mercer taking four 41. There were great celebrations on the Arms Park ground to mark Glamorgan's success.

Pennies began to drop. The touring sides were usually a major attraction and Glamorgan had stuck gold with matches which not only attracted large crowds but were a welcome respite from the rigours of the Championship. The South Africans were here in 1924 under the captaincy of Herbie Taylor but they brought little joy for Glamorgan. Their visit to Cardiff Arms Park coincided with bad weather which prevented play on August Bank Holiday Monday and Tuesday. James Blanckenberg enjoyed Saturday, however, taking eight wickets in the Welsh total of 178, the Springboks ending the day and the match on 15 for one. There was more rain about in 1926 when the Australians were here, the cricket having to be set against the background of the General Strike. That ended after eight days in May, but the miners stayed out for months, South Wales being among several areas to suffer deprivation. At Whitsuntide the tourists gained an innings victory over Oxford University, Arthur Richardson's off breaks claiming eleven wickets.

Meanwhile Glamorgan, now led by Clay, were having an astonishing season. They had finished last in 1925, with only one win and 20 losses – 13 consecutively - in 26 Championship matches but the following year saw a remarkable turnaround. Early in the season they headed the table and they were in second place when the Australians arrived at St Helen's. There was a record crowd of 25,000 on August Bank Holiday Monday, with hundreds of people left outside. Mercer caused problems on Saturday, with five for 74 but neither he nor anybody else could shift Bill Ponsford, who was still there with 143 when the innings closed for 283. Glamorgan's batsmen found the spin of Clarrie Grimmett and Arthur Mailey too much for them to handle. Although the 20-year-old Cyril Walters, later to join Worcestershire and captain England, made an unbeaten 42 they were defeated by 224 runs. The defeat seemed to take the stuffing out of the county side. They failed to win any of their remaining nine games and finished eighth.

Cardiff was the venue in 1927 for the August holiday match against the New Zealanders, who were touring England for the first time. No Tests were played but the Kiwis gave a good account of themselves, with Dempster (Leicestershire), Merritt and James (Northamptonshire) and Charles Dacre (Gloucestershire) going on to make an impact in county cricket. They drew with Oxford University at Whitsuntide, Errol Holmes making 165 for the hosts, and gained a comfortable victory at Cardiff. Mercer and Clay toiled away but Dempster's 167 put the tourists firmly in command. Clay made his maiden century in the second innings but it was not enough. Apart from 1970 that was the last season in England in which no Test matches took place, the West Indies being accorded such status in 1928. At Whitsuntide, Constantine's pace was too great for Cambridge University, while at Swansea the touring captain RK Nunes made a hundred and there were useful contributions from Challenor. Ryan took seven for 52 in the second innings, Glamorgan needing 236, but the match ended in a draw with their score on 101 for three.

The South African tour of 1929 was significant in that it gave Glamorgan two matches against the tourists, at Whitsuntide and August Bank Holiday, for the first time. The first game was at the tree-lined Ynysangharad Park, Pontypridd, where Glamorgan had played for the first time in 1926. The club had been suffering financially and decided to experiment with a move up the Taff Vale in quest of support outside Cardiff and Swansea. More fixtures were scheduled and there were several civic receptions arranged to entertain the South Africans. Out in the middle Mercer offered no such hospitality with eight for 60 and six for 59 but Glamorgan found Cyril Vincent's slow left-arm equally difficult and the Springboks won by 170 runs. Mercer was again among the wickets at Swansea in August, where Trevil Morgan made an unbeaten century, but rain washed out Saturday and the match was inconclusive.

Everything Glamorgan had achieved against the touring teams paled before their performance against the 1930 Australians at Swansea. Maurice Turnbull was appointed captain and guided the side into 11th in the Championship. Australia, heavily defeated by England in 1928-29, regained the Ashes with a 2-1 victory in the series during which Bradman made 974 runs at an average of 139.14. This was the season in which he first entered the holiday matches. As the summer progressed followers of county cricket anxiously scanned the Australian team lists to see if this new phenomenon would be playing and he turned out for both of the Bank Holiday crowds.

In the Whitsun match at Cambridge, the University could make only 145 and 225, Freddie Brown getting 52 in the second innings and Bradman enjoying unusual success with leg breaks, taking three for 35 and three for 68. After tea on the first day, he went out to bat with the score on 13 for one. He stayed 50 minutes for 32 before being caught in the slips trying to cut a very wide ball. On Monday, Bill Woodfull (216) and Stan McCabe (96) enabled the former to declare at 504 for eight, victory being achieved by an innings and 134 runs. At Swansea more than 50,000 people packed St Helen's over the three days, the gate boosted by the news that Bradman was playing. Rain prevented any play on Saturday until 4.20pm and Bradman, going in at 93, had 47 minutes batting overnight, making 27 not out on a dead pitch. Ponsford was out for 53. The hordes arrived on August Bank Holiday Monday, looking on as the pitch offered Frank Ryan's slow left-arm increasing help. Bradman and McCabe took their third wicket partnership to 101 in 86 minutes but once they were separated the last seven wickets added only 49. Bradman's 50 took 104 minutes and he batted exactly two hours for 58 (five fours) before being bowled by Ryan, playing back, at 215 for five. Ryan's six wickets cost 76 but Glamorgan were unable to cope with Grimmett and were all out for 99. Vic Richardson, the Australian captain, went for quick runs and his declaration at 71 for one (Bradman 19 not out) left Glamorgan 218 in 165 minutes. Bates (73) and Turnbull (52) gave them a flying start with 93 in just over an hour and the chase was on. Wickets fell but the runs came and eventually Richardson slowed the game down by using his faster bowlers. Glamorgan ended on 197 for seven, 21 short. A year later, as Glamorgan economised, two of the heroes, Bates and Ryan, both in the veteran stage, were released. The county adopted a home-grown policy and 1932 was to see the start of a new opening partnership which lasted for years as Emrys Davies and Arnold Dyson replaced Bates and Bell at the head of the order.

Meanwhile two holiday fixtures against the 1931 New Zealanders brought some fine batting from Dempster at Cardiff, where the match was drawn, and a comfortable win for the tourists at Swansea. The Indians also found South Wales to their liking in 1932, with the Whitsun match at Cardiff being drawn, Turnbull declaring after Dyson made 100 and setting the tourists 257. Wazir Ali hit 108 but time ran out at 184 for four. In the return at Swansea, Mercer and Clay were among the wickets but Amar Singh's pace wrecked Glamorgan's first innings and they were beaten by 54 runs. It was a disappointing outcome for the Welsh crowd but the Cardiff faction of it received a rare treat in the 1933 Whitsun game, when the West Indies were the visitors. George Headley, still arguably the greatest batsman to emerge from the Caribbean, gave a delightful display, his timing and quick footwork being brilliant. He made 129 in a total of 475 but Dyson, excelling with late and square cuts and drives past cover, responded with 147 for Glamorgan. Glamorgan headed the West Indian total by 18, though on the last day the tourists were handicapped through both their fast bowlers Martindale and Griffith suffering from strains. There was added interest in the season because Turnbull appeared in two of the three Test matches against the West Indies (he made only 28 and four) so his 60 at Cardiff had added significance. At Cardiff everything went the West Indies' way and they cruised home by ten wickets, the main feature being a hard hitting century by Sealey.

This paved the way for another Australian year but there was to be no Bradman, who was injured, at Swansea in August. He played at Oxford over Whitsuntide but never appeared comfortable in making 37 on the Saturday. Len Darling made 100 and Grimmett and Fleetwood-Smith spun the University out twice for an innings' victory. At St Helen's Woodfull was unbeaten with 228 in a total of 440 for seven declared and then Bill O'Reilly and Fleetwood-Smith got among the wickets but the game was drawn.

It was all very one-sided but Glamorgan's followers were to be richly entertained when the South Africans came again in 1935. On Whit Saturday at Cardiff the tourists batted all day for 327 for three, Herbert Wade and Eric Rowan making hundreds and adding 256 for the second wicket. The total reached 401 and on Monday Glamorgan were dismissed in three hours for 142. Following on, Glamorgan, requiring 259 to avoid defeat by an innings, began the last day with four men out for 10. The fifth wicket also went down at 10 and although Cyril Smart offered resistance, the eighth and ninth fell in successive balls from Langton after tea with the score on 114. Smart was then joined by Donald Hughes, a 24-year-old schoolmaster from Ebbw Vale and later headmaster of Rydal School, who was making his county debut as a right-arm fast medium bowler. Hughes not only survived the hat trick ball but launched into an incredible attack on the bowling which produced four sixes and six fours in an unbroken partnership of 131 for the last wicket. Smart joined in the fun, reaching his century with a six and shortly afterwards lofting the ball out of the ground and through the window of the nearby Grand Hotel in Westgate Street. The match ended with Glamorgan 245 for nine; Smart 114 not out (three sixes and 11 fours), Hughes 70 not out. There was more fun in the return at Swansea, when 17,000 attended on August Bank Holiday Monday. Glamorgan needed 251 to win and began well before Dyson was caught at slip by Louis Duffus, a cricket journalist and author from Johannesburg who had played in the Currie Cup and was fielding substitute for Wade. The spin of Vincent and Bruce Mitchell then got the tourists home by 96 runs.

Poor weather over the 1936 Whitsun affected all of the holiday games and India were restricted to an hour's play on the Saturday and none at all on Tuesday at Fenner's. Glamorgan entertained Sir Julien Cahn's XI at Cardiff for Mercer's benefit but rain restricted the attendance. In August they delighted their followers with an innings victory over the Indians at Swansea. Overnight rain prevented any play on Saturday but the pitch suited Mercer (seven for 48) on Monday and the tourists were all out for 112. Smart (58) and Turnbull (50) helped Glamorgan to a lead of 126 and the Indians then collapsed against Clay, who took eight for 14 as nine wickets fell for 49. Jahangir Khan and Mahomed Nissar then added 65, Clay going for 29 in his last three overs, before Dai Davies bowled Nissar for 49. Glamorgan were now getting into the habit of beating the tourists and they recorded a notable double over the New Zealanders in 1937. At Cardiff, Closs Jones, a young off spinner, took 10-94 in the match and Richard Duckfield made a century, the winning margin being six wickets. At Swansea Emrys Davies made 58 in Glamorgan's 229 before the pace of Austin Matthews and slow left-arm from Davies gained a lead of 102. This was consolidated by an opening partnership of 157 by Davies and Dyson, some big hitting from Smart (94) ramming the advantage home. New Zealand, needing 443, fell apart against Davies and Clay and were beaten by 332 runs. If ever there was a man of the match, it was Emrys Davies in this game: 58 and 78 and 9-46 in 24.4 overs.

He was among the runs again when the Australians came to Swansea in 1938, with 58 in a total of 145 for five declared. Although more than 25,000 people turned up on August Bank Holiday Monday, rain ruined the contest. Turnbull declared to enable the spectators to have an opportunity of seeing the Australians bat on the third afternoon on a soaking pitch which was really unfit for play. Australia made 61 for three in 32 overs, Bradman, coming in at 3-1, staying 63 minutes for 17 before being stumped by Haydn Davies off Clay at 43.

In 1939, Wilfred Wooller, the Welsh rugby three-quarter who was to become one of the greatest figures associated with Glamorgan cricket, made his mark on the Whitsuntide game against the West Indies at Cardiff. Wooller, middle order batsman, right-arm medium fast bowler, brilliant close fieldsman and a future captain, club secretary and Test selector, was then 26, having gained a Blue at Cambridge in 1935 and 1936. Turnbull made 60 but six men were out for 156 before Wooller hit two sixes and 13 fours in 111. With Haydn Davies (64) he added 103 for the eighth wicket in 50 minutes. West Indies, needing 282 for victory, fell 73 short, Wooller taking five for 69. The Welsh fervour followed the tourists to Swansea, where the dismissal of 25 men on Saturday for 273 seemed to have ruined the match, Matthews being Glamorgan's chief destroyer with seven for 21. Haydn Davies (seven catches in the game) hit 58 in the second innings and West Indies needed 191. A Bank Holiday Monday crowd of 7,000 saw eight wickets go down for 181 before Constantine, with a six and a four, won the match. It was an entertaining end to the inter-war years.

View of Park Avenue, Bradford in the 1920s

Roy Kilner
5-23 at Old Trafford in 1923 and 5-14 at
Bramall Lane in 1925

Hedley Verity
87 wickets in Roses Matches between 1931 and
1939

Cecil Parkin
6-88 and 8-35 at Old Trafford in 1919

Eddie Paynter
152 at Bramall Lane in 1932

This card does not necessarily include the fall of the last wicket

Surrey County Cricket Club
KENNINGTON OVAL

4 D.

SURREY v. NOTTINGHAMSHIRE
Saturday, August 1st, 1959 (3 Day Match)

SURREY	First Innings		Second Innings	
1 Stewart, M. J.	b Atkinson	15	c Hill M., b Springall	32
2 Fletcher, D. G. W.	b Atkinson	56	c Springall, b Morgan	44
3 Barrington, K.	b Springall	4	c Millman, b Morgan	51
4 Clark, T. H.	c Poole, b Cotton	10	NOT OUT	22
5 Constable, B.	c Winfield, b Springall	21	NOT OUT	25
‡6 Swetman, R.	c Atkinson, b Springall	12		
7 Lock, G. A. R.	b Springall	2		
8 Gibson, D.	b Springall	80	DID NOT BAT	
9 Laker, J. C.	c Millman, b Springall	9		
*10 Bedser, A. V.	c Hill N., b Cotton	31		
11 Loader, P. J.	not out	18		
	B2, l-b , w1 , n-b	3	B , l-b2 , w , n-b	2
	Total	261	Total 3dec. 176	

Fall of the wickets.   Average runs per over   2.30
1—35 2—42 3—63 4—108 5—108 6—111 7—124 8—140 9—219 10—261
1—45 2—128 3—129 4— 5— 6— 7— 8— 9— 10—

BOWLING ANALYSIS	First Innings						Second Innings					
	O.	M.	R.	W.	Wd.	N.b.	O.	M.	R.	W.	Wd.	N.b.
Cotton	21	7	64	2	1		13	2	26	0		
Matthews	32	4	80	0			5	0	22	0		
Atkinson	36	14	66	2			13	3	40	0		
Springall	23.1	11	43	6			13	2	54	1		
Morgan	1	0	5	0			8	1	32	2		

NEW BALL may be taken at the discretion of the fielding captain either (a) after 200 runs have been scored or (b) after 75 overs have been bowled. In the latter case a WHITE disc will be shown on the main score board at the end of the 65th over and will be replaced by a YELLOW disc after the 70th over. At the commencement of the 75th over both discs will be exposed and remain until the new ball has been taken.

Next Match, Thurs., Aug. 6th (1 Day) Lambeth Cricket Club

NOTTINGHAMSHIRE	First Innings		Second Innings	
1 Hill, N.	c Swetman, b Bedser	7	c Barrington b Bedser	27
‡2 Millman, G.	b Loader	1	b Loader	1
3 Winfield, H. M.	b Gibson	7	c Swetman b Bedser	10
4 Springall, J. D.	c Laker, b Bedser	9	b Loader	0
*5 R. T. Simpson	b Gibson	5	NOT OUT	108
6 Poole, C. J.	b Loader	52	b Gibson	63
7 Hill, M.	b Gibson	20	b Gibson	4
8 Atkinson, T.	b Bedser	8	c Laker b Loader	27
9 Morgan, M.	b Bedser	4	c Bedser b Loader	0
10 Cotton, J.	b Bedser	1	b Loader	0
11 Matthews, C. S.	not out	1	b Loader	2
	B4, l-b2 , w , n-b	6	B8, l-b8, w , n-b1	17
	Total	121	Total	259

Fall of the wickets.   Average runs per over   2.18
1—9 2—9 3—25 4—25 5—40 6—76 7—105 8—119 9—119 10—121
1—13 2—30 3—33 4—47 5—152 6—158 7—237 8—237 9—247 10—259

BOWLING ANALYSIS	First Innings						Second Innings					
	O.	M.	R.	W.	Wd.	N.b.	O.	M.	R.	W.	Wd.	N.b.
Loader	16	3	39	2			17.2	3	51	6		1
Bedser (A.V.)	19.3	8	29	5			21	6	64	2		
Gibson	15	3	27	3			15	2	34	2		
Laker	5	1	20	0			12	3	44	0		
Lock							14	1	37	0		
Barrington							5	0	12	0		

*Captain ‡Wkt.-keeper
Umpires—Copson & Langridge   Toss won by—Surrey   Bonus Points—Surrey
RESULT—Surrey won by 57 runs
Hours of Play—1st Day 11.30—6.30. 2nd Day 11.0—6.30. 3rd Day 11.0—5.0 or 5.30. Lunch 1.30 all days

Printed on the ground by the Surrey County Cricket Club Printing Department

A century for Reg Simpson, fifty in each innings for Cyril Poole and five wicket hauls for Alec Bedser and Peter Loader

THE GILLETTE SAFETY RAZOR COMPANY

are once again delighted to sponsor the

ONE-DAY KNOCK-OUT COMPETITION

for the

GILLETTE CRICKET CUP

This card does not necessarily include the fall of the last wicket

Price 6d.

May 28, 30 and 31.

Notts. won the toss

NOTTINGHAMSHIRE v. SURREY

Nottinghamshire

		1st Innings		2nd Innings	
1	Bolus, J. B.	c Tindall b Pocock	54	lbw b Jefferson	8
2	†Hill, N.	c Edrich b Storey	23	c Tindall b Harman	23
3	Whittingham, B.	c Tindall b Pocock	7	Tindall b Jefferson	7
4	Moore, H. I.	Not out	65	c b Barrington	65
5	White, R. A.	c Harman b Storey	36	c Harman b Storey	36
6	Parkin, J.	Storey b Storey	13	c b Barrington	13
7	‡Swetman, R.	Storey b Jefferson	58	c b Bowling	58
8	Taylor, M.	Not out	6	Not out	6
9	Forbes, C.	c b Harman	35	Not out	
10	Johnson, A.				
11	Davison, I.			21	
	Extras			6 8, 1b1, w7, w7	
			260-7		**233-8**

†Captain ‡Wicketkeeper

1st Ins. 1-56 2-74 3-113 4-155 5-174 6-192 7-149 8-229 9- 10-
2nd Ins. 1-7 2-15 3-58 4-90 5-116 6-147 7-232 8- 9- 10-

Surrey

		1st Innings		2nd Innings	
1	†Stewart, M. J.	c Taylor b Davison	4	b Johnson	8
2	Edrich, J. H.	c Moore b Forbes	137	b Davison	24
3	Tindall, R. A. E.	c and b Forbes	19	b Swetman	91
4	Barrington, K. F.	not out	49	c Swetman b White	104
5	Willett, M. D.			c Swetman b Forbes	35
6	Storey, S. J.	c White b Forbes	0	Not out	51
7	Jefferson, R. I.	not out	17	Not out	7
8	Pocock, P. I.				
9	Arnold, G.				
10	‡Long, A.				
11	Harman, R.				
	Extras		13		20
		Inns. closed (65 ov.) 4 wks.	**239**		**391-5dec**

†Captain ‡Wicketkeeper

1st Ins. 1-11 2-74 3-213 4-213 5- 6- 7- 8- 9- 10-
2nd Ins. 1-23 2-54 3-197 4-251 5-313 6- 7- 8- 9- 10-

Bowling Analysis (Nottinghamshire)

	O	M	R	Wk	N	W

Bowling Analysis (Surrey)

	O	M	R	Wk	N	W
Davison, I.	16	2	58	1		
Johnson, A.	15	1	47	0		
Forbes, C.	18	4	74	3		
Taylor, M.	16	4	47	0		
White, R.A.						

Umpires—T. W. Spencer & W. F. Simpson

Hours of Play—1st Day, 11.30—6.30. 2nd Day, 12—7, 3rd Day, 11.30—6 or 6.30.

Lunch, 1st & 3rd Day 1.30 to 2.10 p.m. 2nd Day 2 to 2.40 p.m.
Tea approx. 4.30 p.m.

1st Innings restricted to 65 overs

Next Home Match v. Hampshire June 4, 5 and 6

Scorers A. Wheat and A. Sandham

The last Whit Monday clash between Nottinghamshire and Surrey, 1966

*Jack Hobbs
226 as the First
World War was about
to begin and a further
ten centuries in Bank
Holiday matches*

*David Fletcher
194 in Surrey's total
of 706-4dec at Trent
Bridge in 1947*

*Percy Fender
Great friend
and rival
of Arthur Carr*

*Roger Harman
8-12 for Surrey at
Trent Bridge in 1964*

*A.P. 'Tich' Freeman
(right)
Prolific wicket-taker:
14-119 v Hampshire
in 1927 was typical*

*Harold Larwood
(below)
One of the greatest
fast bowlers*

*Jack O'Connor
(above)
An Essex regular
between the Wars*

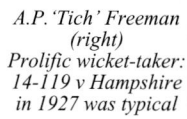

*Philip Mead
(above)
Always in the runs*

*V.W.C.Jupp
(left)
Six doubles for
Northamptonshire*

*Maurice Turnbull
and
Don Bradman
at Swansea in 1938
when only five hours play
was possible*

*Programme for
Glamorgan's match against
the 1948 Australians*

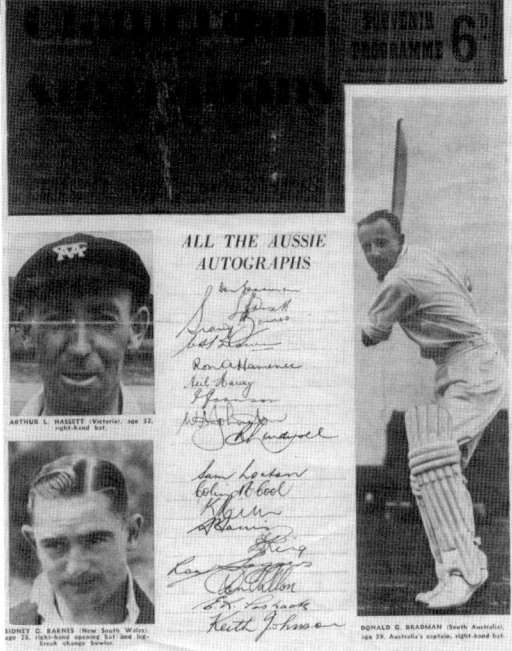

Alan Watkins catches Jack Cheetham
to set up Glamorgan's victory over the South Africans in 1951

The Swansea crowd when Glamorgan defeated the 1968 Australians
on what would have been the original August Bank Holiday

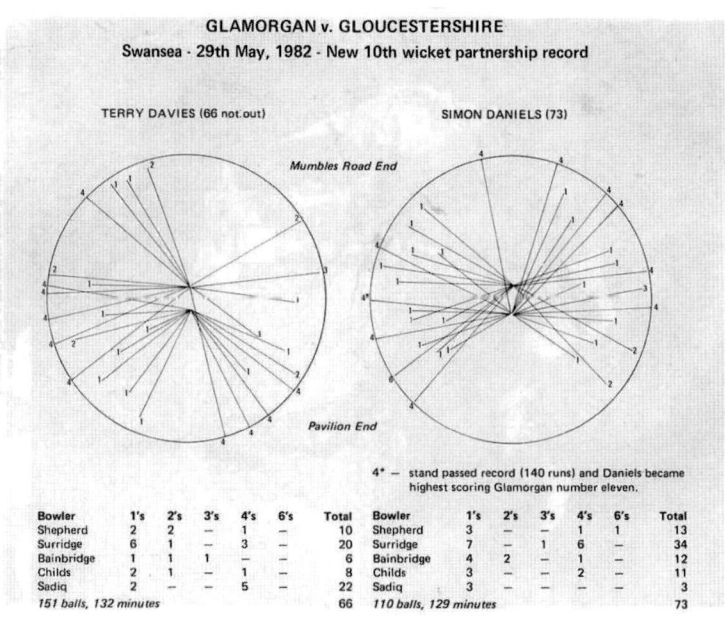

GLAMORGAN v. GLOUCESTERSHIRE
Swansea - 29th May, 1982 - New 10th wicket partnership record

TERRY DAVIES (66 not.out)　　　　　SIMON DANIELS (73)

Mumbles Road End

Pavilion End

4* — stand passed record (140 runs) and Daniels became
highest scoring Glamorgan number eleven.

Bowler	1's	2's	3's	4's	6's	Total	Bowler	1's	2's	3's	4's	6's	Total
Shepherd	2	2	—	1	—	10	Shepherd	3	—	—	1	1	13
Surridge	6	1	—	3	—	20	Surridge	7	—	1	6	—	34
Bainbridge	1	1	1	—	—	6	Bainbridge	4	2	—	1	—	12
Childs	2	1	—	1	—	8	Childs	3	—	—	2	—	11
Sadiq	2	—	—	5	—	22	Sadiq	3	—	—	—	—	3
151 balls, 132 minutes						66	*110 balls, 129 minutes*						73

The record 10th wicket partnership for Glamorgan:
143 by Terry Davies and Simon Daniels
against Gloucestershire Spring Bank Holiday 1982

The record breaking pair: Simon Daniels and Terry Davies

Denis Smith
(left)
Derbyshire player
and coach 1927-1972

Walter Hammond
(above)
After many seasons of
outstanding success a
sad ending in 1951

Charles Barnett
(above)
Rapid scoring
opening batsman

Stan Worthington
(above)
A true Derbyshire
stalwart

Arthur Wellard
(right)
Opening bowler and
hitter of sixes

Leslie Ames
(above)
Both his benefit
matches were Bank
Holiday fixtures

Les Berry
(above)
Scorer of 45 centuries
including 156 v
Northamptonshire in
1931

Harold Gimblett
(above)
135 against
Gloucestershire in
1946

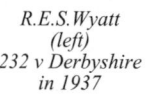

R.E.S.Wyatt
(left)
232 v Derbyshire
in 1937

Reg Perks
(right)
Ever-present from
1930 to 1955

John Langridge and Ted Bowley
stand in front of the Hove scorebox after their opening partnership of 490
against Middlesex in August 1933

LORD'S **GROUND**

MIDDLESEX v. SUSSEX
(DENIS COMPTON'S TESTIMONIAL)
Saturday, Monday & Tuesday, June 8, 10 & 11, 1957   (3-day Match)

	SUSSEX	First Innings		Second Innings	
1	Smith, D. V.	c Moss b Titmus	149	c Compton b Bennett	68
2	Lenham, L. J.	LBW b Hurst	44	c Hurst b Titmus	26
3	Parks, J. M.	b Bennett	7	c Murray b Moss	39
4	Suttle, K. G.	c Warr b Titmus	59	b Titmus	10
5	Foreman, D. J.	b Bennett	0	c Bennett b Hurst	22
6	Willson, R. H.	Run Out	3	c Compton b Hurst	0
†7	R G. Marlar	LBW b Titmus	0	c and b Hurst	0
*8	Webb, R. T.	b Moss	19	NOT OUT	3
9	Thomson, N. I.	LBW b Titmus	1	c Compton b Moss	11
10	Bates, D. L.	NOT OUT	7	st Murray b Hurst	0
11	James, A. E.	NOT OUT	7	c Titmus b Moss	0
...	Langridge, R. J.				

B 2, l-b 1, w , n-b .3
Scoring rate per over 3.21   Total 9 dec. 299

B 1, l-b 5, w , n-b .6
Total 183

FALL OF THE WICKETS
1—98 2—129 3—183 4—196 5—207 6—228 7—260 8—289 9—289 10—
1—77 2—92 3—114 4—161 5—168 6—179 7—180 8—182 9—182 10—183

ANALYSIS OF BOWLING

Name	1st Innings					2nd Innings				
	O.	M.	R.	W.	Wd. N-b	O.	M.	R.	W.	Wd. N-b
Moss	28	4	94	1	...	9	3	32	4	...
Warr	12	3	61	0	...	12	0	42	0	...
Bennett	23	4	59	2	...	9	0	40	1	...
Compton	8	1	28	0	...					
Hurst	2	2	4	1	...	5.5	1	29	4	...
Titmus	13	1	55	4	...	14.5	3	35	2	...

Total 103

	MIDDLESEX	First Innings		Second Innings	
1	Robertson, J. D.	c Bates b James	119	c Smith b Suttle	65
2	Gale, R. A.	b Smith	126	b Bates	4
†3	W. J. Edrich	b Smith	16	c Thomson b Marlar	37
4	Compton, D. C. S.	Run Out	7	c Lenham b James	27
5	Titmus, F. J.	c Marlar b Bates	11	b Suttle	0
6	G. P. S. Delisle	NOT OUT	29	b Suttle	0
*7	Murray, J. T.	b James	62	LBW b Marlar	4
8	Bennett, D.			NOT OUT	17
9	J. J. Warr			NOT OUT	1
10	Hurst, R. J.				
11	Moss, A. E.				
...	Bick, D. A.				

B 5, l-b , w , n-b .5
Scoring rate per over 3.82   Total 6 dec. 515

B , l-b 5, w , n-b 5
Total 7 dec. 161

FALL OF THE WICKETS
1—209 2—265 3—266 4—282 5—284 6—375 7— 8— 9— 10—
1—24 2—107 3—107 4—108 5—108 6—113 7—151 8— 9— 10—

ANALYSIS OF BOWLING

Name	1st Innings					2nd Innings				
	O.	M.	R.	W.	Wd. N-b	O.	M.	R.	W.	Wd. N-b
Bates	25	7	67	1	...	6	0	32	1	...
Thomson	21	3	100	0	...	13	4	27	0	...
James	25	7	85	2	...	9	3	24	1	...
Smith	21	5	88	2	...					
Marlar	6	0	30	0	...	10	1	29	2	...
Suttle	...	...	...	...	...	14	4	44	3	...

Total 98

Umpires—R. S. Lay & A. Skelding   Scorers—E. H. Hendren & G. Washer
† Captain   * Wicket-keeper
Play begins at 11.30 each day   Stumps drawn 1st & 2nd days at 6.30, 3rd day at 6
(Half-an-hour extra on the last day if necessary)

*The match in which Jack Robertson scored a century before lunch
and one of the occasions when Denis Compton ran himself out*

SUSSEX

	Batsman	1st Innings		2nd Innings	
1	G.D. MENDIS	Run Out	15	c Emburey b Daniel	66
2	A.M. GREEN	c Downton b Daniel	6	c Downton b Daniel	99
5 3	C.M. WELLS	b Emburey	29	c Cowans b Daniel	5 (3)
4	P.W.G. PARKER	c Butcher b Cowans	0	Run Out	2
3 5	J.R.T. BARCLAY+	c Downton b Daniel	64	c Sub b Emburey	2 (7)
7 8	G.S. LE ROUX	NOT OUT	46	b Emburey	7 (5)
7	D.J. SMITH*				
6 8	I.A. GREIG	LBW b Emburey	55	c Cowans b Emburey	1
8 9	A.P. WELLS	NOT OUT	12	NOT OUT	45
10	A.C.S. PIGOTT				
9 11	C.E. WALLER			NOT OUT	15
		b6 lb3 wd nb15 Extras	24	b lb3 wd nb9 Extras	12
		TOTAL	251-6d	TOTAL	254-7

Bonus Points

Runs at fall	1 11	2 26	3 26	4 73	5 161	6 2337	8	9	10		
of wicket	1 168	2 178	3 180	4 193	5 185	6 199	7 201	8	9	10	

Bowling analysis:

	O	M	R	W	WB	NB	O	M	R	W	WB	NB
Daniel	14.2	3	61	2			10	1	38	3		
Cowans	19	3	45	1			10	2	43	0		
Emburey	30	5	51	2			19.5	1	79	3		
Hughes	15	2	35	0			11	0	67	0		
Slack	10	2	21	0			4	0	15	0		

MIDDLESEX

	Batsman	1st Innings		2nd Innings	
1	J.M. BREARLEY+	b Greig	58	NOT OUT	100
2	W.N. SLACK	c Le Roux b Greig	27	c Green b Pigott	1
3	K.P. TOMLINS	c Smith b Le Roux	5		
4	R.O. BUTCHER	c+b Waller	32	c Pigott b C.M. Wells	33
5	C.T. RADLEY	c Barclay b Le Roux	6	NOT OUT	0
6	J.E. EMBURY	b Greig	44		
7	P.R. DOWNTON*	c Le Roux b Pigott	47		
8	R.G.P. ELLIS	b Waller	50	c Green b Waller	55
9	S.P. HUGHES				
10	N.G. COWANS	NOT OUT	1		
11	W.W. DANIEL	LBW b Greig	16		
		b3 lb6 wd1 nb8 Extras	18	b3 lb4 wd nb2 Extras	9
		TOTAL	304-9d	TOTAL	198-3d

Bonus Points

Runs at fall	1 45	2 140	3 144	4 174	5 192	6 192	7 275	8 303	9 304	10	
of wicket	1 1	2 108	3 197	4	5	6	7	8	9	10	

Bowling analysis:

	O	M	R	W	WB	NB	O	M	R	W	WB	NB
Le Roux	20	5	64	2			5	1	16	0		
Pigott	10	1	50	1			7	0	41	1		
Greig	32	8	85	4			7	1	43	0		
Wells C.M.	8	2	24	0			23	0	13	1		
Barclay	7	1	17	0								
Waller	29	20	46	2			11	0	68	1		
Green							1	0	8	0		

Middlesex won the toss & elected to bat

A three-wicket win for Sussex
despite an unbeaten century by Mike Brearley in his final season for Middlesex

The toss: John Barclay and Mike Brearley at Hove, August 1982

*Mike Brearley
and
Wilf Slack
going out to open for
Middlesex at Hove,
August 1982*

SUSSEX SHARKS

CLUB FOUNDED 1839

Farnrise Construction

MAJOR SPONSOR

SUSSEX v GLAMORGAN

at Hove from 27th to 30th August 2010 - LV County Championship Division 2

Sussex		1st Innings		2nd Innings	
1	EC Joyce [24]	lbw b Harris	56	NOT OUT	24
2	CD Nash [23]	lbw b Harris	19	c Wallace b Waters	0
3	BC Brown [26]	b Allenby	59	c Wallace b Waters	10
4	MW Goodwin [3]	c Allenby b Harris	28	NOT OUT	58
5	MH Yardy [20]*	lbw b Waters	18		
6	LJ Wright [10]	b Waters	8		
7	AJ Hodd [19] +	lbw b Cosker	26		
8	Yasir Arafat [29]	lbw b Cosker	8		
9	OP Rayner [22]	c Wallace b Waters	6		
10	MS Panesar [7]	lbw b Allenby	17		
11	CD Collymore [32]	NOT OUT	0		
12	RG Aga [28]				

JE Amya

	b 4	lb 5	wd	nb 2	11	b	lb 1	wd	nb	1
	Overs 67.3		Provisional Total		250	Overs		Provisional Total		93
	Pens	Wkts		Total		Pens	Wkts 2		Total	

Fall of	1st	1-39	2-111	3-166	4-179	5-192	2nd	1-4	2-14	3-	4-	5-
Wickets	Inns	6-203	7-211	8-229	9-250	10-255	Inns	6-	7-	8-	9-	10-

Bowling	Ovs	Md	R	Wk	wd	nb	Ovs	Md	R	Wk	wd	nb
Harris	16	6	37	3		1	9	4	14	0		
Waters	20	7	71	3			9		35	2		
Allenby	8	0	33	2			1	0	2	0		
Harrison	12	2	61	0								
Cosker	10.3	0	38	2			5	1	21	0		
Cosgrove	1	0	1	0								
Maynard							3	0	20	0		

Glamorgan		1st Innings		2nd Innings	
1	GP Rees [28]	c Wright b Panesar	12	c Hodd b Yasir Arafat	20
2	MJ Cosgrove [4]	b Yasir Arafat	142	c Nash b Yasir Arafat	9
3	WD Bragg [22]	lbw b Wright	44	lbw b Yasir Arafat	5
5 4	TL Maynard [33]	c Yardy b Collymore	12	lbw b Wright	76
4 8	BJ Wright [29]	b Yasir Arafat	16	c Goodwin b Collymore	25
6	J Allenby [6]	c Hodd b Amya	13	c Hodd b Amya	8
7	MA Wallace [18]*+	lbw b Collymore	8	c Hodd b Wright	16
8	JAR Harris [9]	lbw b Amya	0	NOT OUT	14
9	RDB Croft [10]				
10	DA Cosker [23]	NOT OUT	9	b Wright	2
11	DS Harrison [20]	c Yardy b Amya	25	b Wright	5
12	HT Waters [17]	did not bat		c Hodd b Amya	4

	b	lb 7	wd 2	nb 10	19	b 5	lb 8	wd 7	nb 6	26
	Overs 80.2		Provisional Total		300	Overs 64.5		Provisional Total		210
	Pens	Wkts 9		Total	300	Pens	Wkts 10		Total	210

Fall of	1st	1-44	2-164	3-218	4-239	5-239	2nd	1-29	2-38	3-43	4-112	5-127
Wickets	Inns	6-256	7-259	8-266	9-300	10-	Inns	6-174	7-191	8-193	9-199	10-210

Bowling	Ovs	Md	R	Wk	wd	nb	Ovs	Md	R	Wk	wd	nb
Yasir Arafat	15	0	67	2	1	2	21	6	64	3		2
Collymore	18	4	57	2			13	2	52	0		1
Panesar	22	3	70	1			13	3	38	0	3	
Amya	15.2	1	52	3	1		10.5	2	19	2		
Nash	4	0	6	0								
Wright	6	0	41	1		3	7	2	24	4		

UMPIRES :
B Dudleston
P Willey

SCORERS :
MJ Charman
AK Hignell

HOURS OF PLAY
11am to 6pm

Lunch - 1pm - 1.40pm

Tea - 3.40pm - 4pm
or when 32 overs remain
to be bowled,
whichever is later*
(* Days 1 and 2 only)

Additonal time - up to 30
mins additional time may be
added at the end of play to
offset any time lost during
that day's play

BONUS POINTS
(Only in the 1st Inns,
and the first 110 Overs)

Batting (Max 5pts)
1pt on achieving 200, 250,
300, 350 and 400 runs

Bowling (Max 3pts)
1 pt for taking 3, 6
and 9 wickets

Toss won by
Sussex
who elected to
field

RESULT
Match drawn

Sussex 8 points
Glamorgan 9 points

August Bank Holiday Weekend 2010

Chapter Twenty-Four
Wartime Holidays

In the darkest days, Herbert Morrison, the Home Secretary, made the point that total war might not mean total misery. Thus after Dunkirk in July 1940, Ernest Bevin, the Minister of Labour, anxious that some recreation should be provided to ease the strain of the war effort, asked that a cricket team should be sent to the industrial north. There was no Championship from 1940 to 1945 but two new teams – London Counties and the British Empire XI – were formed, providing valuable relaxation for players and spectators and raising money for charity. Thus after a week in May 1940 during which Winston Churchill became Prime Minister following the Commons debate over the debacle of the Norwegian campaign and Germany invaded the Netherlands, solace could be found in cricket over the Whit weekend: MCC v Westminster School on the Saturday, Cambridge University defeating the British Empire XI on Saturday, Monday and Tuesday (Norman Yardley, JR Thompson, JR Bridger and ER Conradi made hundreds and a Freshman from Sherborne, HJC Bashford, took six for 36 in the second innings) and, on Saturday and Monday, Leicestershire v Northamptonshire and Nottinghamshire v Derbyshire. There was one major victim. Sir Pelham Warner, MCC's deputy assistant secretary, planned a two-day match for the Whit holiday at Lord's, Over-30s v Under-30s, but the match was cancelled after the Hitler offensive.

The most competitive cricket was played in the leagues, notably the Lancashire League and the Bradford League, where, in 1943, 80 first-class cricketers appeared. With men on leave or engaged in essential occupations such as coal mining, the Bradford League, the only one still to pay its professionals, found itself awash with talent. It was a similar story in the Birmingham League, although not quite to the same degree.

League cricket had always been popular and the Bank Holidays were key dates, although in 1940 August Bank Holiday was cancelled as the Government appealed for continuous working that week, some cricket still being played. At Whitsun there would be matches on Saturday and Whit Monday. Eddie Paynter played for England against the West Indies in 1939; on Whit Monday 1940, he scored 150 not out in the Bradford League for Keighley against Lightcliffe.

In the Bradford League, the Priestley Cup was the top attraction on August Bank Holiday Mondays. Sometimes the semi-finals took place on the Monday and the final later in the month. In 1945 this changed to the final at Bradford Park Avenue ground on the holiday Monday. Roy Genders, a player with vast experience of league cricket, said it was known as Priestley Cup Final Day. "All that week talk in the Men's Clubs, coming out of chapel, on the various cricket grounds and in almost every home in Bradford, and for miles around too, has the Priestley Cup Final as the chief topic. Nobody in Bradford goes away for August Bank Holiday, neither mother, wife nor girl friend dare suggest such a thing. A week at Blackpool or Scarborough later in the summer, maybe, but not this weekend, for Bank Holiday Monday is Priestley Cup Day whichever side is playing. For this is the cricket followers' very own day, when out comes the new summer suit and the new cloth cap pulled well down over the eyes to shade the sun. In most buttonholes is a carnation or rose or sweetpea and all carry a box of sandwiches and a bottle of beer. For the ladies it is a flask of tea, for the youngsters it is a lemonade."

It was a similar story in other competitions. The Nottinghamshire and Derbyshire Border League's Bayley Cup Final was played on August Bank Holiday Monday, continuing throughout the war. Big crowds attended - 1941 at Heanor for example, start 2.30pm, admission 7d - and Reg Simpson said the league laid the foundations of the mental toughness required to make centuries at Test match level. As a teenager, he made hundreds of runs for Notts City Police before beginning his Nottinghamshire career but two run outs taught him valuable lessons, one in a league game while gardening and the other in the 1937 cup final while backing up at the non-striker's end. It is customary to issue a warning first but the bowler, Frank 'Tinny' Riley, did not do so. "I remember the Police team was a bit incensed about this," Simpson said. "I hadn't strayed very far at all but Tinny was a hard competitor and, of course, he was within his rights. Both of the run out incidents taught me lessons I never forgot. They probably stood me in good stead when we met the Australians years later."

The Bayley Cup finals were played to a finish, a system which could cause problems if the weather was unkind. Such an occasion, in 1954, was to become the catalyst for change. The game began on August Bank Holiday Monday and finished shortly before 9pm on Wednesday. Play did not start on Monday until 3.15pm, Openwoodgate closing at 340 for six. There was no play on Tuesday evening and when the match resumed on Wednesday evening, the innings ended at 372, Tommy Tomlinson making 172. Their opponents, Jacksdale, were all out for 144 (Tomlinson five for 49) and after two more matches had spanned 48 hours, over-limit finals were introduced in 1961.

Midway through 1942, Ernest Bevin wrote to civic heads, including Alderman Tiptaft, the Mayor of Birmingham, asking for daylight entertainment to be provided for factory workers. The Mayor delegated the task to Councillor Reginald Ivor 'Rusty' Scorer, a 50-year-old businessman from Moseley who had played occasionally for Warwickshire between 1921 and 1926. Lieut-Col Scorer, who served 16 years on the Rugby Union committee, was also running the Queensbury All Services Club in Hurst Street, Birmingham and was in the Home Guard. He set about tidying up the neglected Edgbaston ground with the intention of staging a festival of cricket as part of the holidays at home drive.

The Birmingham Festival, which took place during the August Bank Holiday weeks from 1942 to 1945, was an unqualified success. Warwickshire and Worcestershire opened the 1942 event, followed by the Birmingham League against Coventry and District and Warwickshire (Wyatt 171 not out) against Civil Defence Services. The ground was lent free of charge; such players as Stewart Dempster, Frank Lee, Harold Gimblett and the Langridge brothers turned out – as did Scorer himself - and the festival raised £450 for the Lord Mayor's War Relief Fund. There were prizes for the biggest hits and the best bowling and fielding performances and entertainment by the band of the 30th Warwickshire Home Guard.

Poor weather failed to dampen enthusiasm during the 1943 festival, 20,000 people turning up over the four days, with the fund benefiting by £1,036. Wyatt,

Eric Hollies, Cyril Washbrook, Gimblett and Roly Jenkins were to the fore but the event excelled itself during glorious weather in 1944. It spanned seven days; more than 42,000 spectators watched the play, the attendance on Saturday exceeding 10,000 and there was a profit of £2,514. Test and county cricketers graced the teams and there was a stunning finale when the RAF defeated the Festival XI by seven wickets. Reg Simpson made 47 and 71 for the Festival team but an unbeaten hundred from Dennis Brookes in the first innings and superb batting by Wally Hammond and Leslie Todd in the second got the RAF home. "While I was waiting for a posting I played a bit of cricket, including the Birmingham Festival, in 1944 where I scored quite a few runs just before I went to India," said Simpson. He shared in two opening partnerships of 171 and 146 with Dempster but it was not just about the cricket. Each scorecard contained on the reverse a diagram of the fielding positions, Scorer kept the crowd informed with some comment and humorous observations over the public address system and schoolboys and wounded soldiers were not forgotten. Hammond was also seen at his best in the same period when he thrilled a Worcester crowd of 5,000 with 117 for RAF against the home county. Reg Perks took five for 79 but RAF won by 97 runs, a cheque for £387 being sent to the RAF Benevolent Fund.

The war in Europe was over by the time of the 1945 Birmingham Festival and rain fell on five of the seven days. Hammond, Learie Constantine and Bill Edrich were among the leading players. During its four years, the festival attracted 140,000 spectators and raised £10,000 for wartime funds. In his final broadcast Scorer said: "And so my wartime festivals come to an end – for me happy memories of wonderful sportsmen, great cricket and happy crowds bringing money for those who need it. I give you a toast – to Cricket." Birmingham was the only city which held an annual festival in wartime, although Jack Appleyard, the Leeds and District League secretary, organised some successful Bank Holiday Festival Weeks at Roundhay Park in Leeds.

Several counties arranged matches, usually of one or two days. Derbyshire and Nottinghamshire met at Trent Bridge (where the Notts secretary HA Brown played a notable role in organising wartime cricket) and Ilkeston during the Bank Holidays and Essex became involved in the Four Counties match at Lord's, initially over the August Bank Holidays of 1941 and 1942. This featured Middlesex and Essex against Kent and Surrey under the captaincy of Gubby Allen and Errol Holmes and in 1941 more than 15,000 attended, the proceeds going to King George's War Fund for Sailors. Rain ended the game but not before Edrich registered a splendid century. The match became a feature of the Lord's wartime calendar and the gate rose to 22,000 in 1942, with a century for Holmes and a glimpse of England's future with Denis Compton, Edrich, Trevor Bailey, Godfrey Evans and Alec Bedser on view.

Cardiff Arms Park became a military training centre and St Helen's was taken over by the ARP although the squares were protected to allow matches to take place. In 1943 two were arranged at Cardiff for the August Bank Holiday period: Glamorgan meeting an Army team and Glamorgan of The Future, the latter including the 17-year-old Gilbert Parkhouse. Matches against a British Empire XI and The Army took place at Cardiff and Newport in the 1944 holidays, when news came of Major Maurice Turnbull's death at the age of 38 in action in Normandy. In happier circumstances another of the great names of Welsh cricket, Johnnie Clay, took ten wickets in a match against the Royal Australian Air Force at Cardiff over Whitsun in 1945. The stylish Parkhouse provided more evidence of burgeoning talent with two fine innings against the Army at Swansea during August Bank Holiday.

Gloucestershire, with the county ground at Bristol occupied by the Services for most of the war years, largely hibernated, although a number of fixtures were played around the county. With ports such as Southampton and Portsmouth in regular use, Hampshire attempted nothing before 1945, when matches were played at Southampton against Southampton Police at Whit and Southampton and District in August. Special matches were arranged in Kent on August Bank Holidays, when Alderman C Lefevre, the Mayor of Canterbury, provided hospitality which managed to keep alive the spirit of the Week In 1945, 7,000 people saw the Kent fast bowler Norman Harding take all ten against The Rest. Two years later Harding was dead, a victim of polio at the age of 31.

Old Trafford was requisitioned by the army and during the 1940-41 winter it suffered from the Luftwaffe as Manchester endured its share of the blitz. There were a number of charity games arranged in the county, notably over the 1943 Bank Holidays when elevens representing England and the West Indies met at Longsight, Manchester at Whit and North Western RAF played AA Command at Blackpool in August.

At Leicester, Aylestone Road was used by the National Fire Service before the US Army Pioneer Corps moved in. After the Americans left, Leicester Corporation took over the ground for an extension to the adjoining electricity works. Leicestershire had aimed to use Grace Road while Aylestone Road was renovated but because this was now the sports ground of the City of Leicester School plans had to be changed. It meant the county could only stage games when the ground was not required by the school. It was to be 1966 before Leicestershire bought Grace Road and built a new pavilion. During the war the county maintained the holiday fixtures with Northamptonshire, although the home game had to be played on the village ground of Barwell, which was barely adequate for county cricket. The reverse fixture took place at Spinney Hill, about a mile from the County Ground at Northampton, where the pavilion was requisitioned by the National Fire Service. A dozen matches saw honours even; perhaps the most notable coming in August 1944 at Spinney Hill, when a large crowd saw Dennis Brookes and Emrys Davies (Glamorgan) open the Northamptonshire innings with a partnership of 143.

Taunton was used by the army but August Bank Holiday Saturday in 1941 saw a whiff of the old rivalry when Somerset and Gloucestershire Services met, Somerset winning after some lusty hitting by Jack Meyer, Cambridge blue and founder of Millfield School. On Whit Monday 1945, Somerset defeated West of England by ten wickets in the first match played at Bristol since 1939. Bill Andrews took seven for 31 as West of England were dismissed for 67 and then, batting on after the runs were obtained, Gimblett hit 65, including 22 off an over from Sinfield, who finished with five for 74.

Surrey lost The Oval, first for a searchlight site and then a prisoner of war camp for parachutists who never arrived. The club restricted itself to Colts' matches and the Four Counties' games at Lord's. Sussex, facing no such obstacles, could show more ambition. A combined Royal Navy and Royal Air Force team defeated the Army at Hove in a two-day August Bank Holiday match in 1942, Eric Bedser making a hundred and Maurice Tate taking five for 51. On Whit Saturday 1943 the Australian Keith Miller gave an indication of his all-round powers with an unbeaten 134 and seven for 36 as United Services defeated Sussex. Hove was the venue for another August fixture in 1945, when a South African left-hander DR Fell hit 120 for Sussex against a New Zealand XI. In Yorkshire, The Army met Major AB Sellers' XI at Headingley during August Bank Holiday 1942 and although rain prevented play on the Monday, Harry Halliday and Charles Palmer made some attractive runs.

Lord's was the focal point for wartime cricket. August Bank Holiday 1943 saw an encounter between England and The Dominions, who included six Australians, three West Indians and one each from New Zealand and South Africa. Leslie Ames made a sparkling 133 and Denis Compton 58 before Walter Robins declared with England 324 for nine. Keith Carmody and Miller carried Dominions to 93 for two but the rest collapsed against Compton (six for 15) and the innings closed at 115. England did not enforce the follow on and four wickets fell for six before Robins and Errol Holmes staged a recovery, the declaration setting Dominions 360 in four and a half hours. They made a brave attempt, Dempster playing beautifully for 113 and Carmody making 49. Constantine hit 21 before falling to a brilliant catch off Alec Bedser by Leslie Compton, left-handed and at full stretch while leaning on the pavilion rails, both his feet being within the boundary. The catch was fair but there was some criticism because the ball, which cleared the rails, was over the boundary. There was no argument from Constantine, who said: "That is cricket." With seven down for 218, Dominions looked well beaten but the wicket-keeper Stan Sismey and Bertie Clarke added 108 before Clarke was bowled by Denis Compton for 52. Fourteen were needed when Robins brought on Jack Robertson, the Middlesex opener who bowled occasional off breaks. Sismey took a couple of twos on the leg side but was then well caught low down at mid-on by Alec Bedser for 70. Trevor Bailey caught Roper at extra cover off the next ball and England got home by eight runs. On Monday the teams were presented to the Duke of Gloucester before lunch. The numbers paying for admission were 23,993 on Monday and 14,217 on Tuesday, the proceeds going to the Red Cross Fund. An entry on the second innings' scorecard heralded the future: KR Miller c Evans b Bedser 2. England would not often escape so lightly.

Lord's now had a taste for such matches and in 1944 England defeated Australia in a one-day match on Whit Monday, Australia having beaten The Rest on the Saturday in preparation for the clash. The paying attendances were 26,415 on Saturday and 25,680 on Monday. The Australians were at some disadvantage for only Miller would go on to make a name for himself in Test cricket while Gubby Allen's England team included ten such players, the exception being Tony Mallett. When the teams convened on August Bank Holiday Monday, 16,000 spectators saw Hammond (105) at his best. Miller hit a sparkling 85 but the rest could not cope with Doug Wright's leg spin and England got home by 33 runs.

Cricket had been overtaken by events when England and Australia met at Lord's during Whitsuntide in 1945. On Tuesday 8 May the nation celebrated VE Day, the war in Europe being at an end although it still raged in the Far East. Sir Pelham Warner's Lord's programme had included two two-day games over the holidays but these simple arrangements grew like a snowball after VE Day. Five three-day unofficial Victory Tests were scheduled, the teams being captained by Hammond and Lindsay Hassett. England fielded a strong side in the first at Lord's: Hutton, Washbrook, Robertson, Hammond, Ames, Edrich, Robins, Stephenson, Billy Griffith, the wicket-keeper, Wright and Gover. Australia, although a powerful outfit, had only Hassett and Miller with a future in big cricket. Nevertheless, they had the best of it when play started on Saturday 19 May 1945. England batted on a pitch green after overnight rain, with the outfield slow. Ames (57), Robertson (53) and Edrich (45) were the chief scorers in a total of 267, Australia reaching 82 for two by the close.

Whit Monday's crowd of 30,000 saw Miller (105) and Hassett (77) master the bowling. Despite an interruption for rain, Australia piled up 455, with useful contributions down the order. Stephenson took five for 116 but all the bowlers suffered punishment. More rain fell in the evening and on Tuesday England, 188 behind, batted on turf drying in sunshine. Robertson did well with 84 and Edrich got 50, Australia needing 107 in 70 minutes or what turned out to be 22 overs. Wickets fell and with 12 minutes remaining, 31 were wanted. After two run-outs Cecil Pepper hit an unbeaten 54, including a mighty on-drive for six. Australia won by six wickets, just on seven o'clock. Gover and Stephenson had bowled unchanged and Hammond came in for some criticism for not giving one of them a rest and trying Wright. About 17,000 saw the finish, while altogether 67,660 paid the shilling admission during the three days. The proceeds of £1,935 went to Red Cross and Australian charities, entertainment tax absorbing £957.

The euphoria continued. In July, Labour swept to victory in the General Election, Clement Attlee becoming Prime Minister in succession to Winston Churchill. People stoically queued for bread but made the most of August Bank Holiday and their one-week's holiday with pay. The LMS carried more than 102,000 to Blackpool, in London's Liverpool Street, 35 trains headed for the seaside. At Lord's, where the fourth Victory Test began on August Bank Holiday Monday, 34,000 squeezed into the old ground, with some 10,000 locked outside. Australia now led by 2-1 but England again had a strong side: Laurie Fishlock, Hutton, Robertson, Hammond, Washbrook, Edrich, George Pope, Griffith, Dick Pollard, Wright and the Lancashire slow left-hander Bill Roberts. On Monday, when 34,000 attended, Sismey, with Australia seeking to protect their lead, spent four hours over 59 but a blow on the thumb prevented him from keeping wicket. Miller, although troubled by Pope for a time, made 118 and Pepper hit 57. Australia took seven hours over 388, the innings closing at lunch on the second day. England made a rousing reply, 249 for three by the close, and the declaration came on Wednesday at 468 for seven: Washbrook 112, Hammond 83, Edrich not out with 73 and Fishlock 69. There was little chance of a win and Australia finished the match, which attracted 93,000 over the three days, at 140 for four. On the second day Mr Attlee was present and Field Marshal Montgomery also attended for a few hours on one afternoon. Warner recalled: "As his car entered the members' gate he was at once recognised, and on his way to the committee room he was cheered to the echo, the pavilion standing up to welcome him." England went on to level the series by winning at Old Trafford.

Half-a-world away, two atomic bombs dropped on the Japanese cities of Hiroshima and Nagasaki during the week hastened the end of the 1939-45 war. Returning to his desk after active service, Bill Connor began his Cassandra column in the Daily Mirror: "As I was saying before I was interrupted..." There was also a refreshing desire to return to normality when the 1946 first-class fixture list was announced, the Whitsuntide matches due to start on Saturday 8 June reading Derbyshire-Warwickshire, Essex-Worcestershire, Glamorgan-India, Hampshire-Kent, Leicestershire-Northamptonshire, Middlesex-Sussex,

Nottinghamshire-Surrey, Somerset-Gloucestershire and Yorkshire-Lancashire, with the reverse fixtures beginning on Saturday 3 August.

Chapter Twenty-Five
Middlesex v Sussex

Poor weather turned the first post-war Whitsuntide at Lord's into something of an anti climax. Middlesex had started well and were third in the table on the eve of the holiday. Sussex were locked at the bottom, a fate they shared with three other counties.

Things were not going well for Denis Compton. He missed the Victory Tests because he was serving in India but had made a lot of runs on the sub-continent. After a good start to the 1946 season his form slumped to such an extent that one Test and eight Championship innings produced 27 runs, with average of 3.37. What is sometimes forgotten is that in the midst of this run and in the match immediately preceding Whit he made 202 at Fenner's. Guy Willatt, later to captain Derbyshire, got a hundred for Cambridge University and both *Wisden* and Willatt are in agreement that the contrast could scarcely have been greater. "I had to be patient and take the runs when and where I could but Denis made it all look ridiculously easy," said Willatt.

In spite of Compton's bad trot he was still averaging 65, with more than 900 runs in credit, by the time the Whitsun game began. It was Jim Sims's benefit match but the weather was miserable and cold. On Whit Monday, when Field Marshal Alexander attended, Robertson and Edrich added 192 for the second wicket but Compton was bowled by James Langridge before he had scored. George Cox batted well for Sussex against the spin of Sims and Ian Peebles but thundery showers had the last laugh. The weather relented for the Hove return, with Middlesex still chasing the leaders Yorkshire and Lancashire and Sussex trying to avoid the wooden spoon. The Sussex batting was strong; the two Langridges, the Oakes brothers, Harry Parks, Bartlett and Cox but Billy Griffith, the captain was handicapped by a poor bowling attack with only Jim Langridge returning anything like reasonable figures. Compton, now back to his best, took full advantage with 121 and Middlesex were left with a comfortable task. Sussex occupied last place in 1946, Griffith handing the captaincy over to Bartlett and Middlesex finished runners-up for the fifth consecutive season.

They went one better in the scorching summer of 1947. Britain was then an austere, grey world of queues, restrictions and rationing. The winter had been the worst in living memory. Heavy snow which fell in January left huge drifts, causing road and rail chaos. Fuel was scarce, with electricity off for long spells and gas at quarter pressure. Heavy rain then accompanied the thaw which led to floods in some areas. The cricket-loving public yearned for a vintage season and Middlesex – and Compton and Edrich aided and abetted by Robertson and Syd Brown - provided it. Runs came at such a rate that Robins had plenty of time to deploy his attack, the pace of Gray and Edrich, slow left-arm of Jack Young, leg spin from Sims and Robins himself and unorthodox left-handed googlies and chinamen from Denis Compton.

Winter's misery soon faded; Whit Saturday found 17,000 at Lord's to see Edrich (106) and Compton (110) share a third wicket partnership of 223. At the close, Sussex had lost four wickets for 43 in reply to Middlesex's 380 and on Whit Monday, when the crowd was nearly 30,000, they followed on. Cox and James Langridge fought hard but Middlesex were home and dry by the end of the second day. The Hove game was allocated to James Langridge for his benefit and it provided a perfect illustration of the type of cricket which brought the title to Middlesex. Robertson and Brown gave them a flying start, Edrich, Compton and George Mann maintained the pace and Robins was able to declare at 401 for four. Sussex followed on but Bartlett and Charles Oakes halted Middlesex's progress with some clean and powerful strokes. They added 138 in 95 minutes for the sixth wicket, leaving Middlesex to make 111. Rain caused some anxiety on Tuesday but Brown took 17 from Jack Nye's first over and Robertson and Edrich finished the job, knocking off the remaining 87 in 45 minutes. Sir Aubrey Smith, by now well-known as a film star, attended the game and at lunch Jack Holmes, chairman of the Test selectors, toasted him as the senior living county captain.

The holiday fixtures became a natural choice for beneficiaries; Laurie Gray at Lord's and, jointly, Harry Parks and John Langridge at Hove in 1948. Denis Compton's benefit match took place at Whitsuntide in 1949. Rain prevented play until 2pm on Saturday, when Compton won the toss and took a wicket in his first over, Sussex making 269. On Whit Monday the gates were closed after 35,000 people had been admitted on a bright, sunny day. In his autobiography *End of an Innings* Compton said that he felt more taut and nervous than usual when he went out to bat to the generous applause of the crowd. He continued, "Usually a beneficiary gets one off the mark; but the usual thing didn't happen that day – and I make no complaint about it; plainly Hugh Bartlett, in assessing the situation, had said to himself: "This is the best chance we have of getting this chap out – and we badly want him out." The fielders crowded round me and got after me right from the start." Compton spent 16 minutes getting off the mark but went on to make 182, his last 79 coming in 44 minutes. His brother Leslie then hit an unbeaten 59 while their 69-year-old father looked proudly on from the members' stand. John Langridge deprived Middlesex of any chance of victory. During the three days 55,000 people were present, of whom 49,194 passed through the turnstiles. Compton's benefit realised £12,200.

Middlesex were joint champions in 1949 and Sussex only 14th but there was a remarkable turnaround at Hove in August. Sussex did well enough to make 302 but Jim Wood's fast medium left-arm bowling accounted for seven Middlesex batsmen for 34 as the visitors were bundled out for 91. Set 148, Sussex lost four for 37 before Hubert Doggart and James Langridge shared an unfinished stand of 114. But it was impossible to keep Compton out of the headlines. During the 1949-50 football season, when he suffered from problems with his right knee, he was in the Arsenal team which defeated Liverpool in the FA Cup final at Wembley. In the Lord's match at Whitsuntide he made 50 but next day was admitted to the London Clinic for a knee operation which put him out of the game for a large part of the season. Typically at Hove he arrived in plimsolls, having overslept. Robins put him on to bowl as a punishment and he responded with a couple of wickets. Middlesex won that game by 24 runs but, apart from Compton's antics, it was notable for the performances of young batsmen weaned on the pitches at Fenner's: John Dewes, the left-handed opener who made two hundreds in the match, David Sheppard and Hubert Doggart.

Jim Parks, who played in 44 Sussex-Middlesex games, recalled Whit Monday at Lord's in 1955, a joint benefit for Harry Sharp and Alex Thompson. There was no play on Saturday but 20,000 saw an incredible display by Compton on the second day. Going in when two wickets had fallen at four, he soon lost Edrich but went on to make 150 out of a total of 206 against an attack including Thomson, James, Marlar and Oakman in a total of 206. Only two other batsmen reached double figures, John Warr's 13 being the next best effort. "He never played and missed," said Parks. "He eventually holed out and I can see it now, Ken Suttle catching him off Robin Marlar in front of the grandstand. It was magnificent."

Parks also had good cause to remember the Lord's game in June 1954, which was for Leslie Compton's benefit. Middlesex had won their first six Championship matches but Sussex were at the bottom of the table when they arrived at headquarters. Sheppard, Doggart and Suttle batted well and Parks was unbeaten with 92 when the declaration came at 263 for eight. Six Middlesex wickets then fell for 96 when Leslie Compton came in to join his brother. "We caught them on a wet pitch," said Parks. "We batted well on Saturday and then it rained and, of course, pitches were left uncovered in those days. Once again Denis played a marvellous innings. About the only thing he didn't do well was run between the wickets. Bill Edrich reckoned that instead of calling you had to negotiate with him. Leslie came in and you usually gave the beneficiary one off the mark. I was at cover point when Leslie played the ball there and we gave him the single. The very next ball Denis played straight to me and Les had just crossed so he was run out by his brother in his benefit game for 1. Fred Titmus had been run out for 14 earlier and when the last man, Alan Moss, strolled to the wicket, he said 'there's one thing certain – he'll not run me out'. Shortly afterwards the scorecard read Moss run out 2. Again, Denis never played and missed in making 72 not out in a total of 144." Crowds of 20,000 looked on but rain washed out the third day. Middlesex ended the year in seventh place, Sussex finishing ninth. The run-out incident involving the Comptons was also recalled by David Sheppard. "Les was calling out, 'He's done it again,' when he was only halfway down the pitch."

Middlesex and Sussex continued to attract the crowds and the beneficiaries generally reaped the rewards. Sussex won a thriller at Hove in 1952 in what was a field day for the fast medium bowlers: Wood, Cornford and Ian Thomson for Sussex and Alan Moss, John Warr and Don Bennett on the visitors' side. Sussex finished 13th that year; in 1953 under the inspiring captaincy of Sheppard they were runners-up to Surrey. Sheppard, Ken Suttle, Jim Parks, Cox and John Langridge made most of the runs and the leading wicket takers were Thomson, Ted James, Wood and Alan Oakman. They were beaten at Lord's and the August fixture at Hove found them in second place to Middlesex in the table. Edrich won the toss, put Sussex in on a damp pitch and Moss rewarded him with seven for 35 in a total of 118. By the close Middlesex were 104 for two, an unbroken partnership by Edrich and Compton having added 94. On Bank Holiday Monday conditions were much better when a record 15,000 crowd attended. Middlesex occupied seven and a half hours – nearly 150 overs – in making 346 but Doggart, Parks and Suttle ensured Sussex were safe from defeat.

As the seasons passed there was little evidence of a decline in popularity. The first two days at Lord's in 1954 attracted 20,000 before rain washed out the final day and the Hove fixtures remained well attended. Sussex continued to even up the score, with a win by an innings at Lord's in 1956 and victories at Hove in 1954 and 1957. The latter year marked the end of Denis Compton's career.

Operations on his knee meant that he was never as fluent after 1949 as he had been previously but he still headed the county's batting averages in his final season. In the Whit match at Lord's he was overshadowed by Robertson and Bob Gale, who both got hundreds in an opening partnership of 209, and Don Smith who hit 149 for Sussex. But he was seen at his best in the Hove game. First he took five for 40 as Sussex were dismissed for 243. He made only 16 as Middlesex trailed by 65, Robin Marlar's off breaks bringing about a collapse. Sussex were in a strong position as Smith and Suttle added 94 but again Compton, five for 71 and match figures of 10-111, bowled his side back into the game. They needed 266 but only Compton (44) showed much enterprise and they went down by 99 runs.

Parks said: "I think the saddest thing for me was Denis's final season in 1957. In the first innings at Hove I caught him at cover off Ted James. I've never been so sad at catching anybody out. He was such a lovely man. During the whole of my career the Middlesex and Sussex teams got on extremely well. I remember coming in as a young player and Leslie Compton, who was keeping wicket, saying 'good luck son.' There was keen competition but the matches were always played in a sporting manner."

Compton played in 30 matches for Middlesex against Sussex, scoring 2,032 runs at an average of 53.47 with seven hundreds. Edrich was not far behind; 31 matches, 1,967 runs, average 47.97 and five centuries.

By the end of the 1950s, the great days seemed to have passed as both Middlesex and Sussex had the look of teams from which the glory had gone. But a new generation of Middlesex batsmen led by Peter Parfitt and Eric Russell emerged and Ted Dexter was coming to prominence for Sussex. At Lord's during the 1959 Whitsun, Russell played well for 52 and 32 and was awarded his cap during the course of the match. Middlesex gained a lead of 90 after Sussex broke down against the off breaks of Titmus. Parfitt made 60 but Don Bates struck back for Sussex and by the close of Monday's play – 13,000 attended on a cool day – they had made a useful start in quest of 229. On the final day Sussex, although without their opening batsman Les Lenham, who returned to Brighton with torn ankle ligaments, made good progress. Don Smith got 90 and Dexter, also capped during the game ten months after receiving one for England, 58 and with four wickets down for 209, only 20 were needed. Moss and Warr, with the new ball, then brought about a startling breakdown, although Suttle remained at the crease. The fast bowlers began to tire but when Suttle was joined by his captain Marlar only ten were required. For 25 minutes the runs accrued before Marlar suddenly hit Warr back over his head to the pavilion. One to tie and Suttle to face Moss. Five straight good length balls yielded no run and before the sixth Warr, the Middlesex captain, dropped two men back on the leg side. Moss dug in a short, fast one and Suttle, swatting at the ball as it passed over his head, was caught behind by John Murray. Middlesex had won by one run – having beaten Kent by two runs in their previous game. Four years later, in Titmus's benefit, Sussex avenged this defeat with a win by a similar margin. Middlesex needed 112 but Oakman, little used as an off spinner by that time, took six for 53, the last three in the extra half-hour and the last with four minutes remaining.

Roger Moulton has fond memories of Whitsuntide matches at Lord's. "In 1957 I saw Jack Robertson reach his century with a four off the last ball before lunch. He then took an hour to make another 18 runs. After the Robertson-Gale opening partnership of 209 the stage was set for Edrich and Compton but Edrich only made 16 and Compton ran himself out for seven. In 1958 at Lord's 20 wickets fell on the first day. Sussex were all out by lunchtime and Robertson made 99 out of 189 – the only batsman to cope with the green wicket. Sussex were 0-0 at close of play. In 1959 Jim Parks was out to the first ball on Whit Monday and Les Lenham damaged ankle ligaments when he tripped over the boundary board in front of the Warner Stand and had to be carried off. The 1960 match was absorbing until Sussex decided not to go for the runs on the last afternoon. At all these matches I remember large crowds all round the ground."

People now came to Hove to watch the batting of Dexter and Parks just as they came to the same ground in the high summers of Ranji and Fry. The Bank Holiday masses saw Dexter, now captaining Sussex, at his lordly best. At Lord's in 1960 he responded to a Parfitt hundred with 105 and an unbeaten 78, 15,000 seeing him become the first batsman to complete 1,000 runs for the season. At Hove he made 157 in the first innings during which he drove with power and grace. Middlesex, set 329 in five hours, were 121 for six when a storm held up play. This was a crucial match, with Middlesex third in the table and Sussex fourth. Play resumed with an hour remaining and Dexter, who had taken three wickets for a single before the stoppage, got two more with consecutive balls at the same score. It was time for the dead bat and 82 deliveries were sent down without a run being scored before Ron Hooker pushed Thomson to cover for a single. Dexter then had Warr brilliantly caught by Ron Bell at backward short leg and Sussex had won by 202 runs with 13 minutes to spare, leapfrogging their rivals into third place. In the final reckoning Yorkshire were champions, followed by Lancashire, Middlesex and Sussex.

Not everybody was happy, however. At Hove in 1963 Russell spent four hours 20 minutes in making 105, four spectators demanding and receiving the return of their admission fee. The following year, 1964, was the last occasion the August Bank Holiday took place on the first Monday in the month. Umpire Ron Aspinall no-balled the Middlesex seamer Pat Lawrence twice for throwing at Whitsuntide before the August game provided another thriller. Sussex were set a target of 261 in just over three hours but nine wickets were down for 208 before Mike Griffith and Bell played out the final 25 minutes.

Chapter Twenty-Six
Lancashire v Yorkshire

For the hordes descending on Bramall Lane at Sheffield on Saturday 8 June 1946 the world was as it should be. The war had ended, the Whitsuntide Roses match was about to begin and the old rivals were back in their rightful place, occupying the top two places in the Championship table.

Whitsuntide was late in 1946, which meant the season was well under way by the time of the clash. Lancashire headed the table with 52 points from six matches; Yorkshire had a game in hand and were 12 points – the allocation for a win – behind. The status quo had returned but so had the all-too typical North Country Whitsun weather. Despite the forecast, 14,761 paid £1,370 gate money to see two and a half hours cricket on Saturday. It was even worse on Whit Monday when rain flooded the pitch. On Tuesday Yorkshire batted on for half-an-hour, Brian Sellers declaring at 171 for three under an arrangement with his Lancashire counterpart John Fallows that the Red Rose declaration would occur immediately after the lead was obtained. As it was 80 overs were used up in making 127 for four before a storm put a merciful end to proceedings.

Throughout June and July Lancashire remained at the top of the table but they had to take account of the fact that Yorkshire had games in hand. On the eve of August Bank Holiday, Yorkshire took over and although Middlesex were hanging on to third place a two-horse race was taking shape. Such was the interest that vast crowds had to be locked out of Old Trafford for the return game. Yorkshire began badly, losing half their side cheaply before Smailes and Sellers stopped the rot. Nevertheless 180 was no sort of total and nobody really came to terms with the flighted spin of Roberts, who took five for 56. Alec Coxon soon dismissed Washbrook and Ikin but Place and King made hundreds and Yorkshire, 216 behind, lost Hutton and Barber on the second evening. Five men were out for 120 and Lancashire scented the victory that would take them back to the head of the table. Then Sellers and Leyland, in his last significant innings for Yorkshire, came together in a splendid display of White Rose obstinacy which added 100 without them being separated. Yorkshire were never deposed after this and Lancashire faded into third place behind Middlesex in the final table.

More titanic battles followed although for a few years their influence on the outcome of the Championship was minimal. To the faithful, this in no way diminished the Roses fixtures. In 1947 Yorkshire slipped to eighth place and although Lancashire, now captained by Ken Cranston, finished third they never mounted a serious challenge to Middlesex and Gloucestershire. But big crowds attended the two games; 20,000 on each of the first two days at Old Trafford, 22,000 on the Saturday at Bramall Lane, with 15,000 on August Bank Holiday Monday despite a wet morning and 15,000 on the third day. Again both encounters were drawn, although Lancashire were hanging on at Sheffield, where the 20-year-old left-handed Gerry Smithson defied Roses convention and earned himself a place in the MCC party which visited the West Indies the following winter by hitting four fours and a three in one over in making 98 (a five and 13 fours). Normality was restored in 1948 when Washbrook, Eric Edrich and Hutton made centuries at Headingley, where 33,000 turned up on Whit Monday. Ted Lester went one better with two in the match at Old Trafford. Hutton also registered three figures and so did Washbrook and Ikin in adding 244 for the third wicket. Then, in the hot sun of 1949, Yorkshire tied with Middlesex for the Championship. At Whitsuntide Hutton struck three sixes, a five and 19 fours in a flawless 201 at Old Trafford. Fred Trueman, playing in his first Roses match, said Hutton had been unjustly criticised for scoring slowly on a rain-affected pitch on the Saturday, when he was 60 not out. "On the Monday morning Len asked me to go out and bowl a few to him in the nets. He returned to the dressing room, changed his shirt, had a cup of tea and then went out and hit the first ball of the day straight back over Bill Roberts's head for six. He went on to make 201 of the most fantastic runs I have ever seen. In the second innings, feeling unwell, he batted lower down the order and was 91 not out when Norman Yardley declared."

Lancashire, bracketed 11th that season, saved the follow-on by one run and, as it happened, the match after fine batting from Wharton and Ken Grieves. They also frustrated their rivals at Headingley, where Jack Ikin got a century as Lancashire had slightly the better of things. On October 7 1949 a dinner was held at the Grand Hotel, Sheffield to celebrate 100 years of Roses matches, attended by famous players from the past including EB Rowley, RH Spooner, CS Marriott, Ernest Tyldesley and Harry Makepeace.

By 1950 both counties were back in contention for the title and at Whitsuntide, Bramall Lane produced the first outright result since before the war. Yardley won the toss and put Lancashire in but rain restricted matters on Saturday. Lancashire were indebted to Wharton (93) and Geoffrey Edrich (70) for their total of 257, made against an attack comprised of Trueman, then in the raw stage of his career, Coxon, Johnny Wardle and Brian Close. Lancashire's most potent weapon in 1950 was spin: Roy Tattersall (off breaks) and Bob Berry and Malcolm Hilton (different shades of slow left-arm). When Yorkshire batted after lunch on Whit Monday, a fascinating contest developed between Hutton and his new young opening partner Frank Lowson and Berry, Tattersall and the leg spin of Grieves. Yardley declared 64 behind on the third morning, Close and Wardle then dismissing Lancashire on a venomous pitch for 117. It would have been much worse but for a typical Australian display of aggression from Grieves, who made 52 in under an hour. The pitch had eased a little when Yorkshire set about their quest for 182, with 16,000 people transfixed. Hutton made 45 and in company with Yardley looked to be setting Yorkshire on course for victory before falling to a catch by Ikin close in off Tattersall. Yardley continued to resist and with Close batting well, the outcome still favoured Yorkshire. Then Yardley declined a call for a second run and Close, in turning, slipped and was run out by a sharp return from Berry. Seven were down for 125 when Yardley was joined by Wardle. In little more than quarter of an hour, 27 runs came before Wardle was caught and bowled from a full blooded drive off Berry. Thirty needed but the wicket-keeper Don Brennan soon fell and with Trueman at the crease it was really all down to Yardley. He reached 51, declined singles from each of the first three balls of an over from Berry and then, attempting to turn the ball around the corner for one to retain the strike, lobbed a simple catch to Ikin, close in. Tattersall finished with five for 60, Berry four for 67 and Lancashire won by 14 runs. It was their first victory over Yorkshire since 1937.

August Bank Holiday 1950 found Lancashire heading the table with 13 wins from 21 matches. They were 20 points ahead of Yorkshire with Surrey third, another 12 points behind. Brian Statham made his Roses debut at Old Trafford, skidding and falling down twice before knocking over Lowson's off stump with his sixth delivery. Within six overs Yorkshire were 13 for four, Lester and Watson also falling to Statham. Such pace was a rarity in the Championship and at the other end Hutton, so often on the receiving end from Lindwall and Miller, had food for thought. Yardley remained defiant and was last out for 119 in a total of 226; Statham 21-4-52-5. Washbrook made 88 to guide Lancashire into a seven-run lead with the last pair together, Coxon and Wardle each taking five wickets and then Hutton and Willie Watson helped Yardley set up a declaration which left Lancashire to make 276 in 205 minutes. Washbrook made 74 out of 102 for the first wicket with Place but the game fizzled out. Statham's bowling in this match led to his going to Australia as a reinforcement in 1950-51.

In 1951 Yorkshire were second and Lancashire third to Warwickshire. Both Roses matches were drawn, the August weather allowing only Saturday's play at Bramall Lane. The Roses counties were similarly placed in 1952, when Surrey began their seven-year run as champions. At Headingley, Hutton and Lowson ended a rain-shortened Saturday on 170 and they carried their first wicket partnership to 245 on Whit Monday. Declarations left Lancashire to make 233 in 150 minutes. They accepted the challenge but Close got among them and it was left to Washbrook, with a heavily bandaged bruised thumb, and the wicket-keeper Alan Wilson to defy Yorkshire in the last half hour with eight wickets down. There was another thrilling finish at Old Trafford in August. Rain prevented play until four o'clock on Saturday but on Monday 20,000 people saw 23 wickets fall for 234 runs. First Berry took six for 52 as Yorkshire were dismissed on a drying pitch for 200. Then Trueman and Eric Burgin, an in swing bowler who had a successful career in league cricket, shot out Lancashire for 65. Close hit 61 and a declaration set Lancashire 299 in 225 minutes. With half-an-hour left they were 157 for seven when Trueman and Burgin took the new ball. Trueman bowled Statham and Tattersall but the wicket-keeper (and jazz musician) Frank Parr and the last man Berry held out for a draw.

A lean year for Yorkshire in 1953 failed to dampen the enthusiasm for the Roses game, more than 60,000 attending the Bramall Lane match in August. On Whit Saturday 1954, 29,000 packed Headingley to see Yorkshire, runners-up that season, make 348 for seven. On Monday 20,000 people waited in vain for the rain to stop but there was no further play. At Old Trafford in August, Vic Wilson made an unbeaten 130 in a total of 248, Statham taking six wickets. Lancashire were then completely bamboozled by Wardle, who took full advantage of a helpful pitch. His nine for 25 marked the most outstanding bowling feat since George Hirst's nine for 23 at Headingley in 1910. Following on, Lancashire collapsed again, this time to Bob Appleyard and Yorkshire, by an innings and 38 had gained their first Roses win since the war and consolidated their title challenge.

They promptly won again at Old Trafford in 1955 and were then robbed by the weather at Sheffield, where Watson made 174. Lancashire took due revenge at Headingley over Whitsun a year later, Tattersall taking six for 47 and eight for 43 to return a match analysis of 56.3-31-90-14. More than 66,000 watched an exciting game, Yorkshire chasing a target but failing against Tattersall. There was another fine match at Old Trafford in August 1956 when Lancashire finished

70 short with one wicket in hand, Hilton defying a hostile final over from Trueman. Each side escaped with a draw in 1957, Alan Wharton recording Lancashire's first Roses hundred since 1949 and although rain handicapped the 1958 matches Lancashire gained an eight-wicket victory at Headingley, where Statham took six for 16 in the first innings.

In 1959, a vibrant, young Yorkshire team emerged but it came a cropper at Old Trafford, where Lancashire won with five minutes to spare. Whitsuntide was early and Lancashire set the pace. The left-handed Geoff Pullar made 76 and 105, Doug Padgett responded with a hundred for Yorkshire but Lancashire gained their first Roses victory at Manchester for 32 years. By August Bank Holiday, Yorkshire were chasing Surrey and Warwickshire with Lancashire out of the picture. Bramall Lane in that hot summer provided a batsman's paradise for the Roses encounter, Pullar and Close making hundreds and Yorkshire gaining a lead on the first innings at 3.30pm on the final day. Aficionadoes of the 1920s nodded in approval.

Yorkshire, thrillingly, won the Championship during the glorious summer of 1959 and they were soon in the forefront again in 1960 under a new professional captain in Vic Wilson. Lancashire, too, had a new skipper, Bob Barber succeeding Washbrook who had retired. At Whitsuntide, Lancashire gained a crushing victory by ten wickets, Yorkshire collapsing against the leg spin of Tommy Greenhough and Bob Barber and, in the second innings, Jack Dyson's off breaks, on a dry, dusty pitch. Pullar made his third hundred in successive Roses matches, having made another against them in the Champion County v The Rest match at the end of 1959. The match ended on the second day, 20,000 having watched the White Rose fade away.

Nevertheless, Yorkshire headed the table going into the 1960 August Bank Holiday fixtures which pitted first against second – Yorkshire v Lancashire at Old Trafford – and third against fourth – Middlesex v Sussex at Hove. Seldom had the holiday games been so crucial to the Championship's outcome and the Roses clash on July 30 and August 1 and 2 was one of the finest in the long rivalry's history. The match involved true sons of the rival shires. Only two of the 22 players, Lancashire's Ken Grieves (Sydney, Australia) and Ken Higgs (Kidsgrove, Staffordshire), were born outside the counties' boundaries.

Both teams were immensely strong. Yorkshire had batting of quality: Brian Stott, Ken Taylor, Doug Padgett, Brian Close and Phil Sharpe, depth in the middle order, Ray Illingworth and Vic Wilson, a wicket-keeper who was one of the best in the country in Jimmy Binks, pace from Fred Trueman, supporting seam from Mel Ryan and slow left arm from Don Wilson. Lancashire's batting was not quite so good but the left-handed openers Geoff Pullar and Bob Barber, Alan Wharton, Grieves and Peter Marner each made more than a thousand runs and Jack Dyson, Roy Collins and the wicket-keeper Geoff Clayton added substance to the middle order. But the bowling had the edge; Brian Statham and Higgs with the new ball, leg breaks from Barber, Grieves and Tommy Greenhough and off spin from Dyson. Each side excelled in the field. Binks assisted in 108 first-class dismissals, Clayton in 89. On the Yorkshire side, Close, Sharpe, the two Wilsons, Illingworth and Trueman were high in the list of the fielding tables with Grieves and Marner as their Lancashire equivalents.

Fourteen – eight from Yorkshire, six from Lancashire – appeared in Test matches during their careers, Illingworth, Trueman, Padgett, Pullar, Statham, Barber and

Greenhough playing for England against South Africa in 1960 and Statham captaining the Players against the Gentlemen at Lord's. Furthermore the Lancashire team lacked two other Test players in Hilton and Tattersall, out of the side and close to the end of their careers, the match being allocated for their joint benefit. Tattersall was 12th man and Hilton was playing for Lancashire Second XI at Scarborough. The umpires were John Langridge and Syd Buller.

Immediately, Lancashire took a firm grip on the match after Barber had won the toss and decided to field. On Saturday splendid bowling by Statham, five for 43, and Higgs, four for 48, dismissed Yorkshire for 154, only a sound display from Close (63) preventing a complete rout. Close got rid of Pullar at 26 but Barber reached his half-century before the close when Yorkshire were 97 without further loss. On August Bank Holiday Monday, Barber (71) and Wharton (83) carried their second wicket partnership to 131 which took Lancashire into the lead with only one wicket down, although keen bowling and fielding denied them bonus points. At 187 for three Lancashire were in a strong position but following a heavy storm just after lunch Trueman (four for 65) and Ryan (three for 69) were able to make the ball fly and the innings closed at 226. Yorkshire, 72 behind, lost two men for 19 before the day ended and on Tuesday, with Statham (four for 23) taking full advantage of the pitch, half their side had gone for 36 before Sharpe (46) and the two Wilsons resisted. The innings closed for 149, leaving Lancashire to make 78 in two hours.

What could Yorkshire do? They considered starting with spin but it was discarded as carrying too many risks. They decided on a pace attack, making every possible use of the lift that was in the pitch to give the batsmen as much trouble as possible, with a defensive field setting. They would try to force Lancashire into mistakes while cutting off as many scoring opportunities as possible.

Trueman takes up the story. "We could not reasonably expect to bowl them out but we could hope to put them under pressure when they got behind the clock. Above all, we wanted to prevent a Lancashire win. Well, don't tell anybody who saw that Tuesday afternoon's play that defensive cricket can never be exciting because I'm pretty sure no one who saw it will ever forget the next two hours."

His partner was Mel Ryan, who did not have a settled place in the team, playing only a few matches each season, and as Trueman said: "His experience of bowling 'tight' was limited but he bowled magnificently."

Lancashire began steadily but Barber was run out after 40 minutes by a brilliant return from Padgett. Gradually the task became increasingly difficult. Wharton fell to a good catch by Padgett, Pullar was bowled by a devastating ball from Ryan and Trueman bowled Marner for a duck. Suddenly 16 without loss became 32 for four. Lancashire were now under pressure. A fifth wicket (Collins) fell at 43 and then Statham was caught at the wicket off Ryan before he had scored. Six down for 43; Grieves and Clayton now together.

At 60 Grieves was missed off Trueman by the usually safe Vic Wilson at deep mid-off and 29 runs were added in 25 minutes as Lancashire struck back. Clayton hit ten off Ryan's final over, including two lucky fours, but with the total 72 Grieves had gone, caught behind off Ryan for 27. Lancashire, with seven wickets down, needed six from the last over of the game to be delivered by Trueman. Clayton pushed a single off the first but the second bowled Greenhough, leaving

Higgs padded up in the pavilion at 73 for eight. The third ball went away to leg off Dyson's pads. They ran two and Dyson stopped the fourth dead in his blockhole, setting off on a run when he saw Clayton hurtling towards him. Clayton scored another single behind the wicket from the fifth ball and so it was Dyson, the Manchester City footballer, who, at 5.15pm, faced the last ball from Trueman with the scores level at 77 for eight. Trueman recalled Clayton giving Dyson all kinds of instructions which he probably didn't hear.

The bowler walked back to his mark. He suspected that Dyson feared a bouncer but instead he decided to bowl a yorker to the bottom of the leg and middle stump. "It was as good a yorker as I have ever bowled but Dyson countered with the only possible effective answer. He shuffled forward, bat and pad close together, and somehow he got an edge. It was an edge just thick enough to deflect the ball wide of Jimmy Binks's outstretched glove and away the ball went to the fine-leg boundary." Lancashire, 81 for eight from 31 overs, had won by two wickets. Clayton was unbeaten with 15; Ryan's figures were 15-4-50-5 and Trueman's 16-4-28-2. During the three days, 74,000 spectators saw this red-blooded encounter in which Lancashire completed their first Roses double since 1893.

Lancashire now headed the table and Sussex's victory at Hove meant they moved ahead of Middlesex. The top four on August 2 read: Lancashire played 23, points 176, average 7.65; Yorkshire 24, 176, 7.33; Sussex 23, 154, 6.69 and Middlesex 19, 126, 6.63. Lancashire won their next game to maintain the lead but their last six Championship matches were disastrous for four were lost and two drawn. In the end they were hard pressed to finish second to Yorkshire, with Middlesex third and Sussex fourth. Trueman wrote: "Twenty years later I think of the 1960 season not as one when we won the Championship but as the time we were beaten twice by Lancashire – and a thick edge off my last ball brought the winning runs. Such wounds are slow to heal."

Trueman had made his England debut against the Indians in 1952 and he said he found the pressures of Test cricket nothing like those of the game against Lancashire the previous weekend. He was to the fore in Yorkshire's dominance of the Roses encounters before the holidays changed course, which tended to bring them Whitsuntide victories, with the August matches undecided. In the 1963 game at Bramall Lane, Stott (143) shared a fourth wicket partnership of 249 with Geoff Boycott, whose 145 was his maiden hundred. He promptly followed with two more centuries at Old Trafford in 1963 and 1964 – and then 'failed' with 62 at Headingley in August 1964, when Yorkshire won by an innings despite Sonny Ramadhin's eight for 121.

Chapter Twenty-Seven
Surrey v Nottinghamshire

It was no longer the clash of titans but the Surrey-Nottinghamshire fixture still carried a certain resonance when county cricket was resumed in 1946. Neither club was particularly prominent in the early post-war seasons but this was not reflected in the crowds, who, starved of cricket for so long, hurried to The Oval and Trent Bridge.

Given that the average daily gate at a first-class match was around 3,400, some of the attendances beggar belief. On the August Saturday of 1946, Tom Barling (233 not out) and Bob Gregory (164) shared a third wicket partnership of 267 in under three and a half hours. The gate of 13,000 rose to 17,000, among them Field Marshal Montgomery, on August Bank Holiday Monday, Surrey going on to win by seven wickets. The Whitsun crowds at Nottingham in 1947 saw too much of a good thing. The featherbed Trent Bridge pitches of those days were made for batsmen and they took full advantage. Nottinghamshire's 401 was good enough to win most three-day matches but Surrey replied with a massive 706 for four declared, David Fletcher, Stan Squires, Jack Parker and Errol Holmes all getting hundreds. Inevitably the game was inconclusive but Nottinghamshire won a fine game at The Oval by 48 runs in August, Guy Willatt, the Cambridge captain, making 131.

All the attendance figures paled before that of Whit Monday in 1948. Surrey made 419, Michael Barton getting a century, and Nottinghamshire declared immediately after passing this total, with hundreds from Keeton and Hardstaff. On the Monday the crowd of 35,000 established a new record for the ground and there was another good turnout on Tuesday, when after a Surrey declaration, Nottinghamshire successfully chased 266 in 160 minutes to win with half-an-hour to spare by four wickets. Surrey exacted due revenge at The Oval but in Nottingham captains sought results by setting a fourth innings target. Thus 1949 found Fishlock make two hundreds in the match only to be outshone by Simpson. He made a glorious 200 not out in 280 minutes with 27 fours, delighting a large Whit Monday crowd with some superlative stroke play. A personal memory of the day is boyhood confusion over the two Bedsers, the supposition being that Alec had switched to spin before the reality dawned that it was Eric. On the final day Nottinghamshire, set 206 in two hours, got 209 in 97 minutes. Simpson and Hardstaff giving them a flying start with 120 in 55 minutes and Bill Sime joining in the fun. It seemed remarkable at the time but in those days bowlers got through their overs at a much quicker rate per hour and Surrey actually delivered 36.3 so the rate was just under six an over.

Although 10,000 saw August Bank Holiday Monday's play at The Oval – the match was drawn – the signs were that Nottinghamshire were no longer the attraction of old. The Championship table in 1949 had something to do with this, with Middlesex and Yorkshire sharing the title, Surrey fifth and Nottinghamshire joint eleventh. Surrey threatened for a time and were the only side to defeat each of the joint champions, overcoming Middlesex twice and Yorkshire once. At The

Oval, the Yorkshire match in July attracted 30,000 people, the one against Middlesex 51,250. There was a similar story in 1950, when a late surge by Surrey earned them a share of the Championship with Lancashire. Surrey won both of the holiday games with ease, Nottinghamshire coming in for some mild barracking for some unenterprising batting on a good pitch at The Oval. Hardstaff and Fishlock batted attractively but new blood – Peter May, Jim Laker and Tony Lock – was now coming to the fore.

Their arrival heralded the great years of Surrey as they won seven consecutive Championships between 1952 and 1958, first under Stuart Surridge's dynamic captaincy and then Peter May. In contrast, Nottinghamshire were bottom of the table in 1951, 1958, 1959 and 1961 and not far away in some other years. In 1953 it was decided that the Trent Bridge pitch was so doped with marl that the only solution was to dig up the square and bring in fresh soil. For a few memorable seasons the leg spin and googlies of the Australian Bruce Dooland helped improve fortunes, with fifth place achieved in 1954. But between 1950 and 1960, with May in splendid form and Alec Bedser, Peter Loader, Laker and Lock at the heart of perhaps the finest county attack of all time, Surrey won 16 of their 22 games against Nottinghamshire. The only match Nottinghamshire won was in 1956 at Whitsuntide, although they forced Surrey to follow-on at The Oval in August 1956 and lost by only six runs at The Oval in 1953. Two years later at Trent Bridge umpire Alec Skelding ordered the removal of a brass band preparing to play during the lunch interval because its instruments were reflecting the sun's rays and dazzling the fieldsmen. Alec Bedser took eight for 18 and Laker six for five in 16 overs on helpful Oval pitches; Roger Harman eight for 12 in 17 overs at Trent Bridge and May, John Edrich and Ken Barrington joined the list of double centurions.

Whitsuntide 1957 can be put forward as a perfect example of Surrey's power. A fierce storm ended Saturday's play with Surrey 147 for two and they soon lost Mickey Stewart on Whit Monday. By then May had already made his intentions clear and his determination to force the pace in the pursuit of victory remains in the mind's eye more than half-a-century later. He made 83, adding 103 in an hour with Fletcher (53 not out). Ken Smales and Dooland suffered heavy punishment from beautifully timed drives which rocketed through the covers before May closed the innings at 303 for four. Trent Bridge then became a killing ground for Lock and Laker, with the hawks Stewart, Barrington, Lock himself and the wicket-keeper Arthur McIntyre seeking prey. First it was Lock (32.2-13-49-7), with left-arm spin who enmeshed the batsmen and when Nottinghamshire followed on it was the turn of Laker's off breaks (15.5-10-16-7), Surrey winning by an innings on the final day. As a result of this victory they went to the head of the table and nobody leaving Trent Bridge held any doubts that they would remain there.

Another example of Surrey's dominance had been provided in 1955, when Nottinghamshire, 43 behind on the first innings, went in a second time at 5.25pm on Monday. By the close they were 30 for nine, Laker having a spell of four for one in six overs. Ten runs were added on Tuesday morning before Surrey won by an innings and three runs. Roger Moulton, a frequent visitor to The Oval for the holiday fixtures, said: "I didn't see this but a school friend did and he was still full of it the following term."

Roger's memories also include an enormous crowd on a gloomy Monday in 1958 at The Oval. "In 1959, although Nottinghamshire lost on the Tuesday I enjoyed an excellent century by Reg Simpson and a quick-fire 50 from Cyril Poole, who always seemed to do well in these matches. In 1960 Notts were caught on a wet wicket which was fully exploited by Tony Lock and there was some more big hitting by Poole. I also remember Poole again and a Barrington hundred in 1961."

Some great names, but what of the average bread-and-butter county cricketers who played in these matches? John Clay was one such, a reliable batsman and slip fieldsman who captained Nottinghamshire in 1961, his last and best year with the club. His matches against Surrey took place from 1949 to 1961, the years of their pomp and his memories, unsurprisingly, tend to centre on Messrs Bedser, Loader, Laker and Lock.

"They were all England bowlers, world-class bowlers, in fact. Just imagine being able to put two men on to bowl and then if the pitch wasn't suiting them, replace them with the other two. What a luxury!

"Those holiday games were always special to me. As a youngster I would go to Trent Bridge at Whitsun with my father. Surrey always seemed special even then – chocolate-coloured caps, for instance, when everybody else seemed to be wearing blue. On the field, in the matches I played against them, they were a very hard bunch and a fine team. But they were probably the one side, to a man, that at the end of the day were in the Trent Bridge Inn with us. They were very good socially and always joined us for a drink at the end of the day.

"The senior players, such as Joe Hardstaff, Reg Simpson, Alec Bedser, Jim Laker and Laurie Fishlock, would tend to congregate because they had been on overseas tours together but there was a good spirit of friendship between the sides. I enjoyed playing at The Oval. People always talk about Lord's but I found there was something special about the atmosphere at The Oval, even more so than Lord's. The approach to the ground and the ground itself – it always seemed to be such a massive place.

"We travelled by train to London, then by coach for a time and finally, as the years passed, by car. Over the years we stayed in various hotels, mainly one near Lord's, and we tended to use the same hotels for the games against Sussex and Middlesex or if we were playing at Blackheath, for instance.

"We were usually on the receiving end against Lock and Laker etc., but I recall one day at The Oval in 1953. Reg Simpson and I shared an opening stand of 159 and I remember one or two of the Surrey players getting a bit niggled. They were not used to that sort of thing. It was a memorable game for me. I made 89 and 58 but they won by six runs."

Clay had another good match when he captained Nottinghamshire to a 28-run victory at Trent Bridge in 1961, making 71 and 63 himself. Simpson got a hundred and Clay's declaration left Surrey 291 at 90 an hour. Edrich and Barrington kept them up with the rate but Carlton Forbes transformed matters with three quick wickets. To their credit, Surrey continued to go for the runs and lost their last wicket three minutes from the end of extra time. "Nobody battled more fiercely than Tony Lock in that game," said Clay, "but after it was all over he was the first person to come into our dressing room and say 'well done'. Naturally these games remain the memory. Everything went our way for a while and it was lovely to feel that for a change we were doing so well against one of the best sides in the country.

"I think probably the finest innings I saw in these matches was Peter May's 211 not out at Nottingham in 1954. That was on the Saturday and it rained for the next two days. It was one of the few days when I found myself fielding in the covers – there was no point in having a slip because nothing was getting past the bat. Freddie Stocks and I were both in the covers and the balls were going past us like bullets. He was very powerful and had a fine cover drive and on-drive. Tom Graveney was a fine player but I regard May as the best post-war batsman of my time, remembering that Hutton and Compton developed before the war.

"Times altered and I suppose Notts were no longer Surrey's most important opponents. But I have fond memories of playing against one of the best county sides of all time, on big grounds and before large crowds. There was always a special atmosphere to the games and a good social side too."

Chapter Twenty-Eight
Derbyshire, Warwickshire and Others

In the old days, the County Ground at Derby boasted a concrete stand to the right of the pavilion, with a bar and seats for 300 people. Next to it was a smaller wooden structure. Both were open to the elements and neither was particularly impressive but they offered raised views from behind the wicket.

The stands were magnets for youngsters during the school holidays and also attracted visiting supporters. It was here, on Whit Monday 1950, that a group from the Birmingham area applauded the Warwickshire team after Derbyshire had been dismissed for 190. Rain had curtailed play on Saturday but the New Zealand-born fast bowler Tom Pritchard took six for 78 as the local urchins in the stands fell silent. Warwickshire had made a fine start to the summer; indeed, by the third week in June they were to head the table. It didn't look good for the home team, who were without the injured Cliff Gladwin, a tall young amateur, Tom Hall, sharing the new ball with Les Jackson. No matter. Jackson sent back Fred Gardner and Alan Townsend and Dick Spooner was bowled by Hall. Warwickshire had lost three wickets for one run and all before lunch.

There was much to ponder during the consumption of the egg sandwiches and lemonade. Warwickshire's captain Tom Dollery had just come in and everybody knew that Dollery always made runs against Derbyshire. He had done so before the war and in the first season afterwards, 1946, he got a hundred at Edgbaston, although Derbyshire won. It was even worse in 1948; 167 at Derby, defying Bill Copson who took seven wickets and then a Whit Monday gate of 8,600 had to endure more good bowling from Pritchard and Eric Hollies en route to a Warwickshire victory. Dollery 'failed' at Edgbaston in August with 90 – his side had the best of a rain-affected draw when Derbyshire were leading the Championship - but he delighted the Birmingham crowd at Whitsun in 1949 with another century. In the second innings, when Warwickshire were set 207 to win, Jackson had him caught behind by George Dawkes for four, but Jimmy Ord stayed nearly four hours for 75 and made the winning hit with one wicket remaining. Rain affected the Derby return in August, Dollery making 59 in a total of 359.

Thus, under the alternating system of the fixtures, Dollery was back at the County Ground in 1950 for Whit. And after lunch it was a different game. Hall accounted for Martin Donnelly and bowled Derief Taylor but Dollery launched a magnificent assault on the bowlers, Jackson, Hall, Derek Morgan and Bert Rhodes being put to the sword in turn. He hit three sixes and 12 hours in two hours 55 minutes and each stroke, particularly on the offside, was greeted with Brummie cries of 'Good old Tom' from the away contingent. When Morgan had him caught for 163 he had placed his side in an unassailable position, declaring at 300 with a lead of 110. All this after being one for three! It was a long journey home for the Derbyshire youngsters. The match was drawn and Jackson and Gladwin shared 18 of the 20 wickets at Edgbaston in August, when Derbyshire won by eight wickets. But a personal memory of 1950 is not so much Ramadhin and Valentine and the calypsos but 'Good old Tom'.

In 31 matches against Derbyshire Tom Dollery scored 2,444 runs, average 50.92 and made nine hundreds, six at Edgbaston and three at Derby with 177 the highest. His crowning glory was skippering the side to the championship in 1951, when there were two notable games against Derbyshire. It was a fine team: runs from the openers Gardner and the left-handed Spooner, who also kept wicket, Ord, Dollery, Wolton, Townsend and Ray Hitchcock and possessing a fine attack in Pritchard, Charlie Grove, Hollies and the young slow left-arm bowler Ray Weeks. The fielding was superb, with Townsend breaking records in the slips and Dollery and Gardner also excelling as did Wolton in the deep. Whitsun was early in 1951 and the Edgbaston game developed into a tremendous battle for first innings points. The pitch was slow and on Saturday John Kelly took three and a half hours over his first 50 during a laborious display by Derbyshire, who were 282 for eight at the close, with Kelly on 76. He was a stylish batsman but in this match he sorely tried the patience of the Birmingham faithful and he was still there on 97 after nearly five hours when the innings closed at 313 in 158.3 overs; Hollies's analysis 64-30-69-3.

Kelly's innings was recalled by Robert Brooke, cricket author and a founder of the ACS, in the 1991 summer edition of *The Cricket Statistician*. "Strangely one's memory suggests it was not a boring innings; rather was it similar to one of the Tom Dollery Restaurant's rock cakes – hard, solid, rock like, heavy going but somehow fascinating." At the end of Saturday's play, Brooke, then in a short spell as a schoolboy autograph hunter, asked Kelly to sign his book. The Derbyshire batsman provided the sole example of a player who thanked him for requesting his autograph. "Even in those days many players seemed in too much of hurry and one's interest finally evaporated when one's own county captain and cricket hero invited one to vacate his immediate vicinity ('clear off!')." Although Derbyshire were without Jackson and Gladwin, Warwickshire lost three wickets for 43. Dollery (70) came to the rescue again and there were useful contributions from Wolton and Townsend but Derbyshire gained a lead of 37. Their feeling of well being was eroded by the dismissal of three batsmen for 12 before Kelly and Alan Revill brought about a partial recovery. On the final day, Warwickshire needed 174 in two hours and Dollery accepted the challenge but when he was out for 41 Derbyshire took command. Nine wickets were down for 157 before Hollies played out the last over from Morgan to save the game. Warwickshire took over the leadership on 1 June and stayed there. Their visit to Derby in August was marred by rain when they were well placed; the home batsmen's struggles against Hollies (seven for 67) etched in the memory before the weather closed in.

Charlie Elliott made 50 in that game. "Eric Hollies was always a handful," he said. "There were quite a few leg spinners around in those days and some of us in the Derbyshire team had played alongside Tommy Mitchell but we were often at sea against Hollies. He was different from people like Doug Wright, who bowled leg breaks and googlies at quite a pace and Roly Jenkins who turned the ball a lot. Eric's leg breaks were not extravagantly spun but his length was always immaculate and he did just enough to beat the bat. And, of course, he had the googly and it was this which bowled Bradman for a duck at The Oval in 1948.

"They had a good team in those days but with Les Jackson and Cliff Gladwin in our team we generally gave as good as we got although we had problems getting rid of Fred Gardner and Tom Dollery. There was a fine spirit between the teams. The other big thing which was noticeable to me both as a player and an umpire was the vast improvement at Edgbaston and it was this which brought the return of Test cricket to the ground in 1957."

The Derby crowd developed something of a love-hate relationship with Dollery, Gardner and Hollies and there was a perfect example of this in the 1953 August Bank Holiday game. Guy Willatt and Revill shored up the Derbyshire innings but 233 was nowhere near enough as Hollies had his usual field day: 32-19-38-4. On Monday, 8,000 saw Gardner (143 in six hours) and Dollery add 180 for the fifth wicket before Dollery was run out by Donald Carr from the cover boundary with the scoreboard showing he had made 100. On checking it was found his score was 99. It had been a delightful innings and nobody would have begrudged him the extra run.

At times in 1954 either side looked capable of becoming champions but both of the holiday clashes were ruined by rain in one of the wettest summers on record. Warwickshire stood at the head of the table when they visited Derby at Whit and they took control immediately, dismissing Derbyshire for 172. Jack Bannister, unchanged from the pavilion end, took five for 99 and Hollies four for 39. Gladwin soon got rid of Gardner but Horner and Wolton batted well and Warwickshire were 111 for two by the close. Heavy rain ruled out any play on Whit Monday and there was none until 4.15pm on Tuesday. What was left of the match became a fight for first innings points and the visitors won it with four wickets and four minutes to spare.

By the time August Bank Holiday came around the boot was on the other foot. On the eve of the holiday, Yorkshire led the race with 142 points from 19 games. Derbyshire, who had just completed a stunning victory at Headingley, were second with 132 points from 17 matches and Warwickshire, 128 from 19, came next. Dollery won the toss and batted on Saturday but Warwickshire were well and truly pegged back by some accurate bowling from Jackson, Gladwin, Morgan and Edwin Smith. By lunch the score was 51 for three, with Gardner and Dollery together but Jackson had Dollery caught behind for three and wickets fell regularly. Warwickshire took over four hours to make 106, occupying 80 overs; had it not been for Gardner, eighth out for 40 after a 230-minute stay, their plight would have been even worse. Jackson took five for 28 and Morgan three for 18. Bannister soon accounted for Kelly but Arnold Hamer and Willatt took the score to 50 before the struggle began against Hollies and Ian King's left-arm slows. By the close Derbyshire were 92 for seven with Carr and Gladwin together and the match evenly poised. On August Bank Holiday Monday rain held up play until 4.15pm, when Carr (62) and Gladwin (38) took their partnership to 82 before the innings closed for 158. Warwickshire ended the day on 41 for the loss of Horner, still 11 behind, but rain prevented any play on Tuesday. Ominously for both counties, Surrey found time to beat Nottinghamshire and Yorkshire crushed Lancashire by an innings. Surrey were champions in 1954, Derbyshire ending third and Warwickshire sixth.

Hollies embarked on his final season in 1957 (Dollery finished in 1955) but he was not yet done with Derbyshire. They came to Edgbaston at Whitsuntide at the head of the table on the back of six consecutive victories but the 45-year-old had a match analysis of 10-99 as Warwickshire won easily. He bowled well at Derby in August, when Bannister took 11 wickets in the match and Horner and Warwickshire's new skipper Mike Smith made hundreds, but the home side escaped with a draw. In 36 matches against Derbyshire, Hollies took 159 wickets at 18.41; memory can still recall the good-humoured Revill cheerfully groping forward in a desperate attempt to smother the spin and the fair-haired, likeable bowler smiling at him down the pitch. Gardner continued to make runs; a hundred in the 1958 Whit match at Derby and 65 at Edgbaston, when Gladwin routed Warwickshire's second innings to set up a seven-wicket victory.

Whitsuntide 1959 brought change as Derbyshire met Leicestershire and Northamptonshire faced Warwickshire in a fixture switch. Maurice Hallam made 200 at Grace Road; Willie Watson added 150 at Derby to his century at Whit, Carr also getting a hundred in the August game. Warwickshire were beaten at Northampton, where there were hundreds for Townsend and Raman Subba Row, and drew the Edgbaston return. In the latter Mike Smith hit 142 not out in a total of 252, Frank Tyson taking five for 59. This was a fascinating game for Warwickshire came into it joint top in the Championship with Surrey, who, however, had two matches in hand. After Mick Norman made his first hundred in county cricket, Raman Subba Row declared on Saturday at 257 for nine, Tyson dismissing Jim Stewart before the close.

Season after season, Tyson was condemned to bowl on Northampton pitches which favoured spin and offered him little. This and the passage of time and recovery from a recent ankle injury meant he was below the lightening pace which caused such havoc in Australia five years earlier but he was still very hostile and could swing the ball sharply and late. In the second half of the 1959 season he regained some of his former fire and on August Bank Holiday Monday Warwickshire were on the receiving end at Edgbaston. Nine wickets were down for 174 – four of them to Tyson – when Ossie Wheatley joined MJK Smith, who was having the season of his life: 3,245 runs, eight centuries – including one for England - and an average of 57.94 placing him at the head of the national averages. He was on 74 when Wheatley came in; now with a superb exhibition of farming the bowling and stroke play he guided Warwickshire to 252 for nine, just six away from a first innings lead and bonus points. But Tyson, in his fifth over with the new ball, bowled Wheatley for 10 with a near-yorker on the leg stump. The pair had added 78 for the last wicket and Smith's innings included 18 fours and three sixes.

The next three seasons, 1960, 1961 and 1962, saw Derbyshire meeting Northamptonshire and Warwickshire facing Leicestershire as the variation continued. The Courtaulds' ground at Coventry was the venue for the 1960 Whitsuntide match, which found Warwickshire hanging on for a draw after a fine innings by Smith and they had the better of two close finishes in 1961, by 37 runs at Leicester and by two wickets at Edgbaston.

There was drama aplenty for Derbyshire and Northamptonshire in 1961. At Northampton, Mickey Allen's left-arm slows brought match figures of 13-98, Northamptonshire winning by 129 runs. When the teams reconvened at Derby in August, Carr declared at 279 for six early on Bank Holiday Monday and Harold Rhodes was then no-balled three times in succession by the square-leg umpire Paul Gibb for alleged throwing. Carr took Rhodes off but used him subsequently from the other end, Arthur Jepson, standing at square-leg, finding nothing wrong. These were the years of the great throwing controversy which dominated world cricket and Rhodes was also called by Gibb in 1960 and Syd Buller in 1965, both in matches against the South Africans. His action – his arm had an unusual backward extension of the elbow joint – was eventually declared fair after what amounted to an eight year trial but by then his hopes of a prolonged Test career as the heir-apparent to Statham and Trueman had been dashed.

Leicestershire fell foul of Jackson (13 for 73) in the 1962 Whitsuntide game at Derby and were beaten by 165 runs despite a fine hundred from Watson. The Midlands' holiday merry-go-round had now begun in earnest, with Warwickshire back as Derbyshire's opponents in 1963 and winning both (Smith 144 not out at Derby in August) and Northamptonshire and Leicestershire sharing the spoils. In 1964 the pitch at the County Ground, Derby was turned east-west, spectators seated on the old racecourse grandstand terrace now having a view from behind the bowler's arm. The first Championship match on the newly-aligned pitch was against Northamptonshire match during Whitsuntide, 16-19 May.

This was the last full year of the traditional Bank Holidays, Derbyshire meeting Northamptonshire, Essex-Warwickshire and Leicestershire-Worcestershire. The old order was changing.

Chapter Twenty-Nine
Hampshire v Kent

Canterbury's St Lawrence ground was clearly in need of repair when county cricket resumed in 1946. The old wooden gates were replaced by new iron ones and chestnuts were planted as an avenue up the drive. Over in Hampshire, the County Ground at Northlands Road, Southampton – the club's home since 1885 – also bore signs of wartime wear and tear but the crowds cared little after their long years of deprivation.

Kent had the better of things in the first two seasons. Rain ruined the Whitsuntide game at Southampton in 1946 but there was enough time for Charlie Knott's off spin to trouble the visiting batsmen. These were the years when England launched an increasingly desperate search for a fast bowler as the pre-war exponents aged and the Kent trio Jack Martin, Fred Ridgway and Norman Harding had their advocates. Martin was not playing at Canterbury in 1946 but the latter pair failed to trouble the Hampshire openers Johnny Arnold and Arthur Holt who posted 156 before a wicket fell on Saturday. Hampshire's inconsistency was legendary in 1946 – they were the only county to beat the champions, Yorkshire – and nobody else reached double figures in a total of 229. Kent seized their opportunity. Leslie Todd and Bryan Valentine made hundreds, Godfrey Evans got 72 and then the 24-year-old Tony Pawson, the Winchester captain of 1939-40, came to the middle. Pawson, who had spent four years in the Rifle Brigade on foreign service, was appearing in his first county match. He recalled how as he walked down the pavilion steps he heard a voice proclaim loudly: "It's ridiculous the committee allowing untried youngsters to play in Canterbury Week." Pawson struck 12 fours in making 90 before he was last out attempting a sharp second run after pulling to midwicket. Kent's 477 and some fine bowling from Ridgway and Harding was enough to bring victory by an innings. A collection for Joe Murrin, Canterbury groundsman for 41 years, realised £261.

The Southampton game of 1947 was almost a replica. Arnold and Neville Rogers began with an opening partnership of 126; Hampshire made 367 and then Leslie Ames hit 27 fours in scoring 179 faultless runs. Martin's pace proved too much for Hampshire in the second innings and Kent eased home by nine wickets. They carried their form to Canterbury – Todd's benefit match - where in glorious weather Valentine was able to declare at 445 for seven, Arthur Fagg 123, Ames 94 and the captain himself 81. The Hampshire innings was notable for the performances of the type of occasional amateur so often associated with August. Lieut-Commander John Manners had last appeared for the county in 1936 and Canterbury was to be his solitary appearance in 1947. His innings was a delight, 121 out of 192 in two hours 40 minutes, perfect stroke play of drives, cuts and hooks bringing him 17 fours. Rev John Bridger, a wartime Cambridge blue, got 65 but Doug Wright, although punished, took five wickets and Hampshire had to follow on. Bridger made 43 but Manners ran himself out and the last six wickets fell for 27. Wright had match figures of 10-158 as Kent won in two days. On August Bank Holiday Monday 13,267 paid for admission.

Hampshire surprised everybody by making such a fine start to the 1948 season that they were fifth by mid-July, although they tailed away afterwards. Kent were among their victims, the Whitsuntide match resulting in a two-wicket victory off the third ball of the final over, Valentine and Ames for Kent and Johnny Arnold and Neil McCorkell for Hampshire, getting hundreds and Martin's pace almost bringing victory. These were, indeed, golden days and big crowds saw two Kent successes in 1949. On August Bank Holiday Monday, when 14,000 were present at Canterbury, the Duke of Edinburgh was introduced to the two teams. He was accompanied on to the field by Lord Harris, Kent club president, and Lord Cornwallis, Lord Lieutenant of Kent. Wright carried off the bowling honours with 11-170, including the seventh hat trick of his career.

One of Wright's hat trick victims was Derek Shackleton, who had been given a trial as a batsman in 1947 when he had been playing Army cricket. He never reached a century in the first-class game but he became the acknowledged master of seam bowling at a little above medium pace, with an annual haul of 100 or more wickets in 20 consecutive seasons. In 1950 he was joined by Vic Cannings from Warwickshire and the pair, in dressing room parlance Shack and Vic, rivalled Derbyshire's Jackson and Gladwin as the best contemporary new ball attack in county cricket. They soon made their mark but first in 1950 there was drama at Southampton. It was a game of low scores and Hampshire needed 153 in the fourth innings. Ten minutes before lunch on the final day, Knott, the last Hampshire batsman, joined Cannings with 22 required. Seven were added before the interval and afterwards Knott levelled the scores with a late cut for two. Next ball Knott fell to a slip catch by Fagg off Wright's bowling and the match was a tie.

It was the following season, 1951, that Shackleton began to make a real impact on the Kent-Hampshire fixtures, with ten wickets in the match at Southampton. Kent were a long way now from their glory days and only a fighting maiden century by Richard Mayes kept them in this game. Ridgway, making the ball fly, routed Hampshire in their second innings but Shackleton and Cannings proved too much. The major problem facing Hampshire's captain Desmond Eagar was how to avoid overbowling them but they were a permanency at the Pavilion and Bannister Park ends in the 1952 game at Southampton. Saturday's play was limited to three hours, which saw Hampshire struggling against Martin and Ray Dovey and the slip-catching of Fagg. On Whit Monday Kent, replying to 135, were caught on a rain-affected pitch off which the ball rose alarmingly or skidded through. Nine wickets were down for 18 before Martin struck a six and a four but the innings closed for 32. Peter Hearn batted throughout for an undefeated 12; Shackleton took six for 22 and Cannings four for 10. Martin again proved a handful before Eagar declared 247 ahead and although Evans (34) showed courage, Shackleton and Cannings were again in hostile mood. The innings ended at 91 after 90 minutes, Hampshire winning by 156 runs in two days. On the second day 29 wickets fell, Shackleton having match figures of 21.4-3-67-12 and Cannings 20.1-3-55-8, the pair bowling unchanged.

These were lean times for Kent. In 1951, 1953 and 1956 they were only one place off the bottom and in 1952 they were 15th. Hampshire by contrast, were generally comfortably placed with highs of third in 1955, sixth in 1956 and runners-up in 1958. During Canterbury Week in 1953 committee members were canvassed for their views about the captaincy of Bill Murray-Wood. As the second game – a defeat by Middlesex – drew to a close the committee issued a statement saying Murray-Wood was to be relieved of his post. Doug Wright was appointed as the county's first professional captain until Colin Cowdrey took over in 1957, with Ames as manager. Wright celebrated his first season of leadership in 1954 with match figures of 12-120 – eight for 37 in the second innings – as Kent won the Whitsun game by 18 runs.

The die was now cast for a series of close-run things in the Hampshire-Kent series. Wright and Ted Witherden saved the 1955 match at Southampton with a stubborn eight-wicket partnership when all seemed lost; Cannings took the final Kent wicket with the last possible ball at Canterbury in August, when Cowdrey, opening at the request of the Test selectors, made 45 and 67, and there was an exciting finish to the August match in 1956. Kent chased 146 in 105 minutes; needing six off the last ball with one wicket remaining Ridgway's attempt at a big hit brought only two.

In 1958 Hampshire surprised even their most ardent supporters by mounting a serious challenge for the title under the inspiring captaincy of Colin Ingleby-Mackenzie. On Whit Tuesday that year Cowdrey set Hampshire 305 in four and a half hours. Their West Indian opener Roy Marshall, one of the most attractive batsmen in the country, rose to the challenge and shared a second-wicket partnership of 207 with Ingleby-Mackenzie after an opening stand of 75 with David Blake. Marshall made 131; Ingleby-Mackenzie reached three figures in 98 minutes and Hampshire – 148 behind on the first innings - won by five wickets with half-an-hour to spare. Then to August, with Hampshire, 156 points from 19 matches, leading the Championship from Northamptonshire 140 from 20 and Surrey 134 from 19. John Arlott painted a vivid picture, the marquees of I Zingari, the Old Stagers, the Buffs, the Band of Brothers, The Men of Kent and Kentish Men, the Mayor of Canterbury and the East Kent Yeomanry pitched in the same place every year. "Round the ground, motor cars, ranked along the sloping banks give their occupants a view of the game from beneath their own travelling roofs at a price not unreasonable for such a luxury." The Canterbury hotels had been booked up for The Week months ahead, yet Arlott understood that for some years past there had been suggestions that Kent should find more exciting opponents than Hampshire for their most attractive date of the summer. ACS member David Harvey, with boyhood memories of Canterbury Week from the late 1930s, has similar recollections. "In those days Hampshire were not a particularly exciting team and there was sometimes a feeling of 'not Hampshire again' although Gloucestershire and Somerset had been our Bank Holiday opponents only a few years earlier. We would have welcomed some variety, with more attractive opponents, both before and just after the war."

Ingleby-Mackenzie declared at 378 for seven on the Saturday and on August Bank Holiday Monday 15,000 turned up, much to the delight of Ridgway who was the latest Kent professional to choose this fixture for his benefit. They saw Shackleton (seven for 71 unchanged from the Nackington Road end) bowl Kent into following on but they fared better thanks to 127 from the left-handed Bob Wilson. Hampshire needed 80 to win in 97 minutes but they lost six wickets for 48 to Ridgway and Dave Halfyard before Mike Barnard and Leo Harrison got them home. Northamptonshire lost to Leicestershire and, by defeating Nottinghamshire, Surrey moved into second place, 22 points behind Hampshire. The positions were to reverse in the final table.

Kent did their old rivals no favours in Hampshire's Championship year of 1961 but the Southampton match produced some superb cricket. Centuries from Wilson and Cowdrey enabled Kent to declare at 390 for nine on the first day and although Ingleby-Mackenzie entertained with a hard-hit 90 Hampshire were 158 behind. Cowdrey's second declaration left Hampshire the whole of Tuesday's play to score 375 at 70 an hour. Henry Horton led the assault with a century but the last wicket fell in the final minutes of the extra half-hour with Hampshire 28 short. They were leading the Championship when they arrived at the St Lawrence ground in August but, despite a rapid hundred from Marshall, they seldom appeared likely to get anything from the game. Cowdrey made 156 and Kent, gaining the lead, continued their innings until almost lunchtime on the third day and although Hampshire collapsed against spin a finish was never on.

Notwithstanding the relative positions of the two counties the prospect of Cowdrey in full flow was mouth watering for the spectators. The 1962 match at Southampton broke no records but it provided a perfect example of the contest-within-a contest which makes cricket the most fascinating of games. Kent were left to score 216 at 96 an hour against Shackleton, Butch White and the slow left-arm spin of Alan Wassell. Cowdrey and Peter Richardson, his former opening partner for England, hit 50 in 25 minutes for the third wicket before Richardson fell for 43. Cowdrey got 76 and although Shackleton took some punishment his six for 88 proved decisive, Hampshire winning by nine runs with two minutes left.

There was opportunity for more sublime batting from Cowdrey (99 and 100 not out at Canterbury in 1964), not to mention Richardson, Mike Denness, Marshall and Horton before the old style holiday games ceased, with Hampshire marginally ahead in the post-war series.

Chapter Thirty
Gloucestershire v Somerset

On Saturday 4 August 1951, Gloucestershire followers made the journey to the Ashley Down ground at Bristol with more than the usual degree of anticipation for the traditional Somerset match. It had been announced that Wally Hammond would play for the county after being absent for five years.

Hammond had made a successful return to first-class cricket after the war but he had led an ageing England side to defeat in Australia in 1946-47. He was 43, putting on weight and troubled by ill health. It was time to go and he left with a superb record but an unhappy legacy of one tour too many. Then in 1951, at the age of 48, he was persuaded to reappear in an attempt to boost the county's membership recruitment drive.

Gloucestershire's top five looks formidable. George Emmett, Arthur Milton, Tom Graveney, Hammond and Jack Crapp all played for England but Graveney and Milton's best years lay ahead and, as was soon to be demonstrated, Hammond's were emphatically in the past. Emmett (110) and Milton (120) began with 193 and although Graveney failed, Hammond arrived at the crease with his side in a strong position. Much had changed since 1946. On expert advice sand was added to the high clay content of the Bristol pitch to balance the texture. It created a killing ground for the off breaks of Tom Goddard and the slow left arm of Sam Cook in 1947 but it had calmed down by now and there was plenty of time for the great man to play himself in and then, perhaps, unleash some of those glorious strokes of fond memory.

Bomber Wells, then a 21-year-old off spinner of promise doing his National Service in the RAOC, played against Somerset. He recalled the packed ground and the queue which stretched to the Grace Gates, but his main memory is of meeting Hammond. "When I was introduced to him, I almost bowed, for this was the man who when batting in Gloucestershire – and elsewhere no doubt – shops and offices closed so that the staff could see him."

Hammond received a tremendous ovation when he went out to bat. When he was dismissed Wells remembered that "many Somerset and Gloucestershire supporters, knowing full well they would never see him again, unashamedly wept. The vast crowd stood as one as the ageing giant, making his last appearance for the county which he had graced so magnificently for so many years, slowly made his way up the steps of the pavilion. I can tell you now there was a lump in my throat."

Hammond had taken guard against an old foe, the tubby little slow left-arm bowler Horace Hazell, whose own career would end a year later. Hammond had once been heard to say during a Gloucestershire-Somerset game: "I wish I had that little chap in our side – he's as good as anyone in the country when it comes to slow left arm." On this day Hazell would bowl unchanged for four hours ten minutes; 51.3 overs, eight wickets for 101.

It soon became clear that Hammond was a mere shadow of the man who took 2,483 runs off Somerset's bowlers in 28 matches, making 10 hundreds and averaging 73. He survived a confident appeal when Hazell's first delivery rapped his pads and there was a near run-out when Milton called for a quick single and turned to see his partner well short of his ground as the throw missed the stumps. Hammond played and missed, his timing was gone and he was in trouble against Hazell. "And I wasn't even spinning the ball in those little fingers of mine," said the bowler. "I didn't like what was happening. It upset me. I was pitching the ball up to Wally, subconsciously wanting him to show us those wonderful cover drives just once more." It was not to be. Hammond managed to scratch together seven singles in 50 minutes before he was bowled all over the shop coming down the pitch to Hazell. It was his last innings in first-class cricket and although Gloucestershire won, he cut a forlorn figure at slip for a time on Monday before retiring with lumbago.

In later years, Hazell liked to tell how he had fed Hammond half-volleys outside the off-stump out of sympathy but Somerset's Eric Hill (Stephen Chalke, Only Yesterday, *Wisden Cricket Monthly* July 2003) remembered Hazell hitting him on the pads and appealing loudly every time Hammond missed. "He hit him several times on the pad. They looked unlikely but Horace screamed at them all. Whenever Hammond missed, Horace appealed - and he wasn't that sort of bloke usually." Hazell had suffered against Hammond in the past and Hill remembers the bowler's words at the bar: "I owed that bugger one." Hill added: "It was all rather embarrassing. There he was. A great giant who had bestridden everything, struggling like a starter. Just struggling. Looking awful."

John Mortimore recalled that a lot of people in the pavilion had not been able to watch until Hammond got off the mark and Tom Graveney said that he just sat in the dressing room and couldn't watch any of it. Despite Hazell's satisfaction, players on both sides were in subdued mood in the bar during that Saturday evening.

It had all been so different in 1946. The years of war appeared to have taken nothing from Hammond's batting as he began the season in prime form. Rain spoiled the Whitsun fixture at Taunton but the Monday crowd could reflect on a superb display from Hammond; five sixes and six fours in 104. An outrageous chip for six off Bill Andrews resulted in the bowler stopping in midwicket to applaud. Bunty Longrigg, his captain, told him to restrict the hero-worship and get on with the bowling. Hammond was more restrained at Bristol in August, occupying six hours 10 minutes in making a flawless 214. On the Saturday he was on 178, made out of 415 for four, and on Monday Hammond and Basil Allen (132 not out) took their fifth wicket partnership to 242, the declaration coming at 550 for five. Somerset, no strangers themselves to 500-plus totals in 1946, were in some danger although Harold Gimblett played a valuable innings of 133. Nine men were out for 280 on Tuesday before Bertie Buse and Hazell put on 92 for the last wicket and with only two and a half hours remaining on Tuesday, Gloucestershire did not enforce the follow on. A crowd of 17,500 watched the cricket on August Bank Holiday Monday. Normal holiday interest was spiced by the high places the teams occupied in the table - Gloucestershire fourth and Somerset sixth at that point; they were to finish fourth and fifth respectively.

If honours were even in 1946 they were markedly in Gloucestershire's favour during the following summer. Somerset disappointed. A false dawn, a one-wicket victory at Lord's over Middlesex, the eventual champions, found

Maurice Tremlett erroneously heralded as the answer to England's fast bowling prayers; instead, he was to become a batsman of quality and the county's first professional captain. Poor batting and an ageing attack resulted in a fall to joint 11th.

They lost the Whitsun game at Taunton, although Tremlett ensured they went down with all guns blazing; an undefeated 85 in 93 minutes including six sixes and five fours. Gloucestershire were level with Middlesex at the top when the August match began at Bristol but they made a bad start, losing five wickets for 117. Billy Neale and Andy Wilson restored respectability and the total reached 244. When Somerset batted, George Lambert bowled one over with the new ball before he was replaced by Goddard, who promptly rubbed the ball in the dirt. Charlie Barnett took three wickets with his cutters from the other end, Johnnie Lawrence, the little Yorkshire-born leg spinner, hit a six and five fours in 34 but Goddard took seven for 61 and only some lusty blows from Wellard enabled Somerset to avoid following on. Hazell caused problems in turn before a Monday gate of 12,000 before Allen declared with a lead of 342. Somerset were in immediate trouble, losing four wickets for six to Lambert and Barnett. Frank Lee resisted for a time; Goddard came on at Lambert's end and then at 24 for five Cook replaced Barnett for his first over of the match, a maiden. Goddard then took four wickets in his next over, including a hat trick, for no runs. Cook, in his second over, was pushed for one by Buse and then had Hazell leg-before. Somerset were all out for 25, Goddard five for four and 12-65 in the match; Cook, his co-executioner that summer, one for one in the ten deliveries he sent down. Somerset's captain, Jack Meyer, said it was like batting on the beach at Weston-super-Mare. Gimblett was absent from this match but the Sherborne schoolteacher Micky Walford, who used to turn up in August and make hundreds of runs, although not many against Gloucestershire, was playing. Gloucestershire finished runners-up with Goddard taking 206 Championship wickets at 15.94 and Cook 120 at 19.90.

So the post-war series settled down, with Taunton at Whitsuntide and Bristol over the August Bank Holiday high on the lists of holiday attractions. Gloucestershire made over 500 at Taunton in 1948 with a hundred from Crapp and excellent support from Barnett and Emmett; Somerset, despite Gimblett's best efforts, could not escape an innings defeat in the face of Goddard and Cook. They thirsted for revenge and got it on a rain-affected Taunton pitch in 1949. On the Saturday Gloucestershire could make nothing of Hazell, who at one point delivered 105 balls – 17.3 overs - without conceding a run. The young Somerset player, Leslie Angell, recalled: "There was a remarkable tension among the fielders as the maidens increased. We were all so anxious not to be guilty of breaking the sequence by any error on our part." A Gloucestershire side including Emmett, Wilson, Crapp, Graveney, Allen and Milton could make only 123; Hazell's figures were 28.3-21-27-8. Goddard struck back with seven for 110 but Hazell was not to be denied with a match analysis of 50.3-29-63-12 and Gimblett ensured there would be no alarms in Somerset's eight wicket victory. The slow left-hander added eight more to his tally at Bristol, where Tom Graveney made a polished 159, but the match was drawn.

If in 1951 both counties occupied places in the lower half of the table it was not reflected in the Taunton match that year. Gloucestershire needed 105 in 55 minutes and got them with six minutes to spare after some fine hitting by Emmett, Crapp and Ken Graveney. Tremlett and Buse delivered 15.5 overs, Jim

Swanton alluding to the 'scrupulous briskness' with which they bowled and the Somerset fielders crossing over for the left-handed batsmen. Ancient rivals they might have been but there was an inherent fairness about the matches.

The matches continued to be well-attended but something of an imbalance set in. These were lean years for Somerset, who occupied last place in four consecutive seasons from 1952 to 1955, rising only to 15th in 1956. Gloucestershire attained mere respectability, although they were third in 1956 and second in 1959. Inevitably there was little joy for Somerset in the derby matches; hundreds for Graveney, Milton (he made ten in 43 matches against Somerset), Emmett and Martin Young and wickets for Cook, Wells, Scott, Lambert, John Mortimore, David Smith and David Allen on the one side, offset only by Gerry Tordoff, Colin McCool and Bill Alley with the bat and Jim Redman, Lawrence, John McMahon, Malcolm Walker, Brian Langford and Ken Biddulph with the ball. There were thrilling finishes, such as Somerset's last pair Jim Hilton and McMahon doggedly playing out the final 48 minutes at Bristol in 1955 and Gloucestershire scraping home by one wicket a year later at Taunton. They needed 161 in 132 minutes and Cook and Peter Rochford, the wicket-keeper, came together with 18 wanted. Cook settled it with ten in an over from McMahon. Variety was introduced, with Bristol at Whit and Taunton during August in 1954 and 1956 while Bath Festival Week replaced Taunton for the Whitsuntide fixtures of 1958 and between 1960 and 1964.

At last, in 1960, Somerset tasted victory again, their first in a derby since 1949, indeed it was only their second post-war success. This was a much stronger team now; runs from Peter Wight, Graham Atkinson, Roy Virgin, the Australians Colin McCool and Bill Alley (3,019 runs in 1961 at the age of 42) and the wicket-keeper Harold Stephenson and with Langford, Biddulph, Alley and Ken Palmer to take the wickets. First, however, there was drama during the second game of the Bath Festival on Whit Saturday when Eric Bryant, a young left-arm slow bowler, was no-balled five times by Hugo Yarnold for throwing. Milton was facing and patted back each delivery, legal or otherwise, finally saying to Yarnold: "Let's get this over finished with, Hugo." At Bristol in August, Gloucestershire chased 232 in 200 minutes and were going fairly well until Graveney was bowled for 47 by Langford, who sent back Mortimore in the same over. The innings subsided for 183, Langford four for 78, and Somerset were home with 48 runs to spare. They promptly won the next three matches before Gloucestershire reversed the trend with a narrow win at Bristol in 1962, the nip and tuck nature of the games continuing until the holiday changes after 1964. In that season Langford, who usually enjoyed Bath but proved time and again that he could spin the ball elsewhere, exploited a dusty pitch to return 10-78 in the match during the first game of the festival. Sweet revenge was gained at Bristol, when Gloucestershire, set 251 in 280 minutes, got the runs with five wickets and 20 minutes to spare, Ron Nicholls hitting 92. As they finished bottom of the Championship, the win was more than welcome for Gloucestershire.

Of the 38 encounters from 1946 to 1964, Gloucestershire won 17, Somerset seven and 14 were undecided. Given that Somerset were 14-1 down after 29 matches, their post-1960 rally was notable.

Chapter Thirty-One
Essex v Worcestershire

Sometimes a random memory helps illuminate a bigger picture. Holiday visits from Essex to the beautiful New Road ground at Worcester enrich such recollections but the one in mind concerns Worcestershire's match against Derbyshire at Ilkeston in June 1950.

It left no statistical legacy. No records were broken and its impact on the Championship was minimal. Nobody hit a century but the scores – Derbyshire 325 and 206 for eight declared, beat Worcestershire 195 and 271 by 65 runs – reflect pleasant days spent watching nearly a thousand runs scored in what might be described as a perfect example of a three-day county match at its best. Worcestershire, having been behind throughout, made a brave bid for victory but were undone, as so many teams were in those days, by Les Jackson.

The point of all this concerns Worcestershire's attack, consisting of Reg Perks (fast-medium), Peter Jackson (medium-pace off breaks), Dick Howorth (slow left-arm) and Roly Jenkins (leg breaks and googlies). Worcestershire delivered 192 overs in the match and all but five from the captain Ronnie Bird were sent down by these four. There was nothing unusual about this. Twelve years earlier, in August 1938, they had bowled Hampshire out at Worcester. The 1950 season, when Howorth was aged 41, Jackson 39, Perks 38 and Jenkins 31, was to be their final year together. Jackson retired; the other three simply adjusted by taking 100 Championship wickets apiece in 1951. Perks, Howorth and Jenkins played for England, Howorth, on three occasions and Jenkins (twice) achieved the double of 1,000 runs and 100 wickets in a season. Perks became captain in 1955 and combined career figures for the quartet of more than 6,000 first-class wickets complete the story.

The mind's eye can see now Jackson's fair hair, Perks's high action, Howorth's easy delivery and high tossed leg breaks from Jenkins finding turn but the pitch not allowing the ball to spin sharply enough to defeat experienced county batsmen. Additional interest was provided by Worcestershire's challenge for the title a year earlier with a team which included some six or seven players who commanded a regular place before the war. Perhaps an average age of 35 meant it could not quite last the pace but Eddie Cooper, Laddie Outschoorn (who was born in Ceylon and taken prisoner at Singapore by the Japanese) and Don Kenyon made their 1,000 runs and Jenkins, Perks and Howorth each took 100 wickets. Two defeats by Middlesex, the joint champions with Yorkshire, proved costly but third place was a glorious swansong for a popular side.

Essex, their holiday opponents, had a less memorable 1949, finishing joint ninth. Jenkins was too much for them at New Road, spinning his side to an innings' victory, although Eric Price's slow left arm bowling brought him eight for 125 in the Worcestershire innings but the boot was almost on the other foot when the August Bank Holiday match took place at Southend's Southchurch Park. Doug Insole and Stan Cray made big hundreds, typically the opener Dickie Dodds hit ten boundaries in making 56 and Trevor Bailey completed the double with some spirited fast bowling. Worcestershire had to follow on 232 behind the Essex total of 456 but a hundred from Cooper saved the day.

In contrast to Worcestershire, who fielded most of their pre-war side when play resumed in 1946, Essex were left mourning the deaths of Ken Farnes and Laurie Eastman. Stan Nichols was too old for first-class cricket and Jack O'Connor, due to retire in 1939, had secured an important post as a coach. However, Tom Pearce continued as captain, Dodds and Sonny Avery became one of the best opening partnerships in county cricket and the cousins Ray and Peter Smith were allrounders who virtually carried the attack, Ray with medium-pace or off breaks, Peter with leg breaks and googlies. Doug Insole came in as a batsman good enough to play for England and, above all else, there was to be Trevor Bailey. Great things had been predicted when he was at Dulwich College; his reputation was enhanced as a batsman and right-arm fast medium bowler at Cambridge and he was in the England team by 1949. Bailey's deeds in the Test arena have sometimes obscured the fact that he could be a match-winning all rounder in county cricket, where his batting was much more attractive. He was appointed assistant secretary to Essex at the end of 1948, this enabling him able to play regularly for the club as an amateur.

Bailey marked his first appearance for the county with an undefeated 97 in the 1946 August Bank Holiday match at New Road. Worcestershire had won the Whitsun game at Chelmsford by five wickets; requiring 358 to win at Worcester they finished 31 short with two wickets remaining from 88 overs, 74 delivered by the Smiths. The issue, frustratingly, was wide open when time was called but there was even more thrilling finish at New Road in the Whitsuntide fixture of 1947. The Cooper brothers, Edwin and Fred, began with a partnership of 163 for the first wicket and Worcestershire made 371, which, despite an unbeaten 137 from Pearce, was enough to give them a lead of 111. The game turned on the final morning, when Worcestershire lost their last six remaining wickets for 109. Essex, needing 284 in four hours, were 63 for four but Pearce (96) remained until the score reached 220 for seven. Ray Smith hit 57 in 50 minutes and then in the last minute of the extra half-hour the wicket-keeper Tom Wade twice swept Jackson to the boundary to get Essex home by one wicket. A demolition job from Perks at Chelmsford brought due revenge for Worcestershire in August. Worcestershire won the August fixture again in 1948 at New Road despite Peter Smith's eight for 123 in their second innings including three in four balls but the real drama that year was at Southend on 15 and 17 May.

Instead of meeting Worcestershire – who faced Glamorgan - at Whitsuntide, Essex entertained the redoubtable 1948 Australians and the match entered cricket history when the tourists made 721 on the first day. Jack Fingleton, in *Brightly Fades The Don*, recalled the glorious weather of that Whit Saturday. He remembered the different smells along the front. He described the crowd thronging "the front slowly, amid varied yells and smells as the innumerable shops emit the odour of their eating wares and attendants advertise them. In quick succession one sniffs curried eels, elks, whelks, mussels, cockles, oysters and the like, and even early in the morning the sounds of community singing float out from the pubs."

A terrific round of applause from the packed ground greeted an off-drive for four by Sid Barnes in the first over. Barnes and Bill Brown opened the Australian innings with a partnership of 145 before Barnes (79) hit his own wicket. Bradman came in 22 minutes before lunch and by the interval he had made 42, taking five fours off the last over delivered by Frank Vigar. The Don reached 50 after 34 minutes and 100 in 74 minutes before surviving a hard chance in the deep off Price when he was 160 in an over in which he again hit five fours. The pair added 219 in 94 minutes before Brown was caught off Bailey for 153 but Keith Miller, sickened by the slaughter, declined to join the party. Coming in at 364 for two he gave his wicket away first ball, Bradman saying: "He'll learn." But that, of course, was Miller.

Fingleton added that the Southend spectators were out to enjoy themselves but the afternoon sun was not long on its downward path before boundaries were being received in complete silence. "The spectators had had too much of a good thing, and no wonder, because 87 boundaries were hit in the day on a field of average size."

Bradman's last 87 came in 50 minutes and a wide variety of orthodox and unorthodox strokes brought him a five and 32 fours before he was bowled for 187, swinging across a straight ball from Peter Smith. It was his sixth and final innings in the holiday fixtures from 1930 to 1948, in which he made 350 runs with an average of 70. Sam Loxton (120) and the reserve wicket-keeper Ron Saggers (104 not out) piled on the runs and the last wicket fell at 721, in five hours 50 minutes. The bowling figures made sorry reading but to their credit Essex sent down 129 overs in the day which reduced the run rate to below six an over. Bailey took heed. Doug Insole said: "He bowled 21 overs for rather more than six runs apiece. He came back to Cambridge mumbling something to the effect that if he had placed his field properly and bowled intelligently he could have cut it down by half, and feeling rather humiliated. He began to look searchingly at his bowling and set about improving it." Bailey said: "Tom Pearce, the captain, had a pre-war approach. The idea was to get the opposition out, not to stop them scoring."

On Whit Monday, the Essex flag was found to be flying upside down before play started and the county batsmen gave a poor display. The side was dismissed twice, failing against Miller and Ernie Toshack in the first innings and Ian Johnson in the second. Bailey did not bat because of an injury but during the follow on Pearce and Ray Smith added 133 before the match ended, the margin of victory being an innings and 451 runs. The attendance of 32,000 – 16,000 on each day - was a ground record. Worcestershire's visit to East Anglia in 1948 occurred in late August and ended in defeat at Clacton, Avery (214 not out) and Dick Horsfall sharing a fourth-wicket partnership of 298.

Since leaving Leyton, Essex usually played their home games in a series of weeks on grounds owned or rented by local clubs such as Brentwood, Clacton, Colchester, Ilford, Romford, Southend and Westcliff before the county bought their headquarters, the Chelmsford ground in 1964. It was Romford's turn for the 1950 Whitsuntide match against Worcestershire and Outschoorn, Norman Whiting and Insole marked the occasion with hundreds; Insole and Don Kenyon emulating the feat at Worcester. Both matches were drawn, which was something of a bonus for Essex who finished last in the Championship against Worcestershire's sixth. Neither side mounted any sort of realistic challenge for the title in the 1950s, although Essex flickered briefly in 1959. Worcestershire's highest placing was fourth in 1951, with 15th in 1953 ad 1955 and 16th in 1957 their lowest. Essex were fifth in 1957 and sixth in 1958 and 1960. Correspondingly, a series of eight drawn games dulled the appetite for the holiday fixtures. Some, such as 1951 and 1952, fell foul of poor weather. Others produced some outstanding individual performances, hundreds for Bird, George Dews, Kenyon, Outschoorn, the brothers Peter and Derek Richardson, Avery, Bailey, Dodds, Insole, Horsfall and Barry Knight and fine bowling from Bailey, Bob Berry, Jenkins and Perks.

There was a memorable finish to the high-scoring 1953 match at Worcester. The home side declared at 355 for seven (Dews 139) and Jack Flavell, now sharing the new ball with Perks, shot out Dodds and Avery cheaply. Essex, 13 for two at the close, were soon 30 for three after Perks got rid of Paul Gibb but this was one of only two wickets to fall on Whit Monday when 479 runs came, Insole (160 not out) and Horsfall (118) putting on 227 for the fourth wicket. Insole, who made seven hundreds in 29 matches for Essex against Worcestershire, declared as soon as the lead was obtained and then Kenyon (120) and Peter Richardson (99) began Worcestershire's second innings (133 at Monday's close) with an opening partnership of 212. Bird set Essex 285 in just over three hours and when Dodds and Paul Gibb added 94 for the second wicket in 45 minutes they were on target but Perks broke through and they needed three off the last ball with two wickets remaining. Bailey tried to hit a boundary but gave a catch to mid-on and the match was drawn.

Essex ended the sequence of draws with a win at Chelmsford in August 1953, Worcestershire avenging the defeat on the same ground two years later. They piled up a total of 450 before declaring with only five wickets down, Kenyon and Richardson beginning with 145 and Outschoorn remaining unbeaten with 150. The two captains, Insole and Perks, kept the match open and Essex accepted a challenge of 260 in 140 minutes but found the bowling of Perks, Flavell, Jenkins and George Chesterton too much. They faced a similar task – 206 in 170 minutes – at Romford on Whit Tuesday 1956 but Geoff Smith and Ken Preston, the last pair, played out the last seven minutes. Essex saved the match and duly noted the promise of Worcestershire's new-ball attack of Flavell and Len Coldwell.

In August 1957 there was a nostalgic return to Leyton after 24 years. Essex beat Middlesex in the first match of a cricket week but Bank Holiday proved that the pitch proved to be as favourable to batsmen as ever. The match against Worcestershire was drawn after 912 runs were scored for the loss of only 23 wickets. Honours were shared at Romford and Worcester in 1958 and Essex began 1959 by winning their first five matches in the Championship, including one at New Road over Whitsuntide. They had fallen away by August when the teams were back at Leyton for another high-scoring draw. After some fine bowling from Bailey, Worcestershire followed on but 212 from Martin Horton and a hundred from Dews (they added 203 for the fifth wicket) saved the game.

Worcestershire now began a period of ascendancy. It was not particularly noticeable in 1960, when both holiday games were drawn – hundreds for Ron Headley and Kenyon and five wickets for Flavell at Romford, centuries again for Dews, Horton and Insole and five victims for Coldwell at Worcester, when Roy Ralph took 24 off an over from Doug Slade as Essex strove for victory – but by 1961 it was evident that a fine side was developing under the captaincy of Kenyon. Peter Richardson had left for Kent but Martin Horton forged a successful opening partnership with his captain, there were plenty of runs from Bob Broadbent, Dick Richardson, Headley, Dews and the wicket-keeper Roy Booth, while Flavell and Coldwell, Horton with off spin and the medium pace of Jim Standen took care of the bowling. Essex also had a decent team; runs from

Gordon Barker, Geoff Smith, Joe Milner, Bailey and Knight and plenty of wicket-taking potential from the seamers Bailey, Knight and Ken Preston and Bill Greensmith's leg spin. Worcestershire won both holiday games in 1961, by four wickets at New Road and by five wickets at Leyton, the latter the fifth in a sequence of seven consecutive victories which carried them to fourth in the final table, two places above Essex.

Tom Graveney, now qualified after leaving Gloucestershire, added style and power to the batting in 1962 when Worcestershire were runners-up to Yorkshire. Rain ruined the August Bank Holiday game at New Road but Whitsuntide had brought a resounding victory for Worcestershire in two days at Romford, Flavell and Coldwell routing the home batting, Booth holding eight catches and Horton, Headley and Graveney making runs. There was a blip in 1963, Worcestershire falling to 14th although reaching the first-ever final of the Gillette Cup in which they were beaten by Sussex at Lord's. Essex, two places above them, nearly pulled off a victory at Worcester when they set a target of 225 in 130 minutes. Such declarations leading to a final day run chase were now part and parcel of the game and there were three such in this game, which ended with eight Worcestershire wickets down for 118. Jim Laker, now with Essex, had seven men crowding the bat in the final half-hour but the batsmen hung on. For Essex, Michael Bear made a hundred before providing Flavell with his 1000th first-class wicket. At Leyton in August, two declarations from Bailey set up an exciting finish which resulted in an Essex victory by 31 runs. The teams did well to fashion a result; the first day was lost to rain and there was a delay at the start when the umpires Bert Rhodes and Lofty Herman discovered that the wickets were eight and a half inches in width instead of nine. They were pulled up and replaced in new holes.

In 1964, Worcestershire won the Championship after 65 years of trying. They had a rare tussle with their neighbours and old holiday opponents Warwickshire, who, after Worcestershire gained the lead in mid-May, held first place apart from a series of games, until 7 August. A strong finish brought the title to Worcester with three matches remaining. They were worthy champions, Graveney having a magnificent season, Headley, Kenyon, Richardson and Horton again among the runs and, above all, a splendid attack under Kenyon's leadership; Flavell, Coldwell, Norman Gifford's left-arm spin, Standen and Horton.

Essex, tenth in 1964, found themselves with Warwickshire as their holiday opponents, Worcestershire meeting lowly Leicestershire. Grace Road at Whitsuntide brought Worcestershire victory by 44 runs, Gifford wrapping things up with seven for 31 after Duncan Fearnley, who made cricket bats with his father in Yorkshire, had given an early indication of his product's quality with 82, then his best score in first-class cricket. The return at New Road saw Worcestershire win by an innings, Graveney making a hundred and Gifford enjoying a reprise of his earlier success. Meanwhile Essex did their old rivals a couple of favours by holding Warwickshire to draws at Ilford and Edgbaston, Bear, Billy Ibadulla and John Jameson making centuries at Whitsun and Warwickshire, then leading the table, ending the August Bank Holiday game 22 runs short of victory with two wickets remaining. Just over a fortnight earlier, Worcestershire had struck a decisive blow with an emphatic win at Edgbaston after the two leading counties had refused to give each other an inch in a dull draw at New Road.

Although the post-war Essex-Worcestershire series contained a high proportion of drawn games it produced much interesting cricket, with Worcestershire having a 9-5 advantage in the 35 games.

Chapter Thirty-Two
Leicestershire v Northamptonshire

Changes to the holiday programme by counties in the Midlands were part of attempts to stimulate the game as interest waned. The concern was justified. Spectator numbers had fallen alarmingly over the past decade and action was needed. Amidst the calls for a brighter or more positive approach some of the clubs tried to freshen up the fixture list with a new menu. The alterations began in the hot summer of 1959. It was a laudable move but what of the members accustomed to traditional Bank Holiday opponents?

Personal recollections are vivid. It seemed unthinkable that any county other than Surrey should be at Trent Bridge over Whitsun, although attendances were in decline. Saturday's close in 1961 found Edrich and Barrington the not out batsmen and an opportunity too good to miss on Whit Monday. There was a fair crowd from the start but no difficulty was experienced in finding a decent seat at the Radcliffe Road end. Edrich did not stay long but his departure brought a brief glimpse of pre-war skills from Bernard Constable, still three years away from the end of a career that was to span 25 years. In 1959, Leicestershire visited Derby in August instead of Warwickshire. Memories relate not to the loss of an old-established fixture but an absorbing battle for a lead on the first innings which occupied Monday's play. Leicestershire appeared to be winning before Donald Carr and Laurie Johnson came together in a big stand, Carr going on to a stylish hundred. He declared once the lead had been secured but the game fizzled away into a third-day draw. In contrast, Northamptonshire were in the driving seat on Whit Monday at Derby in 1960. They gained a comfortable lead and then unleashed Frank Tyson and the giant David Larter – the past and future of England's new ball attack – with the field in attacking positions. Runs came freely, but although he went for plenty that evening it is Tyson's hostility from the Nottingham Road end in what was to be his final season which stays in the mind's eye.

Thus it was the quality of the cricket which became the talking point rather than the variation of opposition, always excepting the Roses matches and the West Country derbies which seemed set in stone. So, too, did the Leicestershire-Northamptonshire series which had survived the war intact and resumed in 1946 with Whit Monday rained off at Grace Road and victory by an innings for Leicestershire at Northampton. Dennis Brookes gave clear indications that had it not been for Hutton and Washbrook he might have enjoyed a long Test career, winning a fascinating duel with Jack Walsh. Northamptonshire were bottom and Leicestershire second-last on the eve of the August match; they finished 16th and 11th respectively and in 1947 Northamptonshire were back in their familiar territory of bottom place. Walsh yet again spun Leicestershire to an easy victory at the County Ground and in August it appeared to be the same old story on Saturday when five Northamptonshire wickets fell for 78 but Brookes and Eddie Davis added 259 for the sixth wicket in a little over three hours. Brookes batted five and a half hours for 210 (14 fours); Davis reached the boundary nine times in 104, his maiden century. The captain, Arthur Childs-Clarke, weighed in with 68, his highest score for the county and the total reached 455. Walsh, scourge of Northamptonshire, again took five wickets but they cost him 157. Leicestershire, bemused by the leg breaks of the West Indian doctor Bertie Clarke, followed on and although Leslie Berry made a hundred, Northamptonshire won with six wickets to spare. It was their first success at Leicester for 20 years. "There was such rejoicing in the Northants dressing room afterwards as would not be fully understood among the more regularly successful counties," wrote John Arlott.

Although conditions at Grace Road were then rudimentary, the local derby continued to attract the spectators and crowds of 8,000, 11,000 and 8,000 watched the Northamptonshire match at Whitsun in 1948. By 20 July, the counties were level pegging at the bottom but Walsh (13-108) was again in devastating form at Northampton, when Leicestershire won by 182 runs. They finished 11th to Northamptonshire's 17th but change was in the air at the County Ground. Childs-Clarke's two-year reign as captain ended and the 38-year-old Freddie Brown, the former Cambridge University, Surrey and England allrounder, was appointed as his successor. A winter job at British Timken Ltd, the roller bearing firm, was guaranteed and Brown took over in 1949. His leadership skills were schooled under Percy Fender and Douglas Jardine and honed under Errol Holmes and Monty Garland-Wells; five memorable seasons with Northamptonshire brought a transformation and of his 22 Tests, 15 were as captain, notably and courageously the 1950/51 tour of Australia.

Brown began his Northamptonshire career by performing the double in 1949 but he could not manage the revival single-handedly. The county qualification rules had been relaxed by introducing special registrations and Northamptonshire took full advantage. From Lancashire came Norman Oldfield, one of the most promising young batsmen in England before the war, and allrounder Bert Nutter, who had both refused post-war terms at Old Trafford. Off spinner Gordon Garlick, his chances restricted in Lancashire's team, joined the staff and two high-class Australians, Jock Livingston, a small, nimble left-handed batsman, and George Tribe, a slow left-arm bowler and an allrounder capable of doubles, arrived from league cricket. Brown was to make an interesting comparison between Tribe and Jack Walsh. Of the three great chinamen exponents of his time, he felt that the Australian Fleetwood-Smith turned the ball the most. "Walsh possessed the biggest box of tricks in that he bowled so many varieties and George Tribe was probably the most accurate."

Northamptonshire famously rose to sixth in 1949; Leicestershire were last but the positions were not reflected in the holiday fixtures, both of which were drawn. A late Whitsun – 4, 6 and 7 June – saw hundreds from Frank Prentice and Eddie Davis and a determined innings from Maurice Tompkin which frustrated Northamptonshire's hopes. In August, Berry (162) delighted the Grace Road faithful and Oldfield responded with a stylish hundred but rain on the final two days disrupted proceedings.

There were mixed fortunes for Leicestershire in the 1950s; joint third in 1953 and sixth in 1952 and 1955 offset by bottom place in 1956 and 1957 and second-last in 1950, 1954 and 1959. Northamptonshire, by contrast, were runners-up in 1957 and fourth in 1956 and 1958; their lowest position was 13th in 1951. Northamptonshire's superiority was not always to the fore in the holiday fixtures, although in 1950 they won a thrilling game at Grace Road by 22 runs. They were only 130 ahead with seven second wickets down but the left-handers Vince Broderick and Bob Clarke added 86 for the eighth wicket. Leicestershire needed 250 and when Berry and Gerry Lester began with 119 they looked capable of getting them. Brown then took a wicket in each of three overs and finished with six for 105, the last one nine minutes from time. Centuries from Berry, Charles Palmer, Leicestershire's captain, Brookes and Livingston (259 for the second wicket) turned the August Bank Holiday return into a high-scoring affair. Northamptonshire, facing 441, gained a lead on the first innings after lunch on the third day. However, Leicestershire just managed to avoid defeat in 1951 at the County Ground, thanks to the efforts of Vic Jackson and Walsh and last pair, Jeff Goodwin and Charles Wooler.

This was one of a sequence of half-a-dozen inconclusive matches, some rain-affected, although Palmer could look back with pride at 119 at Grace Road in 1952 and 201 at the County Ground in 1953. These were heady times for Leicestershire; indeed for three days in August 1953 they led the Championship, a position they had never held before. The Whitsun game at the County Ground was drawn but Leicestershire gained an astonishing win at Grace Road in August. They were 143 behind on the first innings, Bob Clarke's left-arm seamers bringing him seven for 33. Vic Jackson's off breaks and Walsh's usual magic took care of Northamptonshire's second innings and Leicestershire needed 311. They soon lost Lester but Maurice Hallam helped Tompkin add 88 for the second wicket. Palmer and Tompkin then came together in an unbroken third wicket partnership of 212 which carried their side to victory. Tompkin hit 17 fours in a superb 143 and Palmer ten in his 96. It was Northamptonshire's first defeat by a county side that season and one of four wins in five which sustained Leicestershire's title challenge.

Livingston made two hundreds in the 1954 games, Northamptonshire winning at the County Ground by an innings in August, Broderick's slow left-arm bowling bringing him ten in the match and they won again at Grace Road in 1955 despite a Palmer hundred. Earlier that year, at Whitsun, Livingston hit his third consecutive hundred against Leicestershire. The 1956 matches were drawn but Northamptonshire completed a double in 1957, when they were runners-up to Surrey, albeit a long way behind. They completed their third consecutive holiday victory with a win off the fourth ball of the final over (Raman Subba Row an unbeaten 70) at Grace Road in 1958 before Leicestershire stopped the rot with a narrow win at the County Ground in August. Here the home batsmen got a taste of their own medicine on the spin-friendly pitch, John Savage with off breaks returning six for 37 and eight for 62, outbowling Tribe and Jack Manning.

It was 1963 before the counties met again over the holidays, Northamptonshire winning by five wickets at the County Ground with three minutes to spare after Mick Norman had made a hundred in the first innings and 51 in the second. Then Leicestershire, who finished with only Derbyshire below them, caused a shock at Grace Road. The pitch was affected by rain and bowlers had the upper hand, apart from Leicestershire's Clive Inman and Alan Wharton. Northamptonshire were set an unlikely 235 by Hallam and were bowled out by the spin of Savage and Raymond Smith.

During this period, Leicestershire met Derbyshire in 1959 and 1962, Warwickshire in 1960 and 1961 and Worcestershire in 1964. Northamptonshire's opponents were Derbyshire in 1960, 1961 and 1964 and Warwickshire in 1959 and 1962. Of 28 holiday matches from 1946 to 1963,

Northamptonshire won eight, Leicestershire six and 14 were drawn. Perhaps Dennis Brookes and Les Berry can be regarded as epitomising such games; their records, including pre-war, remarkably similar – Berry 42 matches, 2,661 runs, average 42.23 with six hundreds, Brookes 38 matches, 2,450 runs, average 43.75, seven hundreds.

Labelled, often unjustly, as the Cinderellas of the holiday fixtures, Leicestershire and Northamptonshire could count themselves among the pioneers of the attempts to make the game more attractive. In 1960 MCC set up a committee of inquiry which discussed the introduction of limited overs into county cricket. The Gillette Cup was launched in 1963 but Leicestershire were ahead of the game. Mike Turner, their secretary, was an early advocate of one-day cricket and in order to put the experiment into practice in the spring of 1962 he arranged a competition with Derbyshire, Nottinghamshire, Northamptonshire and Leicestershire. The final of the Midlands Knock-Out Cup, with an over-limitation of 65 per side, took place at Grace Road on 9 May 1962, Northamptonshire beating Leicestershire by five wickets.

Chapter Thirty-Three
Tourist Trade

Glamorgan had made history during the 1938 Whitsuntide when they met a county side over the holiday period for the first time since they were admitted to the Championship in 1921. That had been at Worcester and had ended in a draw; by the time of the second occasion in 1948 their fortunes had changed dramatically.

New Road was again the venue, the fixture made possible because Worcestershire's traditional opponents, Essex, were meeting the Australians at Southend, just as they had ten years earlier. Whitsun was early but the weather was fine and warm. Glamorgan had beaten Somerset at Cardiff in their only previous match and they were dominant at Worcester, dismissing the home side for 284 and then running amok with the bat. Allan Watkins made a hundred, Gilbert Parkhouse, Willie Jones and Phil Clift got useful runs and Wilf Wooller was able to declare on the third morning at 485 for nine. Wooller and Norman Hever then took advantage of a cross wind, swerving the ball awkwardly and Worcestershire were dismissed for 153, leaving Glamorgan the winners by an innings and 48 runs.

It was the start of a remarkable season which saw Glamorgan win the Championship for the first time. Wooller's captaincy developed a splendid spirit among the side which was largely unchanged: Emrys Davies, Clift, Parkhouse, Jones, Watkins, Jim Eaglestone, Wooller, Len Muncer, the wicket-keeper Haydn Davies and Hever, plus Arnold Dyson, Stan Trick and, notably at the end, Johnnie Clay. Jones, Emrys Davies and Parkhouse each exceeded a thousand runs, Muncer took more than a hundred wickets with his off breaks but the powerhouse of the side was its fielding and its positive approach.

Glamorgan went to the head of the table in mid-June and remained there until 20 July, when Derbyshire took over. After a defeat by Leicestershire, Glamorgan gained a three-wicket win over Warwickshire at Neath but Derbyshire maintained their lead with a victory over Nottinghamshire. The August Bank Holiday period found Derbyshire at Edgbaston and Glamorgan – back to their traditional game against the tourists - meeting the Australians at Swansea, where there was grave disappointment that Bradman was not playing. On Saturday, the St Helen's crowd saw Emrys Davies and Clift give their side a useful start before Ian Johnson and Doug Ring spun them out for 197. On Monday Miller (84, five sixes and seven fours) gave an aggressive display and shared a partnership of 126 for the third wicket with Hassett but with the score 215 for three torrential rain prevented any more play after 3pm. It carried on raining until after lunch on the final day and the game was left drawn. More than 50,000 people attended and the good news was that Derbyshire had got nothing out of their match against Warwickshire.

Derbyshire stayed top until 10 August and Glamorgan then fended off challenges from Surrey and Yorkshire to win the title by defeating Hampshire at

Bournemouth. Thousands of people greeted the players when they arrived at Cardiff General shortly after 11pm; had the match been played at St Helen's instead of Bournemouth then half of Wales would have tried to get in. But then half of Wales wanted to attend the matches against the tourists over the Whitsun and August holidays, as John Arlott discovered when cricket resumed in 1946. The Indians came to South Wales in June, to be greeted by miserable weather. "A long crowd waited patiently outside the gates at Cardiff on Saturday morning while rain fell steadily," wrote Arlott. "Play started in the afternoon, under grey skies and the threat of more rain. The game was watched by a large crowd inside the ground, and a smaller, but more comfortable, group of spectators who brought armchairs and their tea on to the balconies of the flats that overlook the ground." They saw a mixture of the exotic and the workaday, an unbeaten hundred from Amarnath and more runs from Merchant, Mankad and Hazare. Glamorgan, following on, just managed to avoid defeat against the spin of Sarwate and Mankad. "To see Emrys Davies and Arnold Dyson come out to open the innings is to be reminded of two artisans going out to dig a well or thatch a house," said Arlott, in an assured reminder that all was good and cricket was as it should be after the war. During this match Peter Judge made a king pair, being bowled by successive deliveries from Sarwate. He was last man out when Glamorgan were dismissed and to save time when they followed on, the last wicket pair Clay and Judge remained at the wicket to start the second innings. Judge, who began as an amateur with Middlesex and then became a professional with Glamorgan, was out to the first ball of the second innings.

The weather was much better on August Bank Holiday Monday, when 25,000 went to the match at Swansea: "some came early to get a seat and then stood on it to see the play: the rugby grandstand was full up to a hundred yards from the boundary of the cricket field: uncounted dozens came in over the wall and hundreds turned from the closed gates to the seaside." Clay (seven for 72) bowled Glamorgan to a 35-run lead on the first innings; his declaration set India a target of 273 and they got them for the loss of five wickets after fine batting from Mushtaq Ali and Hazare.

In 1947 the South Africans pulled in the crowds at Cardiff and Swansea, winning the Whitsuntide match by an innings, Bruce Mitchell and Athol Rowan getting hundreds and Tufty Mann thrashing 97 in 55 minutes, and the St Helen's return by 40 runs, despite some splendid bowling by Clay (11-162). A masterly 100 from Tony Harris was the mainstay of the Springboks' batting. Whit Monday 1949 found 17,000 at Cardiff, Wooller and Parkhouse being among the runs against the New Zealanders. On the August Saturday, 20,000 watched Mervyn Wallace make a big hundred for the tourists at Swansea but 14,000 saw only 18 minutes' play on Monday. Glamorgan collapsed against Cresswell's off breaks on a drying pitch when the crowd was admitted free for two hours' cricket on Tuesday.

Such gates paled before August Bank Holiday Monday in 1950 when the all-conquering West Indians arrived. Whitsun at Cardiff had seen the tourists win by an innings, Frank Worrell and Everton Weekes making runs and Hines Johnson and Sonny Ramadhin taking wickets. At Swansea in August the West Indies were dismissed for 211, when nobody could do much against Emrys Davies and Wooller, who bowled at a pace slower than usual. On Monday a record crowd of 32,000 saw Jones (105, including a colossal six on to the rugby stand) and Parkhouse (88) add 132 for the third wicket. Sonny Ramadhin took four for 93 in 30 overs but Glamorgan led by 111. Weekes soon put an end to the nonsense, hitting 147 but heavy rain ended the match after lunch on the final day with West Indies 312 for six.

Since their title success Glamorgan had finished eighth and 11th and 1951 saw them rise to fifth, largely due to the emergence of Jim McConnon, who formed a fine off spin partnership with Muncer. Glorious sunshine on Whit Saturday suited the South Africans, although the spectators had to endure some dour batting from Jackie McGlew (110) and Eric Rowan. Justification could be pleaded by the fact that 330 was enough as Geoff Chubb and Athol Rowan bowled the Springboks to their first victory of the tour. Fearless hitting by Haydn Davies (80 in the second innings) was the only redeeming feature for the Welsh county.

When the teams reconvened at Swansea, Dudley Nourse won the toss and put Glamorgan in on a rain-affected pitch, Percy Mansell and Athol Rowan bowling them out for 111. Nourse must have felt justified but by tea the South Africans had lost seven wickets for 36, with 20,000 spectators in a frenzy. Muncer was causing most of the problems and Nourse even considered declaring at teatime and getting Glamorgan in again on the troublesome pitch. But there was Bank Holiday Monday and an even bigger crowd to consider and he decided to continue. Mansell and Athol Rowan (49 not out) restored some common sense with an eighth wicket partnership of 54 and the scores were tied on the first innings (Muncer seven for 45). Glamorgan closed on 21 for one (Clift, a centurion in Glamorgan's previous match, completed a pair) and the match poised for a second day finish.

Wooller got 46 but the Monday crowd of 25,000 sat in disappointed silence as the tourists, needing 148, reached 54 without loss at tea. A number of people headed for home but must have kicked themselves by the time they got there. McConnon, delivering his off spinners from a good height, dropped on the spot and Muncer was equally effective. Endean, Waite, Nourse and Van Ryneveld fell quickly but at 68 for four, the tourists still had plenty of time and wickets in hand. Then McConnon struck. Cheetham was caught by Watkins at leg slip (his third such catch), Melle tamely defended to Clift at short square leg and Fullerton became the hat trick victim when he was bowled. South Africa were all out for 83, all ten wickets going down in 45 minutes for the addition of 29 runs. They were beaten by 64 runs, the only match they lost to a county during the tour. McConnon, fired by some competitive words from Wooller, took six for 27 and Muncer four for 16. They were toasted in champagne as the ground echoed to the sound of Land of My Fathers and Sospan Fach.

Wooller, who had led by example, standing close at silly mid-on and taking a stunning catch to dismiss Van Ryneveld, was carried shoulder-high from the field and, referring to his rugby days with Cardiff, said: "I never thought to see the day that I would be cheered and chaired on a ground where I have so often been the recipient of other kinds of treatment." The future Glamorgan and England captain Tony Lewis, then aged 13, saw the entire match.

In 1952 Glamorgan almost repeated the success against the Indians at Cardiff. Ramchand's in-swing brought him eight for 33 in the first innings and the tourists were set 118 in 84 minutes. They hit recklessly and eight men were out with 23 minutes left but Hazare and Mantri held out, India finishing on 85 for eight, 33 short. Torrential rain which wiped out the last day ruined the Swansea fixture, with the Indians on top after Divecha had taken eight for 74 in the first innings and Ramchand, Sen and H Gaekwad lifted the score from 154 for seven to 306 for nine declared, 100 coming in little more than an hour.

If 1953 was an Australian year it was overshadowed for a time by Glamorgan's challenge for the title. They headed the table at the start of July but faded away to tenth with only one victory in the last 15 matches. At least the Swansea crowd enjoyed the Australian match in August, when 25,000 attended on each of the first two days. Bill Johnston got among the wickets for the tourists but with a fine display of left-handed batting Watkins (76) enabled the home side to reach 201. The Australians were 93 for one by the close and Neil Harvey treated Monday's crowd to a dazzling display, 180 with three sixes and 28 fours. McConnon took seven wickets in 35.2 overs but went for 165 runs. Glamorgan were 185 behind and lost six wickets for 54 before a combination of Wooller and Muncer (125 stand for the seventh wicket) and rain saved the match.

Whitsuntide had marked a change for the tourists, who easily defeated the Minor Counties at Stoke-on-Trent. Glamorgan had agreed a financial package with the Steel Company of Wales, who had just financed the construction of a sports complex at Margram, close to their Port Talbot works. A holiday game against the Gentlemen of Ireland took place but it was not a success. Rain washed out the first day and the pitch became a nightmare, reflected by the scores: Glamorgan 81 and 81 for six declared, Gentlemen of Ireland 67 and 81 for nine, the last pair surviving the final two overs. Normality returned in 1954 when Pakistan's visits to Cardiff and Swansea attracted more good attendances only for rain to have the last laugh. The weather also spoiled the Cardiff fixture during the South African's 1955 tour but the Springboks avenged their 1951 defeat with an emphatic victory at Swansea, when 20,000 saw August Bank Holiday Monday's cricket. The pace of Peter Heine wrecked the home side's batting in the first innings; 64 all out they required an unlikely 392 in the fourth innings and although Jones got 50 they succumbed to Hugh Tayfield, finishing 226 short.

There was a similar story when the 1956 Australians arrived at Swansea the following August. Ron Archer struck a hurricane 148, Ken Mackay, in need of practice after his torment by Jim Laker, occupied six and a quarter hours for his unbeaten 163 and the declaration came at 408 for four. Jones, with 47 in the first innings and Wooller (70) and Parkhouse (62), who shared an opening partnership of 108 in the second, battled away but the tourists won with an innings to spare. Fine weather - it was better than London, 55F on Monday and Tunbridge Wells where hailstones fell – attracted 48,000 people over the three days. At Whitsuntide, the Australians defeated Cambridge University by an innings, RM James, in only his second first-class match, becoming the first Freshman to make a hundred against any Australian team. Ray Lindwall responded in kind for the tourists. During the same period, Glamorgan beat the Combined Services at Cardiff, mainly as a result of some fine bowling from Don Shepherd (seven for 50 in the second innings). Shepherd, with his classical high action, was one of the finest bowlers in the country, although he never appeared in Test cricket. He changed styles in the 1950s from fast-medium to medium-paced off spin; 2,218 wickets his reward in a career which stretched from 1950 to 1972.

Sonny Ramadhin had been the mystery bowler during the West Indies' tour of 1950; seven years later his mix of off spin and occasional leg breaks without any obvious change of action was rumbled by May and Cowdrey during their epic partnership at Edgbaston. Soon afterwards, however, he baffled Glamorgan's batsmen at Cardiff with a bewildering display, taking 11-70 in the match. Glamorgan made 138 and the visitors then collapsed against McConnon (six for 50) and were 87 for nine by the close. Scenting another Welsh victory over the tourists, 15,000 people crammed into the Arms Park on Whit Monday to see Wes Hall and Tom Dewdney add another 32, the total reaching 119. Ramadhin then struck again and West Indies needed only 97, Rohan Kanhai (52) helping to get them home with five wickets to spare, although there were some tense moments. At Swansea, where 18,000 people attended on the first day, they repeated their success, Ramadhin having a match analysis of 11-131 and Alf Valentine also chipping in.

After rain had ruled out any play on Whit Saturday in 1958, Wooller kept the game open by declaring at 175 for six against the New Zealanders. They responded with 215 (D'Arcy 89, Jim Pressdee's slow left-arm spin six for 77); 40 ahead with only two and a half hours remaining on the final day. Cave, with a spell of 8-8-0-4 then reduced Glamorgan to 19 for six, MacGibbon took over and the innings closed for 69. New Zealand needed 30 in the half-hour of extra time and got them for the loss of one wicket. They also had the better of the draw at Swansea in August, Harford making a hundred and Moir's leg spin troubling the home batsmen. With Wooller injured, Watkins captained a young Glamorgan team against the Indians at Cardiff in 1959 and a maiden hundred for Pressdee enabled them to reach 182. Modest it might have been but it soon looked formidable as the Indians crashed to 96 for seven by the close and 112 all out on Monday. Watkins made 61 and some big hitting from McConnon and Shepherd meant the Indians needed 294. They closed at 51 for one and kept the challenge going on Tuesday, falling 51 short. Due revenge was taken at Swansea, India winning by 114 runs despite Shepherd's 10-134 in the match, Glamorgan fielding the youngest side in their history.

Shepherd was again in fine form at Swansea during the 1960 August match against South Africa but the tourists had by the far the better of the two games. At Whitsun all eyes were on Geoff Griffin, who, after being called for throwing, had spent time at Alf Gover's school. Operating from the River Taff end at the Arms Park he was scrutinised and approved by umpires Harry Baldwin and Emrys Davies, although he delivered only 18 wicketless overs in the match. Baldwin, at square leg, did no ball Don Ward, the off spin bowler on Whit Monday - for having too many fieldsmen on the leg side. Baldwin had been waiting 20 years to find an error from Wooller and when the Glamorgan captain challenged him, he pointed to a man a foot to the on side of the sightscreen on the long on boundary as the sixth player. Wooller, as ever, had the last laugh. "Harry, you clot, that person on the ropes is a bloke with a white coat on selling scorecards." The match was a rout, South Africa winning by an innings, Jackie McGlew and Trevor Goddard each making big hundreds in an opening stand of 256. The result was equally emphatic at St Helen's when Tayfield spun the home side to defeat by nine wickets.

Wooller was missing when the Australians came to Cardiff and Swansea in 1961, his career now all but over. Norman O'Neill and Harvey gave the Arms Park crowd a Saturday treat; Glamorgan followed on and then Pressdee made the first-ever hundred by a Glamorgan batsman against the Australians. Ossie Wheatley's declaration left them 117 in 65 minutes; they ended at 90 without loss. In August some good bowling by Shepherd and Peter Walker reduced the Australians to 192; Shepherd then lashed 51 (25 balls) in 15 minutes (six sixes and three fours) as Glamorgan fell short by 43. A hundred from Simpson and powerful strokes from Benaud set up a target of 306 and with Alan Jones going well on 70, Glamorgan at 124 for two were in with a shout before rain ended play with two and a quarter hours remaining.

They had better luck in 1962 when the Pakistanis were beaten at Cardiff by seven wickets. Hanif made a century for the tourists but Alwyn Harris got 101, Jones 92 and some good bowling from Wheatley and an unbeaten 81 from Bernard Hedges did the rest. Harris was again in good form with 89 at Swansea when he shared an opening partnership of 193 with Hedges who made 144. Glamorgan declared at 363 for six but the rain ruined any hope of a finish.

Cricket was now entering its period of concern over falling attendances but there was no sign of it in 1963 when the West Indies were the visitors. A century from Joey Carew and some devastating bowling from Garfield Sobers brought an innings victory over Whitsuntide and big crowds saw a fine game during the August Bank Holiday. Walker's left arm spin accounted for five visiting wickets in the first innings and then Pressdee top scored with 78 as Wes Hall took seven for 51 to gain his side a lead of 30. A hundred from Seymour Nurse set up the declaration, Jones getting 92 as Glamorgan, needing 274, made 156 for three

So to another Australian visit in 1964 and an August Bank Holiday fixture which aroused more Welsh fervour and attracted spectators in numbers which gave the lie to fears that cricket was dying. But first to Cardiff at Whitsuntide where the tourists revelled in the May sunshine. Most of their batsmen made runs in a total of 361 for seven declared and on Whit Monday the honours went to Gwyn Hughes, a 23-year-old Cambridge graduate who arrived at the crease with five wickets down for 124. Hughes struck 13 fours in his 92 before Brian Booth held a brilliant low catch in the slips. It was to be Hughes's highest score in 22 matches for Glamorgan in which he averaged below 13. Neil Hawke's five for 57, a magnificent hundred from O'Neill and the Australian opening batsman Ian Redpath called by umpire John Langridge for throwing in his only over during a light-hearted end to the match were the other main features.

In August, the Australians arrived at Swansea with the Ashes retained and a St Helen's turner in prospect. The pitch took spin almost from the beginning and with Tom Veivers claiming five wickets with his off breaks, Glamorgan were all out for 197. The tourists then collapsed against Shepherd and Pressdee, losing five men for 21 and ending the day on 63 for six. Some lusty hitting from the left-handed Veivers (six sixes in 51) raised the total to 101; Pressdee six for 58, Shepherd four for 22. On Bank Holiday Monday, more than 25,000 saw Glamorgan consolidate their advantage in a tense atmosphere usually associated with a Welsh rugby international. Some skilfully flighted leg breaks from the Australian captain Bobby Simpson came to his side's rescue and Glamorgan, slumping from 126 for four after some good batting from Tony Lewis and Alan Rees to 172 all out soon after tea, left Australia 269 to win with plenty of time available. Simpson and Bill Lawry made a spirited start, using their feet well to the spinners, but Simpson fell to a catch at silly mid-off at 59. By the close the score was 75 for one.

The match was delicately poised and 10,000 people turned up on the final day to see Shepherd tilt the game Glamorgan's way with two early wickets. O'Neill fell to a superb running catch by Tony Lewis off Euros Lewis but Lawry and Veivers shared a partnership of 77 in 90 minutes to carry the score to 169 for four; 100

needed with six wickets remaining. Veivers hit two sixes and seven fours in his 54 before being bowled by Pressdee to an enormous roar from the crowd. Lawry battled away for four hours and 40 minutes in making 64 before hitting a Pressdee long hop to Rees at mid-wicket and making his disconsolate way up the 70-odd steps to the pavilion. The last four wickets fell for 25 and when Hawke was caught at the wicket, Glamorgan had won by 36 runs. Shepherd took five for 71 in 52 overs, 29 of which were maidens, and Pressdee finished with four for 65. The scenes were incredible and with the National Eisteddfod just down the road, it seemed that half the population of the Principality was there to join in the fun, the songs and the champagne.

Some perspective is required. The pressure was off for the tourists following their success in the Tests, the pitch was treacherous and Shepherd and Pressdee were past masters at exploiting the conditions at Swansea against batsmen unused to its vagaries. Also the Australians lost their next match by nine runs when chasing a target against Warwickshire before going on to draw the final Test. Nevertheless it remained a remarkable achievement for Glamorgan – and one they repeated at Swansea on what would have been the old-style August Bank Holiday in 1968. The earlier victories over South Africa, India and Pakistan had been celebrated – but beating the Aussies was something special.

Chapter Thirty-Four
Changing the Dates

The counties grew alarmed by the fall in attendances. In 1947, the number who paid for admission totalled 2,200,910. In ten years it dropped to 1,174,079 and in 1965 to 659,560. Restlessly some of the clubs sought fresh faces at holiday times but the biggest upheaval to the traditional fixtures was brought about by wider issues which were not of cricket's doing.

In the immediate post-war years, hardly anybody went abroad for their holidays and the tourist industry began pressing the Government to extend the holiday season. Many factories and coal mines had a 'shutdown or factory' fortnight which was often the last week in July and the first week in August. Together with the Bank Holiday, this put pressure on the road and rail systems and the seaside resorts, with a consequent high demand for accommodation over a seven or 10 day period, since few families spent a fortnight away. Whitsuntide created a different problem. The summer half-term usually fell in the holiday week and with many pupils taking exams, difficulties arose. Something more stable than a moveable holiday was mooted.

Thus began the campaign to extend the holiday pattern over a longer period. A Government steering committee for the staggering of holidays was established. Various suggestions were considered – the second week in June, the end of August or the beginning of September and so on – and rejected. By 1960 the weight of statistical evidence was becoming overwhelming. From 1951 to 1959 the number of holidaymakers had risen from 23 million to 27.5 million, with 9.5 million taking their break in August 1959 compared with 7.25 million in 1951. The hotel and travel trade urged the government to move August Bank Holiday to the end of the month and fix a date for a Spring Bank Holiday which did not have to be anchored to a religious festival. It recommended that school exams should be finished by mid-May and school holidays staggered on a regular basis. The Government sought the opinion of the workers and trades unions and set up another working party.

In July 1963 a White Paper on Staggered Holidays was laid before Parliament and views were expressed by a variety of organisations and the public. It was Sir Alec Douglas-Home's Conservative administration which finally bit the bullet. On Wednesday 4 March 1964, Edward Heath, the Secretary of State for Industry, Trade and Regional Development and President of the Board of Trade, made a statement to the Commons. He said the response to the White Paper indicated that everything possible should be done to alleviate the congestion at the peak of the holiday season. "The scope for direct intervention in this field is limited, but the Government consider that they should give a lead wherein it lies within their power," said Mr Heath.

"Our further consultations have confirmed the view that a fixed Spring Bank Holiday and a later August Bank Holiday could make a worthwhile contribution to the extension of the holiday season and to the avoidance of congestion for holiday-makers at peak holiday times. The Government have, therefore, decided, after full consultation with the interests concerned, that the August Bank Holiday for the next two years, 1965 and 1966, should be on the last Monday in August."

There was a minority who would have preferred to see August Bank Holiday moved well into September, but the consensus favoured the end of August. Mr Heath added that they would like to have combined the experiment with a fixed spring holiday on the last Monday in May to replace the present Whit Monday Bank Holiday. "This is not possible in 1965 because of the arrangements which have already been made for school examinations. These cannot now be changed without serious inconvenience. In 1966, the Whit Monday Bank Holiday will, in any case, fall on the last Monday in May."

Mr Heath urged the holiday trades to extend the season and offer inducements to the public to take their holidays at less congested times. His statement was welcomed, although it was pointed out that problems could be caused to diary manufacturers who had pressed for two years' notice of the change. He suggested that a corrigendum slip could indicate the change.

There was a positive response the following day from bus companies, rail spokesmen and Chambers of Trade. Anything which would stagger the holiday period and ease the loading on trains and coaches was to be applauded. Some factories which closed in the final week of July and the first week of August were more guarded, saying they had already added a weekend at the end of September in lieu of August Bank Holiday.

Old habits die hard and it took time to adapt. It rained on what would have been the early August Bank Holiday Monday in 1965 and there was an air of unreality about Monday 30 August which marked the beginning of the experiment. The RAC reported quiet conditions on the roads. "We are now at the end of the main holiday season and most people who were going away have had their holidays. What's more, it will be work again as usual for many factories and other workers which suggest a Bank Holiday rush is unlikely."

Nevertheless the experiment was considered a success. The first Spring Bank Holiday was introduced in 1967, although in June that year the Conservative backbencher Sir William Teeling (since October 1964 the Tories had been in opposition) sought a return to the status quo. He said because Easter had fallen early, there had been a nine-week gap before Spring Bank Holiday and hotels were finding it costly to retain extra staff. But Labour's president of the Board of Trade, JPW Mallalieu, said they shared the view of the previous administration that a fixed Spring Bank Holiday could make a worthwhile contribution to the extension of the holiday season. The Church had been consulted and accepted the change. It was formalised in 1971 when the Banking and Financial Dealings Act, which succeeded the 1871 legislation as the statutory basis for Bank Holidays, regulated the two Bank Holidays as the last Mondays in May and August. Later New Year's Day became such a holiday in 1974 and May Day – the first Monday in May – was introduced in 1978.

So the last of the old August Bank Holiday Mondays fell on 3 August 1964 and the final Whit Monday Bank Holiday on 30 May 1966. Like the 24 May's Empire Day, which eventually became Commonwealth Day, and football on Christmas Day which ceased as a full programme after 1957 (although it was

1965 before the last match of all was played, Blackpool defeating Blackburn Rovers 4-2) they were consigned to history.

Hindsight found flaws. Although nobody can control the weather, it might have made more sense to move Spring Bank Holiday into early June, when it was, on average, warmer and sunnier. Similarly in August, nobody seemed to have considered that sunset was around an hour earlier at the end of the month than at the beginning. There was also a bit of the closing the stable door about the August decision. By the time of the change the number of people going abroad for their holidays had doubled within ten years and would continue to increase, with correspondingly fewer holidaying in British resorts. There was some regret that by removing the Bank Holiday, the quality of Whitsuntide had been eroded, although had it remained as such, some of the traditional local parades and customs would have vanished into the mists of time, as these things do.

But what of cricket? In 1964 the Advisory County Cricket Committee agreed that a new arrangement regarding Bank Holiday matches with the touring team in years when tours were not shared – such as New Zealand and South Africa in 1965 – should be made. It was decided that in 1966 no county should have more than one match against the touring team, in this case the West Indies. This meant that Glamorgan would not play the tourists on both Whit and August Bank Holidays in 1966 and, in turn, some reorganisation of the traditional Bank Holiday matches would be necessary. As an experiment in 1966, a ballot would take place to decide which counties should play the touring team over the two Bank Holidays.

Six counties – Gloucestershire-Somerset, Lancashire-Yorkshire and Middlesex-Sussex – wanted to continue with their traditional holiday matches and would not be entered in the ballot. The eleven remaining counties would meet the tourists over the two holidays or play in a reorganised programme of matches. There were mixed feelings and Rowland Bowen's response in *The Cricket Quarterly* was typically abrasive. The magazine said that the four counties which played two matches against tourists in the last 40 years or so had been Lancashire, Surrey, Yorkshire and Glamorgan. "We have never been able to see why Glamorgan should have both Bank Holiday fixtures, and the only reason – and it is a good one - why she should have one is that large crowds can be obtained from the surrounding industrial and mining areas." As for the other three counties, it urged MCC to reconsider, given the revenue accruing from such matches. Restricting them to only one game per tour would be counter-productive.

"This leads us to a few remarks on Bank Holiday fixtures," the magazine continued. "How absurd it is that there should be a ballot for these games! Has equality ever been more illogical in its pretentions? Can it really be supposed that a Bank Holiday match in Leicester or Northampton can ever hope to provide the gross gate which can be obtained at The Oval or Trent Bridge or Birmingham or indeed Cardiff? The idea has only to be stated for it to be exposed. Here are our administrators anxious to earn money for the game and wilfully throwing it away in pursuit of a non-existent equality of counties. Let there be a rota of counties for Bank Holiday matches, but let it be confined to those who can be expected to provide a sizeable gate. "

In 1966, August Bank Holiday fell on 29 August. The committee felt this was late in the season and therefore not so desirable for big cricket as it had been when it was earlier in the month. If the Government should go back to the original date, then the whole position would be reviewed. Meanwhile, the 1964 matches had continued in their traditional form, the Whitsuntide headlines dominated by clashes between mods and rockers – suit-wearing scooter drivers and black-leathered macho bikers – at Margate, Broadstairs, Hastings and Brighton. The established fixtures for 1965 remained in place. Tony Lewis made big hundreds for Glamorgan against the New Zealanders at Whit and the South Africans in early August, the latter game attracting 30,000 over three days and ending with the tourists hanging on for dear life. Rain interfered with the Whitsuntide games, although it relented at Lord's where 10,000 on Whit Monday saw a fine display by Dexter.

It also curtailed play on what would have been August Bank Holiday Monday, which, with the traditional fixtures still in place, at least, left an impression that nothing had really changed. In some ways nothing had, for many of the agricultural, fruit and vegetable shows also stuck with tradition while others moved forward to the new date. That saw an unfamiliar set of fixtures beginning on Saturday 28 August 1965 – Derbyshire-Warwickshire, Essex-Middlesex, Glamorgan-Surrey, Gloucestershire-Nottinghamshire, Lancashire-Kent, Leicestershire-Hampshire, Sussex-Worcestershire and Yorkshire-Somerset, with the odd county out being Northamptonshire. They also included the final Test against South Africa at The Oval, where England's effort to make 399 on the Tuesday was ended by rain with 109 needed in 85 minutes with six wickets remaining. In addition, cricket also had to compete with football, the league programme being into its third set of fixtures.

The Whitsuntide games of 1966 found Sobers in superb all-round form in the tourists' match at Derby, Don Shepherd taking seven for seven in Glamorgan's victory over Hampshire at Cardiff and Sunday play for the first time in the Leicestershire-Northamptonshire game at Grace Road, where Colin Milburn, Mushtaq Mohammad, David Steele and Clive Inman made centuries. This was a season when each county played 12 matches with the first innings of each limited to 65 overs and Milburn's response was four sixes and 22 fours in a magnificent 171. At Bath, Langford exploited a turning pitch to bowl Somerset to victory over Gloucestershire. And there was a poignant moment in the Roses match at Headingley. Trueman's Test career had ended quietly the previous season; now against the old enemy and at a pace no more than fast medium but with admirable control of length and swing, he returned a pre-lunch spell of four for seven in 11 overs. Lancashire, 57 all out, Trueman 14-6-18-5, were beaten in two days by ten wickets. Attendances in warm, sunny weather were 8,000 on Saturday and 16,000 on Whit Monday.

August 1966 brought an odd mixture of some of the traditional games being played at the beginning of the month and others taking place during the Bank Holiday at the end. Thus the West Indies were at Swansea early on and Southampton at the end. Over the old holiday dates, Yorkshire beat Lancashire by 12 runs at Old Trafford after becoming the first side to forfeit an innings and Worcestershire won at Edgbaston. The Bank Holiday – one of the wettest on record - saw the first County Championship match to be played in North Wales bring victory for Glamorgan over Derbyshire at Colwyn Bay. The New Road crowd was charmed by a huge stand between Graveney and d'Oliveira against Essex, Northamptonshire defeated Gloucestershire by an innings at Bristol, Leicestershire were victorious at Old Trafford, Parfitt, Murray and Suttle made hundreds in the Sussex-Middlesex game at Hove and rain ruined the Warwickshire-Somerset match at Edgbaston.

During that last Whit Bank Holiday in 1966, Nottinghamshire met Surrey in the traditional fixture at Trent Bridge. Edrich and Barrington made centuries for the visitors and Nottinghamshire, set 338 at 65 an hour, ended on 261 for seven, some brave batting by Mike Taylor and Roy Swetman averting defeat. But there was no holiday return fixture at The Oval, Surrey meeting Essex early in the month and entertaining Yorkshire over the Bank Holiday while Nottinghamshire were at Weston-super-Mare and Dover. The Surrey-Nottinghamshire game took place on 3, 4 and 5 August 1966, a midweek fixture ending an 84-year holiday sequence hitherto broken only by the war years.

Inevitably, the weather was the deciding factor during the first Spring Bank Holiday, Monday 27 May 1967. It was so bad on Saturday that for the first time in 11 years not a single ball was bowled in any first-class match in the country. Little could be done on the remaining two days; indeed, with Old Trafford waterlogged the teams never went to the ground, although Mike Smedley, Ken Suttle and Bill Smith found enough time to post undefeated hundreds at Trent Bridge, Lord's and The Oval. It was a dismal beginning to the new era.

There was a departure from the norm in 1968 when a set of games took place over Whitsuntide (1, 3 and 4 June) rather than the official Bank Holiday, with Sunday play on five of them. The second round of the Gillette Cup was allocated to Spring Bank Holiday Saturday, with play continuing into Monday in several matches.

Chapter Thirty-Five
Changing Partners

In time, a generation of cricketers and spectators with no memory of the Whitsuntide and early-August holiday games emerged. After all, Spring Bank Holiday at the end of May bore little difference to Whit Monday and in some years the dates coincided. And as the seasons gradually edged into the second week of September, it followed that they were still in full swing over the late summer holiday.

But although some classic encounters took place after Spring Bank Holiday joined the late August Bank Holiday in 1967 things were never quite the same. Some of Whitsuntide's charm failed to make the transition and as the football season expanded an eye had to be kept on the Spring Bank Holiday weekend's play-offs for the final promotion spots, particularly on the Monday. By August Bank Holiday the new soccer season was under way and crucial Championship matches – and even the final Test - played second fiddle. Within the game itself significant alterations to the pattern and rhythm of the summer occurred. The Gillette Cup, the John Player Sunday League and the Benson and Hedges Cup had to be accommodated. Consequently the Championship was reduced and in 1988 there was an experiment with four-day matches which was fully adopted in 1993. All were absorbed into an increasingly complex and disjointed programme which had few points of reference. Sometimes there was no cricket at all on Saturdays or the Bank Holidays.

At the outset, a desire to continue the Bank Holiday traditions remained. A mixture of old and new emerged. Derbyshire- Nottinghamshire, Essex-Surrey, Gloucestershire-Somerset, Hampshire-Kent, Lancashire-Yorkshire, Middlesex-Sussex, Leicestershire-Northamptonshire and Warwickshire-Worcestershire occupied most, if not all, the holiday dates during the 1970s and 1980s until the four-day matches and, in 2000, two divisions, put paid to the continuity.

Ernest Hemingway closed *Death in the Afternoon*, his classic work on Spain, life and the bullfights, by saying that if it had been enough of a book it would have had everything in it. It would have had the chestnut woods on the high hills, the green country and the rivers, the red dust, the Prado museum of art, with sprinklers watering the grass early in the bright Madrid summer morning, and the cafes where the boys are never wrong and are all brave and there is talk of seasons lost and feeling good because there are no other triumphs so secure.

In this vein, certain things must be acknowledged, such as Middlesex and Sussex, who for more than 20 summers kept the traditional flag flying with an almost unbroken run of holiday fixtures. There must be mention of outstanding performances from John Snow and Kepler Wessels, by Mark Ramprakash in a Middlesex-Surrey derby and of Brian Lara illuminating Lord's before 3,000 spectators on the Monday - far removed from the halcyon days but reasonable enough in modern times - when Warwickshire were the visitors in May 1994. And of the Roses encounters, where the Spring Bank Holiday meeting was sacrosanct but those in August more fleeting. It was enough for Trueman to relish captaining his side to an innings victory at Headingley during the 1968 Whitsuntide and for Old Trafford in 1970 to indicate another sea change in the way cricket was going. Good crowds attended on the Saturday, August Bank Holiday Monday and Tuesday but Sunday was allocated to the John Player League fixture of 40 overs per side. For the first time since 1948 the Old Trafford gates were closed with a crowd of nearly 33,000 watching Lancashire retain the trophy with a seven wicket victory over their old rivals. Then there was some amazing cricket at Southport in the 1994 Spring Bank Holiday game against Somerset. On a pitch which was wearing from the start, John Crawley made an unbeaten 281 and Wasim Akram proved too much for the Somerset batsmen, the match ending after half-an-hour on Spring Bank Holiday Monday. It was a classic example of the lottery of the holiday Monday being the final day – Lord's saw Lara at his best on that same day, Southport the last five Somerset wickets go down for 24. In August 1994, Martyn Moxon's undefeated 274 set up a Yorkshire victory at New Road which was reminiscent of their powerhouse performances of the 1930s.

Surrey and Nottinghamshire met only briefly, Nottinghamshire beginning a series against their neighbours Derbyshire in May 1967 - a holiday fixture which had not been played in the Championship since 1876. There were some close encounters; a bitterly-fought draw at Derby in May 1990, with plenty of bristle involved at a time when the counties jointly led the Championship. In August 1991, Derbyshire, mounting a serious bid for the title, gained a fine victory by four wickets at Trent Bridge and Nottinghamshire won a splendid game at Ilkeston by one wicket in May 1994 – the last first-class fixture to take place on the Rutland Recreation Ground.

Nottinghamshire were at the centre of a history-making performance at St Helen's in Swansea, where they met Glamorgan in a match beginning on Saturday 31 August 1968. Garry Sobers, seeking quick runs to hasten a first-day declaration, struck Malcolm Nash for six sixes in one over. A side-effect of Bank Holiday switching to late August was an opportunity to enjoy the best of two sporting worlds – Saturday's pre-lunch session at the cricket followed by a visit to the football during the afternoon. This took many from St Helen's to Vetch Field half a mile away to watch Swansea draw 0-0 with Workington. More than 40 years on, the decision is still cursed. Nine years later, Nash was on the receiving end again in the August Bank Holiday match against Lancashire at Swansea when Frank Hayes hit him for five sixes and a four in one over, the four coming off the second delivery. In May 1974, Hampshire's Barry Richards carried his bat for 225 at Trent Bridge and there was August success for Nottinghamshire against the 1980 Australians, beaten by an innings and 76 runs.

Surrey found fresh company in Essex, with drama seldom far away, notably at Chelmsford in 1983, where rain ruled out Saturday's play in the Spring Bank Holiday fixture. On the Monday Essex reached 287, Surrey beginning their innings against the bowling of the West Indian allrounder Norbert Phillip and Neil Foster. They got the ball to swing in the humid atmosphere and after Alan Butcher was well caught at the wicket for 2, the next six batsmen to depart were out for nought. Most of them played back to Phillip, who kept the new ball well pitched up. Eight wickets had fallen for eight before a wild slog by Sylvester Clarke produced the only boundary of the innings and averted the humiliation of the lowest-ever first-class total. Surrey made only 14 in 14.3 overs: Phillip six for four and Foster four for 10. An unbeaten century from Roger Knight restored some respectability in the follow-on and the match was drawn. Surrey defeated Yorkshire by an innings during their August drive towards the title in 1971 and they won at Headingley two years later after a Robin Jackman hat trick. Yorkshire avenged these humiliations in 1974, an undefeated 142 from Boycott laying the foundations for a win with an innings to spare.

Mention must also be made of Surrey's 1992 August game at The Oval against Somerset, where Graham Thorpe stayed seven and a half hours for 216, sharing a partnership of 211 in 34 overs for the fifth wicket with the pugnacious Alistair Brown. London derbies with Middlesex took place at Lord's during the 1975 and 1992 Spring Bank Holidays and at The Oval in August 1994 Middlesex won a memorable encounter by two wickets after a Ramprakash century in the first innings. They were set 389 from 88 overs and Mike Gatting (103) and Ramprakash (90) added 178 for the second wicket. John Carr, in the middle of an astonishing run of form, saw them home with four overs to spare, the defeat ending Surrey's lingering hopes of the title.

Derbyshire met their old holiday opponents Warwickshire on only two occasions during the period up to the new century but Mike Hendrick had happy memories of the 1980 Spring Bank Holiday match against the West Indies at Chesterfield, when he ended the tourists' first innings with a hat trick. As for Warwickshire, they were involved in an astonishing match at Trent Bridge in the Whitsun fixture of 1968. They were still 183 behind with only seven second innings wickets remaining when Rohan Kanhai came to the wicket before lunch on the Monday. He was dropped before he had scored by, of all people, Sobers, his Test captain. Kanhai and Billy Ibadulla then shared a fourth-wicket partnership of 402 in six and three-quarter hours, Kanhai hitting a six and 36 fours in 253. Ibadulla was unbeaten with 147 when Alan Smith declared at 435 for four, leaving Nottinghamshire an academic target. Kanhai returned to the pavilion with a remark which underlined to his colleagues just how limitless were his horizons: "That's the third time I've got out in the 250s."

Holiday fixtures between Worcestershire and Essex were rare and Warwickshire soon re-established relationships with their old opponents, Worcestershire. Dennis Amiss was one of the batsmen frequently among the runs but Worcestershire found their own champion in the New Zealand left-hander Glenn Turner. During Worcestershire's second innings at New Road in May 1978, Turner used a crash helmet as a protest against the short-pitched attack of Bob Willis. Then he made an unbeaten 202 at Edgbaston in August in a high-scoring game which saw Amiss make two hundreds. Inevitably, Turner was at the centre of a high-scoring match at New Road in August 1981 when Amiss, Andrew Lloyd and Geoff Humpage made hundreds for Warwickshire, Turner responding with an unbeaten 147 as Worcestershire were set a target of 347 at nearly six an over. The home crowd slow-handclapped Amiss's declaration – one of three in the match – as uncharitable but Turner (139) and Dipak Patel (138) thrashed 200 in 110 minutes and Worcestershire got home by six wickets with four overs to spare. But such feasts were as nothing when compared to the Spring Bank Holiday fixture on the same ground a year later.

Turner was on 99 first-class hundreds when the match against Warwickshire began on a gloriously fine Saturday. His 100th hundred came before lunch and he was unbeaten with 311, the declaration being made at 501 for one. The West Indian Alvin Kallicharran, with a career-best 235on the Monday, helped ensure

Warwickshire avoided the follow-on and the match ended in a draw. And there was drama against the West Indies on Saturday 28 May 1988 when Graeme Hick needed 153 to score 1,000 runs before the end of May. He reached his century and more than 3,000 people were on the ground when at 5.30pm, he cut Curtly Ambrose to the boundary to reach 153. Hick went on to 172 before he was out but rain meant that the last two days were academic.

Gloriously Canterbury Week paid no heed to the August change of dates. It remained in its usual place until the 1990 Week started on Wednesday 25 July and ended on Tuesday 31 July – the first occasion that the festival or some part of it had not been played in August. It continued to host two Championship matches, with a limited-overs game. Since the introduction of a four-day Championship only a single such game and a limited-overs fixture have been played.

In Kent, the main beneficiary of the later August holiday was Folkestone, where the fixtures were part of the Week at Cheriton Road. Never more than 1970, when Kent, last at the start of July, had climbed to sixth on the eve of August Bank Holiday. Folkestone Week began with a visit from Nottinghamshire and an unbeaten hundred from Sobers, the closure coming at 376 for four. On Monday Kent slumped to 27 for five but Brian Luckhurst (156 not out), with support from Alan Ealham and John Shepherd, enabled Cowdrey to declare 66 behind. A further declaration left Kent 282, a target they achieved with three wickets and eight balls to spare. In other important clashes, Derbyshire were victims of Don Shepherd at Swansea, the Roses match was drawn and Surrey lost to Worcestershire at The Oval. Kent, second after the holiday round, moved to the top with victory over Leicestershire in the second match of Folkestone Week and a draw at The Oval secured their first title for 57 years.

 Matches against Hampshire evoked memories, when superb batting by Gordon Greenidge and Trevor Jesty made mincemeat of a target of 312 at Bournemouth in 1978, countered by some notable performances by Derek Underwood on the same ground. And there must be acknowledgement of David O'Sullivan, Hampshire's slow left-arm bowler from New Zealand. At Bournemouth, during the title-winning year of 1973, Nottinghamshire were swept aside during August Bank Holiday by O'Sullivan, 28.5-16-41-11; alas, he was not retained at the season's end, the regulations allowing only two overseas players and Hampshire choosing Barry Richards and Andy Roberts.

Somerset and Gloucestershire continued their traditional rivalry for many years, with duels involving Zaheer Abbas and Ian Botham and a maiden hundred from Viv Richards. Soon Richards would surpass himself with a display in 1977 fit for the Queen's Silver Jubilee when Spring Bank Holiday was delayed until June to coincide with the extended festivities. Somerset, beginning their second innings 196 behind, had lost three men for 76 before Richards turned the game on its head – 241 not out with four sixes and 32 fours. The match was drawn but Richards made the Tuesday holiday memorable. Gloucestershire's Mike Procter struck six sixes from consecutive deliveries during two overs by Dennis Breakwell at Taunton in August 1979. Only Botham could match such goings-on and his day came at Taunton on Saturday 24 May 1980 when he took 107 minutes over his first century and 58 over his second. His peerless 228 in 184 minutes included ten sixes and 27 fours and he shared a fourth wicket partnership of 310 with Peter Denning. Groundstaff and spectators were kept busy retrieving the ball from distant car parks and the groundsman's cabbage patch, some of the sixes landing in the River Tone. Denning said: "For most of the time I just sat on my bat and watched Both get on with it."

Colin Milburn punished the Derbyshire bowlers at Northampton during the 1968 Whitsun but his colourful career received in irreparable setback on the eve of the Surrey match over the 1969 Spring holiday. Following a victory over the West Indies at Wantage Road Milburn attended a party at the Sywell Motel and drove home with Dennis Breakwell and George Sharp. On the narrow lane, his Austin 1800 was in collision with a lorry. Milburn's face went straight into the windscreen, surgeons having to remove his left eye. The right eye was severely damaged and although he attempted a comeback and did reasonably well the handicap proved too much.

Soon the traditional rivalry between Leicestershire and Northamptonshire was resumed, although they were no longer the Cinderellas. Leicestershire were champions in 1975, 1996 and 1998 and Northamptonshire runners-up in 1965 and 1976. In the latter year the August fixtures were crucial. Two matches remained; Middlesex, the leaders with 216 points were at New Road, with Leicestershire (199) and Northamptonshire (198) meeting at Grace Road. After weeks of drought, the West Midlands suffered the wettest August Bank Holiday for 54 years and eleven hours were lost at Leicester. Mushtaq Mohammad declared at 202 for seven after Northamptonshire gained their second bowling point; Ray Illingworth closed the Leicestershire innings at 22 for two to deprive Northamptonshire of a bowling point. Following on they lost three wickets for five runs but Brian Davison and Illingworth played out the last 45 minutes. At Worcester, two inches of rain washed out the last two days, leaving Middlesex with a solitary batting point but they won the title, Northamptonshire finishing second and Leicestershire fourth.

August Bank Holiday 1977 brought more drama at Grace Road. Illingworth put Northamptonshire in and must have been pleased with the outcome: 172 and five wickets for Ken Higgs. Leicestershire then collapsed on a drying pitch and nine wickets were down for 45 when Higgs joined his captain on Monday. They added 228 before Higgs was run out for 98, Illingworth being unbeaten with 119. They were the only batsmen to reach double figures in a total of 273 but an accomplished century by Geoff Cook denied Leicestershire victory. The home supporters found greater cheer in August 1980 when after Wayne Larkins and Richard Williams had shared a second wicket partnership of 322 for Northamptonshire, a brilliant display by Allan Lamb on the Monday enabled Cook to set a target of 381 in 330 minutes. The runs were obtained in 103.3 overs, with David Gower, John Steele and Roger Tolchard the main contributors.

Which brings us to Glamorgan and the tourists, for decades locked in holiday combat at Cardiff and Swansea. No more, although the 1972 Australians won at St Helen's in May and Viv Richards and Joel Garner were to the fore when the 1984 West Indians visited. Otherwise there was no set pattern to Glamorgan's fixtures, with plenty of variety and no little excitement, none more so than the August fixture against Essex in 1969.

Gloucestershire opened a massive lead at the head of the Championship but two decisive victories over their rivals at Sophia Gardens and Cheltenham enabled Glamorgan to close the gap. The August Bank Holiday fixtures, with Glamorgan now leading with a match in hand, were crucial. Arthur Milton's tenth hundred against Somerset and John Mortimore's off spin kept Gloucestershire in the hunt with a victory at Bristol but Glamorgan struggled at Swansea. Massive crowds packed St Helen's and after Glamorgan had trailed on the first innings, Tony Lewis's declaration set Essex 190 in two hours. Nine were down with eight needed when John Lever joined Ray East. Singles were scampered but they still wanted three from the last ball, which East cut towards the third man boundary. Ossie Wheatley sprinted around the ropes and sent an arrow-like return for Eifon Jones to remove the bails with Lever well out of his ground. Glamorgan, victors by one run, went on to win the Championship.

Roy Fredericks (228 not out) and Alan Jones treated the St Helen's crowd to a feast on the 1972 August Bank Holiday Monday with a first-wicket partnership of 330, Frederick remaining unbeaten with 228. Jones had previously forged an opening association with Roger Davis, who was also a fearless and brilliant short leg. On the Saturday of the Spring holiday match at Sophia Gardens in 1971 against Warwickshire, Glamorgan were dismissed for 191. During the visitors' reply, Davis was hit on the side of the head, just behind the ear by a ball which Neil Abberley had whipped off his toes right off the meat of the bat. The fieldsman collapsed and went into convulsions. A doctor in the members' enclosure ran out to offer help and began mouth-to-mouth resuscitation as the player stopped breathing. Thankfully he started to breathe again and was carried off the field and taken to hospital. At first there were fears of brain damage but happily Davis made a full recovery and was playing again by mid-August. Warwickshire's victory, hastened by the spin of Lance Gibbs, seemed academic.

Huge scores from Javed Miandad and a debut hundred for Matthew Maynard were Glamorgan highlights and a hundred for Somerset from Viv Richards and a match analysis of 14-112 by Vic Marks added colour to the fixtures but two uncapped youngsters Terry Davies and Simon Daniels made history against Gloucestershire at Swansea on Saturday 29 May 1982. Nine Glamorgan wickets were down for 165 when Daniels, a young seam bowler, joined wicket-keeper Davies in a partnership of 143. More history was made when Glamorgan flew from Swansea airport instead of undergoing a 190-mile journey to Colwyn Bay for the 1990 Spring holiday fixture with Lancashire.

With no Test matches scheduled during the old-style holidays counties were at full-strength for the fixtures. That changed when the August break was moved to the end of the month. Although the disadvantages to the counties were obvious, at least it offered a glimpse of high quality cricket over the Bank Holiday weekend.

The Oval in 1967 provides an example. By Saturday's close Pakistan, needing 224 to avoid an innings defeat, were 26 for four and on Monday morning the slump continued. Eight were down and 159 still needed to make England bat again when Asif Iqbal took charge with a superb 146, adding 190 for the ninth wicket with Intikhab Alam and although England won comfortably, the crowd could not have wished for better holiday entertainment. But the day did not end happily for England's captain Brian Close, who had been censored for alleged delaying tactics in Yorkshire's match at Edgbaston. After the match finished at The Oval, Doug Insole, the chairman of the selectors, told him that he would not be leading the team to the West Indies. Close said: "I had then to go to a reception, to smile at people, to accept congratulations on winning the series, to make a speech, to make polite small talk with the hierarchy. And all the time I was bleeding inside."

A tradition linking the holiday to limited over internationals or the closing stages of the final Test now emerged. It attracted large crowds who saw some fine individual performances from Ian Botham: his 200th Test wicket and, in 1986, an unbeaten 59 (two sixes and eight fours in 54 minutes) against New Zealand on Monday morning before rain intervened. For the spectators it was a classic case of a holiday ruined by the weather, although the memory of an hour of Botham lingers on when many a full day's cricket is forgotten.

These were contrasting times, ranging from crowd trouble fuelled by alcohol at Edgbaston to the charm of the national Village Championship and women's Test cricket. There were 22,000 people at Lord's when Australia beat England in the Texaco Trophy in 1989 but the focus was on a prolonged streak by a shapely young woman which began at the Mound Stand and finished by the Warner Stand. The period was a boom time for Tests and ODIs. At Lord's on Spring Bank Holiday Monday 1991, 24,871 saw England complete a clean sweep in the three Texaco Trophy games against the West Indies. Neil Fairbrother and Graeme Hick, both found wanting in Test cricket, shared a third wicket partnership of 213 in 31 overs and Denis Compton officially opened the Compton and Edrich stands during the lunch interval.

August Bank Holiday Monday in 1998 brought defeat for an England bemused by the sorcery of Muralitharan and in a Championship fixture which began on a Monday, Phil Tufnell not only discovered that he had been ignored by the England tour selectors but was twice stung by wasps in the Middlesex-Hampshire game at Southampton.

Chapter Thirty-Six
Late Holiday Deal for Durham

The county ranks increased to 18 following Durham's elevation to first-class status in 1992. After a poor start, promotion was vindicated by the opening of the new Riverside ground in 1995 at Chester-le-Street and the winning of two Championships in 2008 and 2009.

Durham were Minor Counties champions nine times – seven outright and two joint – between 1900 and 1984, the first minor county to defeat a first-class county (Yorkshire) in the Gillette Cup and established a record of 65 minor county matches without defeat from 1976 and 1982. In their first-ever match they defeated Northumberland at Ashbrooke Cricket Ground, Sunderland in June 1882 and for most of the 110 years prior to first-class status they engaged in a series of two-day holiday tussles with their neighbours. These took place mainly at Ashbrooke or Northumberland's headquarters at Osborne Avenue, Jesmond, and produced some of the best matches in the Minor Counties Championship from 1901 to 1991.

On Whit Monday and Tuesday 1903, Durham's captain Edgar Elliott made 201, sharing a second wicket partnership of 240 with his brother Henry (104) in a total of 452 for eight declared. Durham won by an innings and 43 runs and there was another notable performance in August 1909 when Alf Morris took nine for 51 at Chester-le-Street's Ropery Lane, not far from the Riverside complex. The margins were narrow in 1919, when they won by two wickets at Jesmond and three wickets at Ashbrooke and there was another close call for Durham, by five wickets at Jesmond in 1920 when Fred Yielder made 50 for the visitors on Whit Monday. A teacher at Bishop Auckland Grammar School, he never played again because he was not prepared to take time off. Northumberland took revenge at Jesmond over the 1921 Whitsuntide with a nine-wicket victory but Durham achieved a double in their championship year of 1926, when 8,000 attended on Whit Monday and Tuesday. There was more high scoring for Durham at Jesmond in May 1939; 503 for six declared with Alan Parnaby making 162 and Bill Barron, later with Northamptonshire, an undefeated 156.

Durham generally had the better of things after the war, dismissing Northumberland for 67 on Whit Tuesday in 1946 at Ashbrooke after no play had been possible on Monday. The former Derbyshire and England all rounder Leslie Townsend top scored with 21 in the Northumberland innings and he enjoyed a measure of revenge at Jesmond in August with 192 out of his side's total of 340, the match being drawn. Northumberland won at Chester-le-Street in 1948, Durham enjoying some consolation from Whitsuntide receipts of £421, then a club record. In 1956, Northumberland were runners-up and Durham third, Northumberland winning the Whitsun encounter at Jesmond by nine wickets and no result being possible in the Ashbrooke return. Durham were champions in 1976 – but Northumberland completed the double in games restricted to a single innings at Chester-le-Street and helped along by declarations at Jesmond. In keeping with the first-class counties, the holiday tradition tended towards inconsistency in the years which followed although it was fitting that the final match between the teams in the Eastern Division of the Minor Counties Championship took place over the old Bank Holiday dates. This was at Gateshead Fell on 3 and 4 August 1991, Durham, led by Geoff Cook, winning by 10 wickets. The match ended on what would have been August Bank Holiday Monday.

Durham's opening first-class holiday fixture resulted in a win for Northamptonshire off the last ball of the match at Stockton in May 1992. It was Durham's fourth match in the Championship and followed a resounding victory at Cardiff over Glamorgan, their predecessors as the junior county. By tea at Stockton on Saturday Northamptonshire were 218 for six but the game resumed in a north-east sea fret during which everybody got soaked. Ian Botham tried to persuade the umpires David Shepherd and Barry Meyer that they would be better off in the dry but play continued. David Ripley and Kevin Curran took full advantage to take the score to 342 for six by the close. Dean Jones made 157 for Durham in the follow-on, but Northamptonshire, needing 92 in nine overs, got home by eight wickets. Phil Bainbridge also battled hard for Durham and he made an unbeaten hundred at Headingley in August 1993 to help save the match against Yorkshire. The August Bank Holiday Monday of 1994 found Durham involved in a similar battle, this time at Portsmouth. Paul Terry's 164 put Hampshire in the driving seat and although John Morris made 149 for Durham they were always chasing the game. Needing 341 on the final day, they were indebted to an unbeaten 159 by Jimmy Daley to steer them to 285 for seven and safety. The Spring Bank Holiday fixture in 1995 failed to reach the final day, Monday, Durham going down to a heavy defeat at Grace Road.

Thus Durham managed to catch the swansong of the holiday games, which, more often than not found the Bank Holiday Mondays restricted to the final day – if the match lasted that long – rather than the first or second as in past times. That did not mean the cricket was lacking in quality: for example the fourth day of the Durham-Gloucestershire match at Chester-le-Street in May 2002 began with the visitors, following on 338 behind, on 44 for two. Seven were down for 177 before a rearguard innings from Jack Russell (78 not out) enabled them to save the game at 261 for eight.

Chapter Thirty-Seven
Dying Embers

So the salad days passed into history. The Bank Holidays still had a role in English cricket but their influence on the Championship was becoming peripheral.

Change was gradual but inexorable. May Day enjoyed its share of holiday fixtures and there was a nod in the direction of the past in 1996 when August Bank Holiday Monday was the final day of matches between Nottinghamshire - Surrey, Worcestershire - Warwickshire and Yorkshire - Lancashire. Graeme Archer and Mathew Dowman followed in the footsteps of the Gunns & Co with hundreds at Trent Bridge but there was little play on the Monday owing to bad weather. At Worcester, Ashley Giles and Tim Munton put on 141 for the last Warwickshire wicket and, after mutual declarations, the visitors, desperate for victory to preserve their slim title hopes, set a target on 268 but after a good start Worcestershire called off the chase. At Headingley, rain allowed only 13 overs on the last day after Craig White and Richard Blakey had made White Rose hundreds.

There was something of a turning point in 1997; a set of Benson and Hedges Cup matches over the May Day weekend, nothing on Spring Bank Holiday Monday and a full round of fixtures during August Bank Holiday week - including the Roses match and Hampshire-Kent – which started on the Wednesday following the holiday Monday. The sixth and final Ashes Test, scheduled for a Monday finish, ended on the Saturday with Australia spun to defeat by Tufnell. By and large now the holiday Mondays were reserved for one-day games, if, indeed, any were scheduled at all, although there were a few flickers as the new century dawned involving festivals at Swansea and Horsham.

Protests were aired. August 2002 saw a round of Championship matches finishing over the weekend and another set beginning on Bank Holiday Tuesday. The Headingley Test ended with a victory for India on the Monday and in the only other scheduled holiday fixture Glamorgan beat Nottinghamshire at Colwyn Bay to move to the top of the Norwich Union 40-over league. A perceptive letter from Angie Tunstall, of Darlington, in the October edition of *The Cricketer International*, described it as "criminal that on August Bank Holiday Monday only one county match was played." She urged the ECB, if nothing else, to arrange a full programme of Norwich Union League fixtures for both Bank Holidays, on a system where each county plays one game at home and one game away for each of two Bank Holidays. Organising a full programme on the Bank Holidays during the season would be a way to get children in and hooked on the game, "whilst boosting counties' revenues with gate money from those of us otherwise left to twiddle our thumbs on these days."

In 2003 the Championship season began on Good Friday, with healthy attendances at the seven county matches, particularly at Bristol for the Gloucestershire-Somerset game. But, with the Lord's Test against Zimbabwe finishing early, there was nothing on Spring Bank Holiday Monday. Gerald Mortimer, *Derby Evening Telegraph* cricket correspondent for 30 years and afterwards a columnist wrote: "Bank Holiday was pleasant where I was, a nice day to watch some cricket. Because of an early finish to the Lord's Test, not a single first-class ball was sent down on Monday. Nor was there a National League (40-overs a side) programme. The Championship season opened on Good Friday, when a combination of excellent weather and people on holiday brought encouraging crowds. For the England and Wales Cricket Board to ignore another Bank Holiday is lunacy. By its nature, Championship cricket cannot attract those who work, especially as Saturdays are often blank. It smacks of a conspiracy to run it down."

These opinions found support and there was a good deal of grumbling in members' enclosures and around the boundary edges. For a retired person, becoming a county member was a passport to a season's cricket. The loss of a Bank Holiday Monday, while regrettable, could be absorbed. For people still at work, such days were precious and there was a feeling that they were being robbed of a day's play. Nothing could be done about days lost to rain but this was akin to being short changed. No attempt had been made at an organised programme over the Bank Holidays, which continued to make do with scraps from the table. There were a few morsels. Glamorgan began a Championship match at Colwyn Bay on August Bank Holiday Monday in 2003 and the holiday crowd saw Michael Powell make a hundred before bad light ended play with nine overs remaining. Test matches and ODIs sometimes offered consolation but the former are dependant on the match going the full course. A Twenty20 between England and Pakistan attracted 14,511 to Bristol on August Bank Holiday Monday 2006; a miserable Spring Bank Holiday Monday in 2007 found England and the West Indies shivering in temperatures of 9c at Headingley – the lowest in which Test cricket had been played since 1965. More than 21,000 attended an ODI between England and India at Edgbaston. In 2009 eight Twenty20 fixtures took place on Spring Bank Holiday Monday, which was, at least, an improvement.

That year's *Wisden* carried an article by its former editor Matthew Engel lamenting the fixture chaos which was destroying the rhythm of the season. It echoed the complaints aired on the county grounds, complaints driven not by nostalgia but common sense. The 2010 fixture list brought hope, with six Championship matches – Nottinghamshire-Essex, Warwickshire-Durham, and Yorkshire-Lancashire and, in the Second Division, Glamorgan-Surrey, Leicestershire-Middlesex and Worcestershire-Gloucestershire – starting on the Saturday preceding Spring Bank Holiday Monday. In addition some Clydesdale Bank 40 League games and the final day of the first Test between England and Bangladesh at Lord's were planned. Similarly August Bank Holiday Monday offered the final days of the England-Pakistan Test at Lord's and Sussex-Glamorgan in the Championship, with Clydesdale 40 League games also featured.

It represented a considerable step towards a happy medium but otherwise the scheduling for 2010 was criticised. A first-class season which opened in Abu Dhabi at the end of March continued with counties in action against the universities on Easter Saturday (3 April). This, the earliest ever start to an English cricket season, was followed by the first round of the LV=County Championship programme beginning on 9 April. Almost a quarter of the four-day competition would be completed by the end of April but fears that those matches which did not fall victim to the weather would be watched by a shivering handful of spectators clad in fleeces and clutching hip flasks proved unfounded. Instead the Championship enjoyed something a mini-Indian summer, during which, a few freezing days apart, matches reached a natural conclusion in beautiful spring sunshine. Good crowds attended the May Day weekend's Clydesdale 40 fixtures and the Whitsun weekend enjoyed glorious weather, with temperatures reaching 28c. Seven Championship fixtures arranged for what would have been the old Whit Monday Bank Holiday (24 May) began in perfect conditions.

A week later the Spring Bank Holiday match at Headingley started with Yorkshire at the head of the table and Lancashire in third place behind Nottinghamshire, who had games in hand. Yorkshire's young opener Adam Lyth, with 853 first-class runs, needed 147 to complete a thousand before the end of May but fell for a second-ball duck on Monday. Bad weather either restricted play or ruled it out altogether in all the matches on the first and fourth days – Saturday and Tuesday – and all six were drawn. Lancashire had the best of the Roses match, Tom Smith registering a maiden Championship hundred, and Phil Mustard, newly-appointed as Durham's captain, also made a century at Edgbaston, where Warwickshire's Pakistani-born leg-spinner Imran Tahir took eight for 114. In the second division James Taylor (206 not out) and Andrew McDonald (176 not out) shared an unbroken fourth-wicket partnership of 360 for Leicestershire at Grace Road, only for Middlesex to respond in style on the Monday. After three wickets had gone for 35 in reply to Leicestershire's 464 for three declared, Owais Shah (156) and Neil Dexter (118) added 266 for the fourth wicket in 68 overs. At New Road, Moen Ali posted a hundred for Worcestershire. In the Clydesdale 40 the Netherlands had mixed fortunes, winning at Derby on Sunday and losing on Monday at Northampton, while Scotland were defeated at Southampton and Canterbury.

Bangladesh followed on at Lord's on Sunday – the fourth day – only for Tamin Iqbal (a sparkling 103) and Imrul Kayes to lead the fight back with an opening partnership of 185. By the close they were 328 for five, 105 ahead and on Monday 9,000 spectators took advantage of MCC's final-day ticketing arrangements of £10 for adults and free for under 16s. People were also allowed to perambulate the ground during the lunch interval; as Michael Atherton wrote in *The Times*: "the sight of the crowd playing cricket, meandering or simply looking at the pitch was almost as welcome as the defiance offered by Bangladesh. Perception is everything and many will have gone away from Lord's yesterday with a different view of what has traditionally been regarded as a stuffy and pompous club." Bangladesh lasted until lunch, England knocking off the 160 needed for victory for the loss two wickets. Jonathan Trott, 226 in the first innings, remaining unbeaten at the end with 36.

England enjoyed sunnier conditions during the afternoon at Lord's but the weather on Sunday and Monday was generally cool and overcast with thick grey clouds and, in parts, a raw wind. On Sunday, 2,250 had braved the conditions at Headingley Carnegie and almost 3,000 turned up on Monday. At Trent Bridge, the attendance was slightly above normal for the Nottinghamshire-Essex game.

It was a similar story on August Bank Holiday Monday when sunny if cool weather greeted a programme of seven Clydesdale 40 matches which produced some excellent cricket. Sadly attention was focussed on the previous day's events when *The News of the World* carried allegations of spot fixing centred on the timing of three no-balls delivered by Pakistan in the Lord's Test. England won by an innings and 225 runs as the last six Pakistan wickets fell in 95 minutes on Sunday morning but the response from the crowd and players alike was muted. The story dominated Monday's newspapers and television news and was the principal topic of conversation around the grounds on Bank Holiday. But it was not allowed to overshadow some fine individual performances, with hundreds from Martin van Jaarsfield, as Kent defeated Hampshire in a nod to the old tradition at Southampton on Sunday, and on Monday from Somerset's Craig Kieswetter at Worcester and Scotland's George Bailey, the Tasmania captain, at Edgbaston. In the LV= County Championship the second division clash between the leaders Sussex and second-placed Glamorgan ended in a draw after the first day had been lost to rain and perhaps the best antidote to the spot fixing allegations was to be found at the seaside resort of Colwyn Bay. Here, in that charming setting, the Unicorns, the ECB's recreational XI run by the Minor Counties Cricket Association, came close to defeating Lancashire in the Clydesdale 40. The Unicorns provide an opportunity for recreational cricketers to demonstrate their talents to the first-class counties in the hope of winning a contract and they set Lancashire a target of 254. After a fine start, Lancashire appeared beaten at 234 for eight with two overs remaining but they scraped home off the last ball.

The cloud hanging over cricket on August Bank Holiday Monday seemed a long way away from Rhos-on-Sea and Colwyn Bay and such matches indicate that as long as Bank Holidays still exist the fixture planners might as well make use of them, even if their heyday is long gone. In the meantime, whether in the Championship, Clydesdale 40 or Twenty20, the ghosts of Hirst, Rhodes, Freeman and Mead might stir in approval at Headingley, Old Trafford and Canterbury.

Bibliography

HS Altham and EW Swanton – *A History of Cricket*, George Allen & Unwin Ltd 1948

John Arlott – *Jack Hobbs, Profile of "The Master"*, John Murray 1981.

John Arlott – *Indian Summer*, Longman's, Green and Co 1947.

John Arlott – *Vintage Summer 1947*, Eyre and Spottiswoode 1967.

Jack Bannister – *The History of Warwickshire County Cricket Club*, Christopher Helm 1990.

Jack Bannister and David Graveney – *Durham CCC*, Queen Anne Press 1993.

Scyld Berry and Rupert Peploe – *Cricket's Burning Passion*, Methuen 2006.

Richard Binns – *Cricket in Firelight*, Selwyn & Blount Ltd c 1935.

Derek Birley – *A Social History of English Cricket*, Aurum Press Ltd 1999 Philip Eden. Weatherwise. MacMillan.

Charles Bray – *Essex*, Convoy Publications Ltd 1950.

Mihir Bose – *All in a Day*, Robin Clark Ltd 1983.

Robert Brooke – *A History of the County Cricket Championship*, Guinness Publishing 1991.

Freddie Brown – *Cricket Musketeer*, Nicholas Kaye Ltd 1954.

Dudley Carew – *To the Wicket*, Chapman and Hall 1946.

Neville Cardus – *The Roses Matches 1919-1939*, Souvenir Press 1982.

George Chesterton and Hubert Doggart – *Oxford and Cambridge Cricket*, Willow Books 1989.

Steven Draper – *Cricket Grounds of Yorkshire*, ACS 1995.

Michael Down – *Archie, A Biography of AC Maclaren*, George Allen & Unwin 1981.

L. Eardley-Simpson – *The Rise of Derbyshire Cricket 1919-1935*, GC Brittain and Sons Ltd 1935.

Matthew Engel and Andrew Radd – *The History of Northamptonshire County Cricket Club*, Christopher Helm 1993.

Alan Edwards – *Lionel Tennyson Regency Buck*, Robson Books 2001.

Jack Fingleton – *Brightly Fades The Don*, Collins 1949.

David Foot – *Sunshine, Sixes and Cider, The History of Somerset Cricket*, David & Charles 1986.

Roy Genders – *League Cricket in England*, T Werner Laurie Ltd 1952.

WG Grace – *Cricket*, Bristol: JW Arrowsmith; London: Simpkin, Marshall, Hamilton, Kent & Co Ltd, 1891.

David Green – *The History of Gloucestershire County Cricket Club*, Christopher Helm 1990.

Duncan Hamilton – *Harold Larwood*, Quercus 2009.

Basil Haynes and John Lucas – *The Trent Bridge Battery, the Story of the Sporting Gunns*, Willow Books 1985.

Andrew Hignell – *The History of Glamorgan County Cricket Club*, Christopher Helm 1988.

Douglas Insole – *Cricket From the Middle*, William Heinemann 1960.

Clifford Jiggens – *Sammy, The Sporting Life of SMJ Woods*, Sansom and Company 1997.

Dennis Lambert – *The History of Leicestershire County Cricket Club*, Christopher Helm 1992.

Harold Larwood with Kevin Perkins – *The Larwood Story*, WH Allen and Company 1955.

Christopher Lee – *From the Sea End, The Official History of Sussex County Cricket Club*, Partridge Press 1989.

David Lemmon – *The History of Middlesex County Cricket Club*, Christopher Helm 1988.

David Lemmon – *The History of Surrey County Cricket Club*, Christopher Helm 1989.

David Lemmon – *The History of Worcestershire County Cricket Club*, Christopher Helm 1989.

Tony Lewis – *Double Century, the story of MCC and Cricket.* Hodder & Stoughton 1987.

Grahame Lloyd – *Six of the Best, Cricket's Most Famous Over*, Celluloid Ltd 2008.

Robert Low – *W.G.*, Richard Cohen Books 1997.

Christopher Martin-Jenkins – *The Wisden Book of County Cricket*, Queen Anne Press 1981.

Ronald Mason – *Plum Warner's Last Season (1920)*, Epworth Press 1970.

Anthony Meredith – *The Demon and The Lobster*, The Kingswood Press 1987.

Dudley Moore – *The History of Kent County Cricket Club*, Christopher Helm 1989.

Patrick Morrah – *The Golden Age of Cricket*, Eyre and Spottiswood 1967.

Ashley Mote – *The Glory Days of Cricket*, Robson Books 1997.

Leslie Newnham – *Essex County Cricket Club 1876-1975*, Vineyard Press Ltd 1976.

RC Robertson-Glasgow – *46 Not Out*, Hollis and Carter 1948.

Peter Roebuck – *From Sammy to Jimmy, The Official History of Somerset County Cricket Club*, Partridge Press 1991.

John Shawcroft – *The History of Derbyshire County Cricket Club*, Christopher Helm 1989.

John Shawcroft – *Local Heroes – The Story of the Derbyshire Team Which Won the County Championship*, SportsBooks Ltd 2006.

Richard Streeton – *PGH Fender – A Biography*, The Pavilion Library 1987.

AJP Taylor – *The First World War*, Penguin Books 1966.

Christopher H Taylor – *Canterbury Cricket Week 1842-1992*, Geerings of Ashford Ltd 1991.

AA Thomson – *The Wars of the Roses*, The Sportsman's Book Club 1968.

AA Thomson – *The Golden Ages*, The Sportsman's Book Club 1962.

David Underdown – *Start of Play, Cricket and Culture in Eighteenth Century England*, The Penguin Press 2000.

BJ Wakley – *Bradman the Great*, Nicholas Kaye Ltd 1959.

Sir Pelham Warner – *Lord's 1787-1945*, George G Harrap & Co Ltd, 1946.

G Derek West – *The Elevens of England*, Darf Publishers Ltd 1988.

Chris Westcott – *Class of '59*, Mainstream Publishing 2000.

Simon Wilde – *Number One, the World's Best Batsmen and Bowlers*, Victor Gollancz 1998.

Jack Williams – *Cricket and England, A Cultural and Social History of the Inter-War Years*, Frank Cass 1999.

LG Wright – *Scraps From a Cricketer's Memory*, Derbyshire County Cricket Supporters' Club 1980.

Anthony Woodhouse – *The History of Yorkshire County Cricket Club*, Christopher Helm 1989.

Peter Wynne-Thomas – *The History of Hampshire County Cricket Club*, Christopher Helm 1988.

Peter Wynne-Thomas – *The History of Lancashire County Cricket Club*, Christopher Helm 1989.

Peter Wynne-Thomas – *The History of Nottinghamshire County Cricket Club*, Christopher Helm 1992.

Wisden Cricketers' Almanack, Cricket, The Cricketer, The Wisden Cricketer, The Cricket Quarterly, Playfair Cricket Monthly, The Cricket Statistician and other ACS publications, county yearbooks, national, evening and weekly newspapers.

Internet sites - *www.cricinfo.com*; *cricketarchive.com.*

Index

A page number in bold indicates an illustration.